Joyce, Bakhtin, and the Literary Tradition

Joyce, Bakhtin, and the Literary Tradition

Toward a Comparative Cultural Poetics

by M. Keith Booker

Ann Arbor

THE UNIVERSITY OF MICHIGAN PRESS

First paperback edition 1997
Copyright © by the University of Michigan 1995
All rights reserved
Published in the United States of America by
The University of Michigan Press
Manufactured in the United States of America
⊖ Printed on acid-free paper

2000 1999 1998 1997   4 3 2 1

A CIP catalog record for this book is available from the British Library.

Library of Congress Cataloging-in-Publication Data

Booker, M. Keith.
    Joyce, Bakhtin, and the literary tradition : toward a comparative
cultural poetics / by M. Keith Booker.
        p.   cm.
    Includes bibliographical references and index.
    ISBN 0-472-10622-8 (hardcover : alk. paper)
    1. Joyce, James, 1882–1941—Criticism and interpretation.
2. Bakhtin, M. M. (Mikhail Mikhaĭlovich), 1895–1975. 3. Joyce,
James, 1882–1941—Knowledge—Literature. 4. Literature,
Comparative—Irish and foreign. 5. Literature, Comparative—
Foreign and Irish. 6. Influence (Literary, artistic, etc.) 7. Poetics.
I. Title.
PR6019.09Z52613 1995
823'.912—dc20   95-40617
                                                              CIP

ISBN 0-472-08521-2 (pbk. : alk. paper)

For Brandy Kershner

Acknowledgments

This study had its genesis during my graduate work at the University of Florida in Gainesville. I would like to thank several members of the faculty at Florida who contributed in important ways to the early development of my ideas about Joyce and literature in general. These include R. A. Shoaf, Alistair Duckworth, and Caryl Flinn. Special thanks are due to Brandy Kershner, who directed my doctoral dissertation at Florida and who served as an important exemplar of Joyce scholarship in his own work. I would also like to thank Dubravka Juraga for her support and advice during this project. Finally, thanks are due to all of those at the University of Michigan Press who helped to bring this manuscript to press, including Susan Whitlock, Ellen McCarthy, LeAnn Fields, Jillian Downey, and Eve Trager.

Contents

Introduction. Joyce and Bakhtin: Toward a Comparative Cultural Poetics

Stephen Greenblatt opens his *Shakespearean Negotiations* with the now-famous declaration that "I began with the desire to speak with the dead" (1). He goes on to suggest that this desire is quite common in literary studies, the central objects of which are the textual traces left behind by past (often long-dead) writers. Literary criticism thus becomes for Greenblatt a sort of conversation between living critics and dead writers, a metaphor that seems particularly appropriate both for Greenblatt's new historical style of criticism and for the study of Shakespeare, whose voice has continued to sound so vividly in western culture during the nearly four centuries since his death.

Greenblatt's vision of criticism-as-séance obviously does not literally apply to the criticism of the works of living writers. It also becomes less compelling as the historical distance between writer and critic decreases, even when those writers are in fact deceased. Greenblatt's invocation of the ghosts of Shakespeare and his contemporaries is thus effective as a metaphor in ways that the invocation of the ghost of a more recent writer like James Joyce cannot be. On the other hand, modern writers like Joyce share with Greenblatt the necessity of dealing with literary voices from the past in their work. Indeed, Joyce's writing is itself very much informed by the desire to speak with the dead, whose voices constitute a powerful element of Joyce's texts. In *Dubliners* Joyce presents a series of stories about a modern city crushed beneath the weight of the dead past, culminating in a final story in which the voices of the dead are so important that they give the story its title. Gabriel Conroy—who will come in the course of "The Dead" to be haunted by the ghost of Michael Furey—might almost be quoting

Greenblatt in advance when he points out in his after-dinner oration that the Irish people "still cherish in our hearts the memory of those dead and gone great ones whose fame the world will not willingly let die" (203).

Of course, Greenblatt's new historical dialogues with the voices of the Renaissance represent anything but a traditional glorification of the past. Similarly, Joyce suggests throughout *Dubliners* that the reverence for the past among the Irish can be crippling and paralyzing in the present. Meanwhile, in *A Portrait of the Artist as a Young Man* Joyce relates the boyhood and adolescence of Stephen Dedalus, still young and very much alive. But Stephen is so haunted by an array of dead voices that he remains radically estranged from life. This estrangement continues in *Ulysses*, in which cultural ghosts like Dante, Augustine, Aquinas, and Shakespeare are joined by the more personal ghost of Stephen's recently deceased mother in haunting the young poet. Numerous other ghosts walk the streets of Dublin in the course of the text as well, ranging from the just-buried Paddy Dignam, to the deceased son of Leopold Bloom, to the personified "SINS OF THE PAST" that arise to remind Bloom of his former indiscretions. Finally, Joyce takes the title of his last novel from a song about a deceased Irishman who rises from the dead the better to be able to participate in the festivities of his own wake.

James Atherton anticipates Greenblatt by suggesting that the complex multivocal texture of *Finnegans Wake* can be likened to a "quasi-spiritualistic séance in which various voices compete" (159). Indeed, the séance metaphor is appropriate for all of Joyce's texts, which closely resemble Greenblatt's description of literary criticism in their constant effort to establish conversations with long-dead predecessors. On the other hand, Greenblatt's fascination with the ability of the voices of dead authors (especially Shakespeare) still to sound in the present comes dangerously close to the kind of immersion in the past that Joyce saw as one of the major sources of paralysis in his contemporary Dublin. Further, Greenblatt's séance model ultimately seems derived from a lingering metaphysics of presence that does not really correspond to our contemporary understanding of textuality. Books are not people, nor do we "speak" with their authors when we read them. Books are cultural productions, and there is no magic required to read the works of dead authors because culture itself continues quite unimpeded after their deaths. Greenblatt himself very effectively demonstrates that Shakespeare's texts derive not from a unique individual genius but from a complex process of cultural negotiation and exchange in Elizabethan England.

This process does not stop after a text is written or after its author dies. Indeed, Joyce's vigorous engagement with the texts of his predecessors should serve as a vivid reminder that literary texts are continually rewritten and renewed. Shakespeare's texts still sound for us today (or for Joyce earlier in this century) not because they magically span the centuries, speaking to us from the past like Hamlet's ghost, but because in a very real sense Shakespeare is, as Jan Kott would have it, our contemporary. By the time of Joyce, "Shakespeare's" plays were not merely the product of Shakespeare's writing; they were also the product of centuries of reading and commentary. The Shakespeare Joyce encountered in his youth was thus to a large extent not an Elizabethan author but a Victorian one, his texts having been thoroughly reconstituted by nineteenth-century readings that produced a Shakespeare suitable for use as the major cultural icon of the British Empire.

In English-language literature, Joyce and Shakespeare are probably the best examples of this phenomenon, which occurs to a greater or lesser extent for all cultural productions. The close complicity between Joyce's writing and its criticism comes about partially because much of his work is so difficult that new readers tend to turn to published explications in search of help and partially because so much published criticism has substantially affected our perception of Joyce. In addition, Joyce himself (unlike Shakespeare) was intensely aware of the important role that criticism would play in the reception of his work, and he often seems to have designed his texts as gold mines for enterprising critics. In his lifetime Joyce frequently fed auxiliary information to explicators like Stuart Gilbert; in one particularly telling instance, the collection *Our Exagmination Round his Factification for Incamination of Work in Progress*, Joyce literally recruited a group of critics to write a series of critical essays on *Finnegans Wake* before the *Wake* was published—or even written—in its full form.

The very existence of this collection says a great deal about Joyce's appreciation of the importance of criticism. Its title derives from a passage in the *Wake* that is also especially revealing: "His producers are they not his consumers? Your exagmination round his factification for incamination of a warping process" (497.1–3).[1] This equation of producer and consumer indicates Joyce's recognition of the way his texts are generated in a very real way in the process of reading rather than being produced as finished artifacts in the process of writing. And the final notation of a "warping process" repeats this identification, referring both to the warping of language in the *Wake* (which was provisionally entitled *Work in Process*) and to the way criticism inevitably modifies, or warps, the reception of literary texts. All cultural productions are, in fact, works in progress, and all of them remain so after publication and even after the deaths of their authors.

The extensive critical attention paid to Joyce's texts has helped to solidify his status at the center of the canon of literary modernism—though in recent years a new generation of critics has placed Joyce's name among the leading figures of postmodernism as well. In short, the modernist Joyce has now become a postmodernist in the same way that the Elizabethan Shakespeare had by Joyce's time become a Victorian. In part this change can be attributed to the complex and multifaceted nature of Joyce's work. Few things are obvious about the writings of Joyce, though one thing that is clear is that different critics have tended to read his work in widely differing ways. For example, one of the most prominent and persistent trends in Joyce criticism over the last decade has been a gradually increasing appreciation of the importance of politics and history in Joyce's work. Of course, the growing "politicization" of Joyce participates in a larger trend toward the politicization of literary criticism in general, and one of the most striking features of the recent career of Joyce's work has been its almost uncanny ability to ride atop whatever critical waves happen to be breaking at the moment. Joyce's works were autonomous, apolitical, aesthetic artifacts during the reign of the New Critics, but they became radical illustrations of the unlimited proliferation of meaning during the heyday of Derrida, and they have remained important for Marxist, feminist, and other socially and politically committed critics who have come to the fore in the past decade or so. Such changes are not epistemological but constitutive. In other words, we are not gaining a better and better understanding of Joyce and coming closer and closer to the "truth" of his texts. On the contrary, Joyce's texts seem different to us now than they did to critics a few decades ago because they *are* different, because criticism has continually rewritten them.

Similar processes might be traced in the critical histories of Homer, Dante, Rabelais, Goethe, Dostoevsky, and any of the other literary predecessors upon whom Joyce draws in his work. These predecessors participate in many different national literatures, they write in different centuries, and their works all continually change and evolve, remaining perpetually contemporary through the rewriting implied by changing critical perceptions of their work. To understand Joyce's engagement with such predecessors, then, we need more than the close and careful attention to a specific time and place embodied in "thick descriptions," even if those descriptions are accompanied by a new historical awareness of the mediating influence of the critic's own cultural perspective. We need a perspective broad enough to ecompass numerous national literatures and flexible enough to attend to historical change.

This is not, of course, to say that Joyce's work is not intensely embedded in its contemporary cultural moment or that close and careful attention to early-twentieth-century Irish culture is not useful or even necessary to enrich our understanding of Joyce's texts. One of the most striking aspects of Joyce's writing is his ability to weave commentary on contemporary Irish social and political issues into the most seemingly "aesthetic" aspects of his work. At the same time, Joyce's texts tend to operate on several levels at once. Joyce's consistent subversive assault on the negative consequences of Catholic hegemony for Irish society also participates in a broader commentary on the status of the Catholic Church as the most powerful worldwide opponent of political progress in the nineteenth century. Joyce's critique of Irish nationalism also refers to the contemporaneous wave of nationalism that swept across Europe. And the antagonism toward British imperial domination of Ireland that is so central to Joyce's work is clearly relevant to the workings of imperialism around the globe. Indeed, the very fact of imperialism constitutes one of the crucial differences between Joyce and his literary predecessors from earlier centuries. In an age of worldwide empires, the kind of local knowledge produced by new historicist close readings of specific cultures can no longer be adequate: by the time of Joyce it makes no sense to speak of Irish culture apart from English culture or to speak of any national culture apart from broader historical phenomena.

In an age of imperialism, then, the geographically localized cultural poetics of new historicism needs to be supplemented by a comparative cultural poetics that can encompass these broader phenomena. Meanwhile, in the age of modernity, a temporally localized cultural poetics is inadequate as well. Joyce's work differs fundamentally from that of predecessors like Shakespeare in the much greater extent of the literary tradition upon which Joyce's writing draws and to which that writing responds. One may be able effectively to read Shakespeare's work almost entirely within an Elizabethan context because Shakespeare writes at the beginning of a modern literary tradition, but a reading of Joyce strictly within an early-twentieth-century context cannot be so effective because it ignores the massive cultural baggage that Joyce inherits from a tradition that is by then several centuries old. A comparative cultural poetics approach to Joyce thus must span different times as well as different geographic locales.

The present study, drawing centrally upon the work of the Russian thinker Mikhail Bakhtin, is an exploration of one form such a comparative cultural poetics might take. Atherton's invocation of the competing voices in Joyce's texts recalls not only Greenblatt but also Bakhtin, whose notions of dialogism and heteroglossia are crucially concerned with the phenomena that occur in the meeting of different social and cultural forces. Meanwhile, Bakhtin's attempts to establish a "historical poetics" are centrally informed by a strong recognition that all uses of language are inevitably colored by textual traces from the past. In particular, for Bakhtin all language has been used before and continues to carry the resonances of former use, so that any utterance involves a dialogic mixture of meanings and intentions. Only the biblical Adam spoke a language untainted by the speech of others, because he had no predecessors. Henceforth,

> Our speech, that is, all our utterances (including creative works), is filled with others' words, varying degrees of otherness or varying degrees of "our-own-ness," varying degrees of awareness and detachment. These words of others carry with them their own expression, their own evaluative tone, which we assimilate, rework, and re-accentuate. (Bakhtin, *Speech* 89)

Such statements, of course, are true signs of Bakhtin's modernity, and it goes without saying that an awareness of such echoes from the past is crucial to the work of modern writers like Joyce. Bakhtin's rich, diverse, and complex meditations on literature and language have provided some of the most exciting and invigorating forces in literary studies of the past quarter century. Bakhtinian concepts and interests like dialogism, polyphony, carnival, chronotope, and Menippean satire have become central elements of the contemporary critical vocabulary, and it would be hard to disagree with Paul de Man's nomination of Bakhtin as a candidate for "hero" in the modern development of the theory of narrative (106–7). Indeed, Bakhtin's work has not only revolutionized critical approaches to literature; it has also transformed our understanding of literature itself, bringing into focus many aspects of literary works that might otherwise have remained invisible. When viewed through the optic of Bakhtin's theories of the novel, for example, seemingly unruly and disjointed works ranging from *Gargantua and Pantagruel*, to *Tristram Shandy*, to *Moby-Dick*, to *Ulysses*, to *Gravity's Rainbow* take on a new coherence of structure, purpose, and genre.

Initial critical receptions of Bakhtin in the West focused especially on his descriptions in *Rabelais and His World* and *Problems of Dostoevsky's Poetics* of the subversive potential of "carnivalesque" images and energies in literature. Drawing on Bakhtin's use of the medieval carnival as a symbol of such energies, numerous critics have attempted not only to explore the significance of carnivalesque elements in specific literary works but to suggest these elements as an important indicator of trends in literary history. Max Nänny, for example, has related both *The Waste Land* and Pound's *Cantos* to Bakhtin's discussions of Menippean satire and of the carnivalization of literature. Moreover, Nänny suggests that such carnivalization is central to modernist literature as a whole.

> It may even be said that one of the major thrusts of 20th century literature (and art) seems to have been toward a kind of recarnivalization in Joyce's and Eliot's wake. . . . The chief modernist works, Joyce's *Ulysses*, Eliot's *The Waste Land*, and Pound's *Cantos* as well as so much post-modern writing may hence be seen as literary expressions of a pervasive carnivalization of 20th century consciousness and culture, expressions whose strongly ludic character demands an active participation in their carnivalesque games. ("*Waste Land*" 534–35)

Nänny's suggestion that a resurgence in carnivalesque energies is central to developments in postmodernist as well as modernist literature is echoed by William Spanos, who includes lengthy citations from Bakhtin to illustrate his argument that postmodernism participates not only in our contemporary historical moment but also in a long literary tradition. For Spanos, postmodernism is the latest incarnation of "a certain marginalized (or colonized) literature informed by the polyglotic 'parodic-travestying' impulse of the lowly folk imagination, a literature that, in the name of contemporaneity . . . has existed from the beginnings of Western civilization" ("Postmodern Literature" 193–94).

Numerous critics in the last decade have concluded that Bakhtin's theories work particularly well when applied to the fiction of Joyce.[2] In a brief 1983 article, for example, David Lodge suggests that the later work of Joyce is paradigmatic of the theories of the novel expounded by Bakhtin:

> the later episodes of *Ulysses,* and the whole enterprise of *Finnegans Wake,* appear not as eccentric digressions from the great tradition of the novel, sidestrains of a maindrain, but the most complete fulfillment of the expressive potential of the novel that has yet been achieved. ("Double Discourses" 1)

In a later study, Lodge describes *Ulysses* as "a kind of thesaurus of Bakhtinian discourse types" (*After Bakhtin* 86) and introduces a quotation from Bakhtin's remarks on *Gargantua and Pantagruel* with the suggestion that in the quoted passage Bakhtin "might be writing about *Finnegans Wake*" (40).

Similarly, Allon White argues in his 1984 article "Bakhtin, Sociolinguistics and Deconstruction" that both *Ulysses* and *Finnegans Wake* exemplify Bakhtin's notion of the carnivalesque and of the importance of mixtures of different discourse types in the novel, concluding that a "full Bakhtinian analysis of *Ulysses* would be an extraordinarily fruitful enterprise" (133). Meanwhile, R. B. Kershner notes in a 1986 article ("The Artist as Text") that "Joyce would seem to be the perfect illustration of nearly all of Bakhtin's major concepts, and was certainly known to Bakhtin's circle in the 1930's" (893, 4n.2). And Kershner follows up on this suggestion with a 1989 book-length study (*Joyce, Bakhtin*), which employs Bakhtin's work as a theoretical framework for the examination of the role of popular culture in *Dubliners, A Portrait of the Artist as a Young Man,* and *Exiles.*

Kershner's study demonstrates that Bakhtin's work can be effectively used to enrich our understanding of Joyce's early work, and numerous other studies, while of smaller scale or employing Bakhtin less extensively, have done the same for Joyce's later work. In a 1988 article, for example, Joseph Valente uses Bakhtin's key concept of polyphony to argue the fundamentally political nature of Joyce's linguistic experimentation in both *Ulysses* and *Finnegans Wake*. A 1989 book-length study by Michael Patrick Gillespie uses Bakhtin's theories of dialogism and polyphony to describe the multiplicity of voices in Joyce's fiction and especially to describe the participation of the reader in the creation of that polyvocality. Another 1989 book, by Zack Bowen, makes use of Bakhtin's descriptions of the carnivalesque aspects of the work of Rabelais to argue the essentially comic nature of Joyce's project in *Ulysses*. And Robert H. Bell draws extensively upon Bakhtin's readings of Rabelais (and other aspects of Bakhtin's work as well) in a 1991 study of the comic dimension of Joyce's work.

Indeed, the applicability of Bakhtin's theories of carnival and of dialogism to Joyce's work has been so widely argued (and accepted) that it seems remarkable that more extensive Bakhtinian studies of Joyce's work—like the "full Bakhtinian analysis of *Ulysses*" recommended by White—have not appeared. One reason is touched upon by Kershner, who concentrates on Joyce's earlier works but acknowledges that "all of Bakhtin's major concepts seem best and most obviously illustrated by *Ulysses* and *Finnegans Wake*" (*Joyce, Bakhtin* 17). It may well be that Joyce's later novels match Bakhtin's ideas so closely and so obviously that most features of those novels that might be identified by reading through Bakhtin can be identified without Bakhtin. After all, one does not need Bakhtin's theories of dialogism and carnival to see that Joyce's works are informed by a multitude of competing styles and voices or to determine that carnivalesque energies inform much of Joyce's comedy. Indeed, even Kershner's very effective use of Bakhtin to illuminate the significance of popular culture in Joyce's early work resonates with a number of other recent studies (Cheryl Herr's *Joyce's Anatomy of Culture* is a good example) that have focused on the importance of popular culture and other aspects of Joyce's contemporary cultural context *without* specific appeal to Bakhtin's work.

In the same way, the importance of dialogue with his literary predecessors is so obviously central to Joyce's writing that Bakhtin's strongly historicized theories of intertextuality at first seem almost entirely redundant as a description of Joyce's technique. After all, we already know a great deal about Joyce's specific processes of composition and about the textual histories of his various manuscripts. We also know quite a lot about Joyce's use of sources (literary and otherwise) and about his practice of patching together his texts from bits and pieces of a variety of other texts. And we certainly do not need Bakhtin's theories to recognize that Joyce draws extensively upon the entire western literary tradition or that predecessors like Homer, Dante, and Shakespeare are of particular importance in Joyce's dialogue with the literary tradition. Still, Kershner's use of Bakhtin does allow him to reach certain conclusions about the implications of Joyce's use of popular culture that might not otherwise be available.

Students of Joyce now have available to them a massive critical apparatus aimed at identifying the various literary and other voices that sound in Joyce's texts. In addition to the myriad individual articles that seek to identify Joyce's specific dialogues with past texts, a number of book-length studies provide sizable compilations of Joyce's references to other texts. By now it would be almost impossible to imagine doing any serious scholarly work on Joyce's texts without recourse to reference works like Weldon Thornton's compilation of allusions in *Ulysses*, Don Gifford's extensive collections of annotations to *Dubliners*, *Portrait*, and *Ulysses*, Adaline Glasheen's "census" of the various personages referred to in *Finnegans Wake*, or Roland McHugh's hefty collection of annotations to the *Wake*. Such studies are valuable—even indispensable—for a delineation of the "what" of Joyce's intertextual sources, just as seminal studies like A. Walton Litz's *The Art of James Joyce* tell us a great deal about the "how" of Joyce's actual procedure of incorporating these materials into his work. But surprisingly little has been done to illuminate the "so what" of Joyce's intertextual poetics, to explore the real implications of Joyce's dialogues with his literary predecessors. It is here that Bakhtin seems particularly promising as a resource because a constant awareness of the social and political implications of aesthetic strategies lies at the very heart of Bakhtin's project.

Still, critics of Joyce have made virtually no use of Bakhtin's work to illuminate Joyce's dialogues with his literary predecessors, even though Bakhtin's theories seem ideally suited for such a task. Indeed, while Joyce criticism in general has been particularly enriched by the many important developments in literary theory in the last twenty-five years, those developments have been used very little to explore Joyce's relation to his great predecessors in the literary tradition, possibly because of a perception that Joyce's relation to figures like Homer, Dante, and Shakespeare has already been thoroughly described. Even when modern critical theory has been used to assess the significance of intertextuality in Joyce, such studies—like Kershner's—have tended to focus on Joyce's use of popular culture or on his relation to more marginal literary traditions such as Menippean satire.

Yet Bakhtin's theories of intertextual dialogue are particularly well suited to treat the kinds of issues of authority that arise when intertextual dialogues involve central figures of the literary tradition. Bakhtin himself resembles Joyce in employing an encyclopedic range of literary works to construct his own texts, but it is also true that both Bakhtin and Joyce rely quite heavily on a few major canonical figures. Bakhtin also resembles Joyce in the way both, despite widespread reputations as enemies of authority, have paradoxically become authorities of sorts in their own right. Moreover, both Bakhtin and Joyce show a certain amount of respect for the authority of the literary tradition. For example, *Rabelais and His World*—the book most responsible for Bakhtin's antiauthoritarian image in the West—begins with an argument for Rabelais's greatness and importance as one of the major writers in the history of European literature. And Bakhtin later identifies Rabelais as one of the very few great "mother-geniuses" in all of world literature, listing him, along with Homer, Shakespeare, and Dante, as a writer whose pioneering work literally led to the birth of entirely new national literatures (123).

It is interesting that Bakhtin includes in this list the three writers who have served as the most obvious intertextual sources for Joyce, though it is also significant that Bakhtin himself does not extensively use Homer, Dante, or Shakespeare to illustrate his own theories. If anything, Bakhtin uses these three major figures as antiexemplars. Homer is inevitably associated with the epic, which functions for Bakhtin as the ultimate authoritarian/monological genre in opposition to which he defines the powerful dialogic potential of the novel. Dante, with his medieval Catholic striving for eternity, figures for Bakhtin as a counter to the intense engagement with contemporary history that gives the novel much of its power. And Shakespeare, along with the entire genre of poetic drama, is rejected by Bakhtin as part of his ongoing attempt to disrupt the kinds of traditional generic hierarchies that have tended to favor poetry and drama over the novel and other prose genres.

At the same time, the writers who are most important to Bakhtin— Rabelais, Goethe, and Dostoevsky—are hardly marginal figures in themselves. And what is particularly interesting is that the three writers who are most important to Bakhtin tend to pair off one-to-one against the three writers who are used most extensively by Joyce. If Homer represents the authority and monologism of the epic, Rabelais represents for Bakhtin the subversive multivocal energies of Menippean satire and other carnivalesque genres. As opposed to his description of Dante's attempts to escape from historicity, Bakhtin figures Goethe as the epitome of engagement with the temporality of everyday history. And the generic denial of polyphony in the works of Shakespeare contrasts with Bakhtin's identification of Dostoevsky as the most polyphonic writer in all of world literature.[3] These pairings of Bakhtin's three great exemplars against Joyce's three great predecessors thus suggest a convenient structure within which to examine not only the ways Bakhtin can enrich our reading and understanding of Joyce but the ways Joyce can enrich our reading and understanding of Bakhtin.

The present study employs this structure. It is arranged as a series of explorations—all of which use Bakhtin as an important theoretical resource—of the intertextual dialogue between Joyce and specific literary predecessors, principally Homer, Rabelais, Dante, Goethe, Shakespeare, and Dostoevsky. This structure allows the use of Bakhtin at an angle, as it were, to Joyce's texts, illuminating aspects of the significance of Joyce's dialogues with his predecessors rather than simply pointing out characteristics of Joyce's texts or instances in which Joyce's work exemplifies Bakhtin's theories. Each chapter focuses primarily on Joyce's relation to one predecessor, which allows a concentration not only on the importance of that predecessor but on the specific literary issues with which that predecessor is inevitably associated if one reads through Bakhtin. Indeed, given the assumption that texts are cultural productions rather than the creations of individual geniuses, it necessarily follows that these chapters are not comparative studies of individual authors but more general discussions of cultural issues. Each chapter also includes extensive dialogues with previous criticism of Joyce to emphasize the fact that Joyce's work—like Shakespeare's—is not accessible to us except through the mediation of criticism.

I begin with a discussion of Joyce's relation to Homer, which—in light of Bakhtin—becomes a discussion of Joyce's attitude toward the cultural authority represented by the Greek epic and by the Golden Age of classical Greek culture. To enrich the intertextual conversation in this chapter, I also bring in the voice of T. S. Eliot, whose specific reading of Joyce's relation to Homer in his description of Joyce's "mythic method" occupies an important early place in the critical tra-dition. Eliot suggests that Joyce relies on Homer to provide the kind of authority no longer available in the modern world and thereby to sta-bilize *Ulysses* as a literary monument in the midst of the fragmentation and degradation of modern culture. Reading Joyce through Bakhtin, however, suggests that Joyce is not so much leaning on Homer's authority as trying to undermine it and thereby to contribute to break-ing the hold that the past exerts on the present of Ireland. To further suggest Joyce's antagonism to traditional cultural authority, I also include in this chapter a comparative discussion of Joyce and the nine-teenth-century Russian anarchist Mikhail Bakunin, whose powerfully iconoclastic voice provides a sort of counter to the quest for authority to be found in Eliot.

In the second chapter, I turn to a discussion of Joyce's dialogue with Rabelais and to the general mode of carnivalesque transgression that Bakhtin associates with Rabelais's work. This chapter, however, suggests that there is far more at stake in Joyce's use of carnivalesque imagery than a mere attempt at flagrant violation of the proscriptions of bourgeois society. Indeed, Joyce consistently employs a strategy that I call inverse transgression by which he attempts to associate transgres-sive images not with violation of authority but with authority itself, thereby suggesting the hypocrisy and duplicity with which official institutions (especially, in Joyce's case, the Catholic Church) further their power. And if Joyce thereby appears less of a wild-eyed Bakunian anarchist than he might, then both Rabelais and Bakhtin perhaps appear by association more soberly responsible as well. Indeed, as Gary Saul Morson and Caryl Emerson have recently pointed out, west-ern critics who have used Bakhtin have tended to focus on certain lib-ertarian elements in his work, especially the work on Rabelais. Such critics have, Morson and Emerson argue, evoked a Bakhtin who does indeed look a lot like Bakunin, a Bakhtin who is "an apostle of freedom and carnival license, who rejoices in the undoing of rules, in centrifugal energy for its own sake, in clowning, and the rejection of all authority and 'official culture'" (43). But, while Morson and Emerson grant that there are such elements in Bakhtin's work, they also argue that an undue emphasis on these elements tends to obscure more central aspects of Bakhtin's thought. Bakhtin, they conclude, is "if anything, an apostle of constraints" (43). My discussion of carnivalesque transgres-sion supports the position of Morson and Emerson here. I also draw extensively on the voices of Gustave Flaubert (especially *The Temptation of St. Anthony*) and of Michel Foucault in the intertextual conversation that constitutes this chapter.

Chapter 3 examines the relation between Joyce and Dante, who may very well be the single predecessor with whom Joyce has the most in common in terms of the technical aspects of his writing. Both Joyce and Dante employ a mode of "sliding signification" to generate richly polysemic structures of meaning. Both authors construct extremely complex and sophisticated texts that include extensive networks of imagery and verbal patterns that link up different parts of those texts in powerful intratextual dialogues. Moreover, both of these writers rely heavily on intertextual dialogues as well, constructing their texts largely as mosaics of quotations from previous texts. In the process, both Joyce and Dante update and renew the texts upon which they draw, illustrating the historicity of both language and literature. On the other hand, Bakhtin's reading of Dante's writing as an attempt to awake from the nightmare of history suggests radically different inter-pretations of the ideological significance of the writing practices of Joyce and Dante. In terms of their dialogues with past texts, for example, one could argue that Dante conscripts these texts in the inter-est of his own strictly monological project, while Joyce engages his sources in dialogue, challenging their authority but allowing them to answer that challenge on their own terms.

The differences between the attitudes toward history shown by Joyce and by Dante are further elucidated in chapter 4 by comparing Joyce to Goethe, whose relation to time and history is, for Bakhtin, so different from Dante's. Goethe, like Joyce and Dante, constructs his works mostly from preexisting textual or historical materials. My examination of parallels between Goethe and Joyce in their use of past texts suggests a reading of Joyce's texts as informed very much by the same close contact with historicity that Bakhtin finds in Goethe. Such readings strengthen the notion of Joyce as an ideological opposite of Dante. They also suggest a recognition in Joyce of the importance of historical constraints and of the impossibility of completely breaking free of the past. This recognition again suggests that Joyce is not the wildly antinomian figure that numerous critics would see in Bakhtin's Rabelais, though Joyce does maintain a consistently critical and oppo-sitional attitude toward official authority in all of his work. On the other hand, reading Joyce in the light of Bakhtin's opposition between

Dante and Goethe helps to bring into focus Joyce's own relation to history, which is far different from the antihistorical escapism of Dante—or of Stephen Dedalus.

Especially in English-speaking cultures, Shakespeare is the most direct literary representative of official authority that one could possibly produce. Reading Joyce's use of Shakespeare as a confrontation with authority (and with history) helps to bring into focus certain aspects of that relationship that have often been ignored by critics. For one thing, Shakespeare is an official icon of *English* culture, while Joyce is an Irish writer intensely aware of the long history of imperial domination of his country by the English. For another, Shakespeare stands as a symbol for Elizabethan England, which has functioned in the imaginations of a number of modern thinkers as a lost past Golden Age of cultural wholeness and integration compared to which modern culture is hopelessly fallen, fragmented, and decayed. Among these thinkers (though in very different ways) are Eliot and Virginia Woolf, whose voices contribute substantially to the intertextual dialogue in the fifth chapter. Joyce's subversive dialogue with Shakespeare strongly challenges such idealized figurations of Renaissance England, a challenge that is supported by the recent work of Renaissance cultural scholars like Greenblatt. Bakhtin's vision of Renaissance culture in his study of Rabelais, as well as Bakhtin's treatment of Shakespeare's works as representative of the genre of drama, also usefully illuminate the implications of Joyce's dialogue with Shakespeare.

In chapter 6 I address via a dialogue between Joyce and Dostoevsky Joyce's engagement with the issue of human subjectivity, an engagement that has provoked widely differing critical responses. Bakhtin's figuration of Dostoevsky as the epitome of the polyphonic novelist suggests numerous obvious comparisons with the work of Joyce. However, in comparing Dostoevsky and Joyce I concentrate on the issue of subjectivity, and particularly on the relationship among subjectivity, narrative, and history in the works of both writers. The numerous parallels between Joyce and Dostoevsky demonstrate that many of Joyce's most modern motifs (problematic subjectivity, awareness of belatedness in the literary tradition, exploration of nontraditional narrative forms, mosaic construction of multigeneric texts) have important predecessors that go well back into the nineteenth century. Moreover, read through Dostoevsky, Joyce's treatment of subjectivity becomes neither an endorsement of individualism nor an attempt to undermine it but an exploration of the difficulty of true individuality in the modern world. In addition, the parallels between Dostoevsky and Joyce suggest the relevance to Joyce's work of the description by Bakhtin and his circle of human subjectivity as an ongoing social phenomenon. Further, Bakhtin's continual insistence on a metaphorical relationship between selves and texts suggests clear parallels between Joyce's exploration of alternative models of subjectivity and his exploration of alternative narrative forms through his experimental writing practice.

Together, the comparative readings in these six chapters suggest a Joyce whose texts are very much in touch with the everyday details of the lives of ordinary people despite Joyce's extensive engagement with the literary tradition. In addition, these readings suggest a Joyce whose works are politically committed, historically engaged, and socially relevant. In short, they suggest a Joyce whose work differs radically from conventional notions of modernist literature as culturally elitist, historically detached, and more interested in individual psychology than in social reality. Many of the issues raised in relation to Joyce's work in the current study are central to contemporary critical debates over the nature of modern literary history and in particular to attempts to describe the character of major movements like modernism and postmodernism. But the resistance of Joyce's work to simple categorization as either modernist or postmodernist on the basis of issues like history, subjectivity, and relation to the literary tradition suggests that such rubrics are more useful as labels for specific kinds of reading styles than for specific kinds of literary texts.

Chapter One

"Reminds One of Homer": Joyce, Homer, and the Myth of the Mythic Method

At one point in the "Circe" chapter of *Ulysses* Joyce's Leopold Bloom assumes the role of political reformer, declaring a program of universal brotherhood that will result in "Free money, free rent, free love and a free lay church in a free lay state" (399). However, that Bloom retains such notions as church and state at all immediately calls into question the real radicalism of his project. As he continues to detail his "schemes for social regeneration" his speech is supported by the appearance of "the new nine muses," who go a long way toward identifying the real nature of his reforms: "Commerce, Operatic Music, Amor, Publicity, Manufacture, Liberty of Speech, Plural Voting, Gastronomy, Private Hygiene, Seaside Concert Entertainments, Painless Obstetrics and Astronomy for the People" (400).[1] In short, Bloom's program (like Bloom himself) is hopelessly bourgeois. But, if Bloom's "radicalism" falls far short of that of political radicals like Mikhail Bakunin and Benjamin Tucker, whose writings influenced Joyce, the fact that Bloom is interested in forward-looking political reform at all places him far to the left of nostalgic modernist reactionaries like Ezra Pound and T. S. Eliot. Bloom thus occupies a middle ground between two opposite political poles, both of which inform modernism in important ways. It has traditionally been more common to associate literary modernism with the ideologies of Pound and Eliot than with those of Bakunin and Tucker, with the more radical innovations of modern art being placed under the separate rubric of the avant-garde. There are, in fact, real reasons why this distinction between modernism and the avant-garde is useful and valid, but at the same time it can be dangerous. Thus, a writer like Joyce, who is almost automatically considered a modernist by most critics, has also sometimes been automatically considered conservative, elitist, and disengaged from contemporary history, with little attention being paid to the real nature of his writing. This kind of reading misses important elements in Joyce's work, as well as illustrating that reading Joyce within certain contexts can powerfully affect the perception of his work. It is possible to read Joyce through Eliot, as did Eliot himself. But it is also possible to read Joyce through Bakunin, which yields a very different picture of Joyce's work.

The dialogue between Eliot and Joyce can perhaps best be joined within the framework of the so-called mythic method, one of the key concepts that has traditionally been used to characterize the alleged modernist flight from history. For Eliot and numerous other critics, modernist artists lean upon the stability and authority of myths and other great cultural artifacts of the past in order to help shore the fragments of their own contemporary texts against the ruins of modernity. According to this reading, myth provides a universal and timeless realm to which the modernist artist can remove her contemporary materials in order to escape the confusion and contingency of history. Joseph Frank's description of this phenomenon is typical.

> What has occurred . . . may be described as the transformation of the historical imagination into myth—an imagination for which historical time does not exist, and which sees the actions and events of a particular time only as bodying forth of eternal prototypes. (60)

Myth, for Frank, clearly serves as an alternative to history. Moreover, in comparison to these "eternal prototypes" from the ideal past, modern culture presumably appears fragmented and degraded, thus giving voice to the well-known modernist sense of crisis in contemporary society.

This model of a modernist escape from the messiness of history can be associated most directly with the conservative Christian ideology of Eliot, who gave the mythic method its name (and reputation) in his reading of Joyce's *Ulysses*. According to Eliot, Joyce uses *The Odyssey* as a scaffold that provides *Ulysses* with an order and stability that the modern world can no longer provide on its own. Paradoxically, however, Eliot proclaimed Joyce's turn to the past to be a revolutionary leap forward in the evolution of literary technique.

In using the myth, in manipulating a continuous parallel between contemporaneity and antiquity, Mr. Joyce is pursuing a method which others must pursue after him. They will not be imitators, any more than the scientist who uses the discoveries of Einstein in pursuing his own, independent, further investigations. It is simply a way of controlling, of ordering, of giving a shape and a significance to the immense panorama of futility and anarchy which is contemporary history. . . . Instead of narrative method, we may now use the mythical method. It is, I seriously believe, a step toward making the modern world possible for art. ("*Ulysses*, Order, and Myth" 681)

By this reading Joyce's juxtaposition of the workaday wanderings of the modern Leopold Bloom to the more heroic quest of the mythic Ulysses works entirely to the advantage of the latter. Bloom is a weak shadow of his epic predecessor, whose strength and heroism stand in stark contrast to the foibles of the all-too-human Bloom. The contemporary historical world is thus disparaged and rejected as a broken image of a nobler past, itself figured in the epic wholeness of the world of Homer.

Eliot's seeming revulsion at the "futility and anarchy of contemporary history" here exemplifies the flight from history that so many critics have identified with modernism. But one certainly wonders whether this flight should be associated with Joyce or with Eliot himself. Indeed, Eliot's delineation of the mythic method serves not only as a description of *Ulysses* but also as a promotion for his own project in *The Waste Land* and as an anticipation of his use of mythic prototypes in later plays like *The Family Reunion*. It is true that myth, as Roland Barthes has argued, generally represents a denial of history by presenting itself as always already complete and by concealing the contingency of its own historical development (*Mythologies* 117). Thus, myth becomes a form of ideology that attempts to pass itself off as absolute truth, as absence of ideology. But this naturalization of myth is accomplished by sealing myth off from history, and one could certainly make a case that Joyce's superposition of history and myth does just the opposite, returning myth to history and to ideology. From this perspective, Joyce does not appeal to Homeric authority but rather undermines it, suggesting that epic heroes were never so grand as we might like to believe, that perhaps Ulysses, like Leopold Bloom, had his human flaws.

Joyce's comparison between the world of modern Dublin and that of Greek myth may well be more in the spirit of Marx's contention that modern technology had rendered myth irrelevant to the real world than of Eliot's belief that modernity had rendered the real world irrelevant to myth. The rhetorical complexity of Joyce's texts is such that one can produce a great deal of evidence (none of it conclusive) to support either the conservative or the subversive reading of Joyce's use of the mythic method. But this method participates in a quite general Joycean preoccupation with ways of dealing with the past, and we know a great deal about Joyce's attitude toward such matters. For example, in a rather acerbic 1903 review of Lady Gregory's *Poets and Dreamers*, Joyce depicts the book as a moribund appeal to the past, as an evocation of a "land almost fabulous in its sorrow and senility" (*Critical Writings* 103). Joyce ends his review with a political twist, hinting that the kind of writing embodied in Lady Gregory's book contributed to the continuation of British imperial domination of Ireland by reducing the Irish to the same level of cultural exhaustion as their vulgar foreign oppressors. Joyce here makes clear his belief that, if there is a path to an awakening from the nightmare of contemporary life in Ireland, that path lies not in a flight from history through an appeal to the past but in an active participation in history as it moves into the future.

Joyce continues this tack in *Dubliners*, a book that is centrally concerned with ways of receiving the past. In particular, he sees Dublin as a city caught in the throes of a spiritual paralysis caused by an acceptance of traditional authority without question. Like the absurd never-to-be-forgotten Johnny circling the statue of King Billy in "The Dead," Joyce's Dubliners repeat themselves endlessly, living sterile and empty lives because of their inability to break free of the gravitational pull of the past. Indeed, Joyce's ongoing criticism of the Irish absorption in the past suggests that to Joyce the problem with the modern world is not a lack of order, but an excess of it, especially as embodied in the authoritarian domination of Ireland by British imperialism and by the Catholic Church.

Eliot's reading of *Ulysses* would seem to cast Joyce virtually in the role of the horse Johnny, circling Homer rather than King Billy. But in point of fact Joyce hardly mentions Homer in *Ulysses*, and his only Homeric allusion that seems relevant to an interpretation of the mythic method occurs in Buck Mulligan's mockery of Yeats's praise for another of Lady Gregory's books: "The most beautiful book that has come out of our country in my time," intones Mulligan sarcastically. "One thinks of Homer" (178). Mulligan does not speak for Joyce, of course, but the conflation here of Homer with the kind of reliance on the past that Joyce so criticizes in relation to Lady Gregory cannot fail to make one suspect that Eliot's view of Joyce's book as idealizing the past arises not so much from Joyce's writing as from Eliot's conservative reading.

That Joyce draws extensively upon Homer in *Ulysses* is undeniable. Indeed, the intertextual relationship between Joyce and Homer has probably been explored as much as that between any other pair of authors in history, and the identification by various critics of Joyce's often ingenious uses of material from *The Odyssey* has taught us a great deal about Joyce's technique in constructing *Ulysses*.[2] Probably the most influential early study of this kind was Stuart Gilbert's *James Joyce's "Ulysses": A Study*, which takes Joyce's own hints at Homeric parallels highly seriously and explores (much in the vein of Eliot) Joyce's use of *The Odyssey* as a structural model for his novel. Gilbert's book (first published in 1930) has taken a great deal of heat from subsequent critics, especially for what many see as an overly pedantic emphasis on Joyce's use of arcane secondary materials like Victor Bérard's *Phéniciens et l'Odyssée*.[3] Moreover, as A. Walton Litz has especially emphasized, many of the background materials cited by Gilbert were used by Joyce only in the final fine-tuning stages as he sought to enrich the texture of what was already an essentially completed work. In addition, Litz notes that many of the Homeric parallels listed in the note sheets Joyce used in compiling material for *Ulysses* never actually appear in the text but were merely used by Joyce to organize his thoughts. Litz thus concludes that, while Joyce may have used Homer "as a ready-made guide for the ordering of his material, the correspondences with the *Odyssey* do not provide a major level of meaning in the completed work" (21).

Litz does conclude, however, that Joyce's goal in the late revisions to *Ulysses* was "to transform the entire novel into an 'epic' work" (34). But Joyce transforms Homer's epic materials radically when he imports them into his novel. Despite numerous critical elaborations to the contrary, *Ulysses* and *The Odyssey* have very little in common in terms of narrative structure, technique, or ideology, and none of Homer's episodes appear in Joyce's novel without having undergone dramatic changes.[4] Thus Fritz Senn, in one of the most useful discussions of Joyce and Homer, describes Joyce's use of texts from the past not as a modernist reliance on the past but as a modernist "reformation of the past."

> Ultramodernist Joyce always turned back to the classics, Aristotle, Homer, Ovid; to medieval figures like Augustine, Aquinas, Dante; and later to Giordano Bruno, Nicolas of Cusa, Pico della Mirandola, or Shakespeare. History, Vico, and *Finnegans Wake* all say that each impulse of new life is a *revival*. (71, Senn's emphasis)

For Senn, Joyce does not use *The Odyssey* as a structural model for *Ulysses*. Instead, Joyce sets up the relatively pure and homogeneous style and language of Homer's epic as a starting point against which he can define his radically heterogeneous text as the antithesis. Joyce's technique in *Ulysses* does not take the novel back to the days of Homer—instead, it "moved the novel away from the Greek groundplan" (72–73). For Senn this movement can change forever the way we read Homer, and he goes on to focus not on the influence of the classics on Joyce but on the influence of Joyce on the classics.

I certainly have no intention here of rehashing the various transformations undergone by Homeric episodes when reinscribed in *Ulysses*, but a brief example might be helpful to indicate the general flavor (and complexity) of these transformations. The "Cyclops" chapter, for instance, appears to be one of Joyce's simplest and most obvious applications of Homeric materials. In this chapter Bloom visits Barney Kiernan's saloon and encounters there a variety of personages, including the chapter's nameless misanthropic narrator and the spiteful "citizen," a staunch Irish nationalist. This chapter includes some of the book's most obvious stylistic parodies of *The Odyssey*, especially in the numerous long (and riotously funny) epic catalogues that make up much of the chapter. For example, a list of great Irish heroes and heroines of the past includes such figures as Dante Alighieri, Christopher Columbus, Charlemagne, the Last of the Mohicans, Napolean Bonaparte, Muhammed, Patrick W. Shakespeare, Brian Confucius, Captain Nemo, Ludwig Beethoven, Herodotus, Gautama Buddha, and the Queen of Sheba (*Ulysses* 244).

That this list serves as a parody of Irish nationalist attempts to romanticize and heroize their past is rather obvious, and one could read this overt mockery as a suggestion of just how unheroic the Irish are relative to their great epic predecessors, the Greeks. On the other hand, such lists could also be taken as a commentary on the ideological functioning of epic heroization in general: perhaps the Greeks also used the epic as a political tool to further their national pride and to solidify the power of the ruling order, whether such pride and power were justified or not. The "Cyclops" chapter also effects a conflation of Irish nationalism and antisemitism and thereby calls attention to certain negative aspects of the Irish nationalist mentality. This aspect of Irish nationalism is made especially clear in the confrontation between Bloom and the citizen, which recognizably follows Homer's narrative of Odysseus's encounter with the Cyclops. Insulted by the citizen's antisemitic remarks, Bloom cannot resist a parting shot as he leaves the bar, reminding his antagonist that "Mendelssohn was a jew and Karl Marx and Mercadante and Spinoza. And the Saviour was a jew and his father was a jew. Your God" (280). Then, just as the blinded Cyclops Polyphemus responds to Odysseus's parting taunts by hurling boulders, the enraged citizen follows Bloom into the street and hurls a biscuit tin at the departing tormentor. The tin misses its mark (as do Polyphemus's boulders), and Bloom rides proudly away, so confident that he has bested his opponent that he metaphorically ascends to heaven on a fiery chariot à la the prophet Elijah.

But Bloom's rhetorical "victory" over the citizen in the bar shows none of the famed cleverness of Odysseus, even if Bloom's parting insult does recall that of his Greek predecessor. In the chapter Bloom does little more than spout clichés of bourgeois sentimentality, his "peak" moment probably occurring when he defines love as the purpose of life and produces as one of his central examples of true love the story (heavily sentimentalized in the popular press at the time) of Jumbo the elephant, who was forced in 1882 to leave his heartsick true love, the female elephant Alice, behind in the London Zoo when he departed to join P. T. Barnum's circus, only to meet his tragic death a few years later. Joyce's narration of the tawdry encounter between Bloom and the citizen in elevated mock heroic language could clearly be taken as a suggestion of the degraded condition of modern Dublin relative to the epic world of Homer, as Eliot would no doubt have it. On the other hand, Joyce's transformation of this episode into an assault on antisemitism and Irish nationalism seems to represent an attempt to engage contemporary history and to comment upon it, not to escape it. In addition, this emphasis on politics reflects back on Homer's text, calling attention to the way Homer uses his Cyclops as an image of individuality and lack of proper communal spirit, thus providing a reminder of the way Homer's authoritarian text consistently seeks to instruct its audience in obedience to the official ideology of ancient Greek society.

In the same way, Joyce in the next chapter of *Ulysses* transforms Homer's Nausicaa into the young woman Gerty MacDowell, held thoroughly in the thrall of masculine fantasies of the feminine that she has absorbed through her reading of male-dominated, but female-targeted, popular culture. Among other things, Joyce's dialogue with Homer in this episode calls attention to the thoroughly patriarchal structure of Homer's text (and society).[5] And so on. As a rule, Joyce's transformations of Homer (and of other texts from the past) shed new light on those texts, which causes us to read them in unprecedented ways. This kind of transformation, of course, is usually the result of what one refers to as parody, especially if one sees parody not in the sense of the mocking of a previous text but in the Bakhtinian sense of "an intentional dialogized hybrid. Within it, languages and styles actively and mutually illuminate one another" (*Dialogic Imagination* 76). In short, effective parody must be transformative; it must change the way we look at the texts being parodied.

Bakhtin's comments on parody are especially germane to the relationship between Joyce and Homer. Despite Eliot's use of the term *mythic method* to describe Joyce's technique, *The Odyssey* is not strictly speaking a myth but an epic. And the relationship between the epic and the novel is central to Bakhtin's theory of the novel as a genre. For Bakhtin, the epic is the ultimate genre of authority, informed in a strictly monological way by the official ideology of the culture in which it arises. In particular, the epic resembles myth in its denial of historicity, presenting itself as a completed form and as a vehicle for the transmittal of the authority of the past. The events of the epic exist in an ideal past time that is strictly sealed off from any dialogue with the present. "In the past, everything is good; all the really good things . . . occur *only* in this past. The epic absolute past is the single source and beginning of everything good for all later times as well" (*Dialogic Imagination* 15). The epic is the genre of sacrosanct and supposedly unchallengeable authority, inherently opposed to the possibility of change. In short, it partakes of very much the same energies that Joyce associates with Lady Gregory's romanticization of the Irish past: "The world of the epic," writes Bakhtin, "is the national heroic past" (13).

For Bakhtin, the epic is the genre of authority and of resistance to historical change. The novel, on the other hand, is the direct antithesis of the epic. It challenges authority; it demands that official ideologies be challenged and questioned; it thrives on change. The novel is the contemporary genre par excellence, distinguished more than anything by its close contact with the historical present and its intense sense of historical change in the midst of that contact. The novel for Bakhtin is a revolutionary and ever-changing genre precisely because it "comes into contact with the spontaneity of the inconclusive present; this is what keeps the genre from congealing" (*Dialogic Imagination* 27). Further, this resistance to "congealing" makes the novel an inherently anti-authoritarian genre, "a genre that is ever questing, ever examining itself and subjecting its established forms to review. Such, indeed, is the only possibility open to a genre that structures itself in a zone of direct contact with developing reality" (39). Reading *Ulysses* through Bakhtin, then, suggests that the confrontation between Joyce and Homer is first and foremost a generic confrontation between the novel and the epic, a confrontation that brings into conflict radically opposed visions of the world.

One could argue that Joyce's parodic use of Homer as a structural model calls the authority of the epic into question, exposing the cracks and fissures in a genre that would seek to pass itself off as a seamless whole. Indeed, Joyce includes in *Ulysses* a wonderful little reflexive parable that strongly suggests a subversive interpretation of the encounter between his text and the authority of the classical past. This parable involves Bloom's fascination with the statues of Greek goddesses in the Irish National Museum. Rather than accept these statues as unquestioned emblems of past aesthetic glories, Bloom applies his practical modern mind to much more prosaic questions. Instead of mindlessly circling these statues, like Johnny circles the statue of King Billy, Bloom circles them with a specific epistemological purpose—"to certify the presence or absence of posterior rectal orifice in the case of Hellenic female divinities" (*Ulysses* 600).

One could interpret this interest as a simple case of Bloom being Bloom (and it is that), but it is probably far more interesting that Bloom here may be mirroring his maker, taking the same attitude toward

Greek statuary that Joyce takes toward the Greek epic. Bloom's attempts at excremental vision may, in fact, be highly significant, since Bakhtin's work on Rabelais has taught us that an emphasis on the "lower bodily stratum" can subvert the pretensions of authoritarian discourse in powerful ways. In particular, Bakhtin argues in *Rabelais and His World* that attempts to view the body as a classical whole represent a denial of history by ignoring excremental and other processes that call attention to the dynamic interaction between body and world. But the "unfinished and open body (dying, bringing forth and being born) is not separated from the world by clearly defined boundaries; it is blended with the world, with animals, with objects" (26–27). Moreover, the dynamic nature of this blending and of the carnivalesque representation of body functions thrusts the subject directly into the contemporaneous flow of history: "The material bodily lower stratum and the entire system of degradation, turnovers, and travesties presented this essential relation to time and to social and historical transformation" (81).

Clearly, Bloom's prosaic attitude toward the statues of Greek goddesses participates in many of the same parodic energies that Bakhtin sees as providing a central impetus of novelistic discourse even as far back as the time of the ancient Greeks themselves. Bakhtin notes how certain seriocomic genres brought the elevated realm of the epic down to earth, where it could be inspected carefully, much as Bloom plans to inspect the statues. Very much, in fact. Bakhtin explains:

> In this plane (the plane of laughter) one can disrespectfully walk around whole objects; therefore, the back and rear portion of an object (and also its innards, not normally accessible for viewing) assume a special importance. (*Dialogic Imagination* 23)

Bakhtin discusses the subversive energies of parodic texts in some detail, noting the way that (even in classical times) such parodies already challenged the pretensions to timeless truth embodied in the epic, so that

> there flourish parody and travesty of all high genres and of all lofty models embodied in national myth. The "absolute past" of gods, demigods, and heroes is here, in parodies and even more so in travesties, "contemporized": it is brought low, represented on a

plane equal with contemporary life, in an everyday environment, in the low language of contemporaneity. (21)

The mythic method—as a subversion of myth—seems to be virtually as old as myth itself. Bakhtin even notes that one of the most common means through which such parodies of high mythic seriousness were effected was through the figure of a "comic Odysseus" (54)—of which Bloom might be seen to be a modern reinscription. It is true that the timeless world of myth is paralleled in *Ulysses* (and in many other modernist works) with the temporal world of contemporary reality, but Bakhtin's work shows that such parallels can often function as challenges to the authority of myth rather than as appeals to that authority.

Bakhtin's focus on genres rather than individual authors provides a salutary reminder that the way one intreprets Joyce's use of the mythic method has implications that go far beyond Joyce's personal attitude toward Homer as a predecessor. For one thing, reading Joyce through Bakhtin calls attention to the fact that Joyce's dialogue with the epic is not limited to Homer but includes a number of other texts in the epic tradition (the *Aeneid*, *Paradise Lost*, *The Voyages of Sinbad*). Moreover, Bakhtin's figuration of the confrontation between novel and epic specifically as a clash between the present and the past places the relationship between Joyce and Homer squarely in the center of critical debates over the modernist attitude toward history. If Joyce is appealing to the authority of Homer to stabilize his own text, then he would indeed seem to be attempting to escape from history and to enter the timeless realm of the epic. But if Joyce is parodying Homer and thereby challenging the authority of the epic with his novel, then he would seem to be attempting to shatter the epic illusion of timelessness and to situate his work firmly within the historical context of the living present.

Again, there is ample support in Joyce's texts for either reading. The interpretive choice a given reader makes here thus says at least as much about that reader and his ideology as about Joyce. For example, one can see a clear relationship between Eliot's determination to read Joyce's use of the mythic method in *Ulysses* as an attempted escape from history and the traditional western (Christian) ideological habit of privileging eternal perspectives over temporal or historical ones, where eternity is associated with ideality (particularly with God) and temporality is associated with the fallen condition of humanity in the physical world. For Eliot, as for St. Augustine centuries before him, the eternal is always to be preferred over the historical, and the Eliotic conclusion that Joyce's use of Homer shows an urge to escape from the fallen world of history arises at least as much from Eliot's own religious predispositions as from Joyce's text. This habit of thought goes back to Plato's preference for being over becoming, though it is with Christianity that this privileging of timelessness takes its most powerful and influential form. Indeed, Christ himself, as the fulfillment of Old Testament messianic prophecies, represents precisely the kind of "bodying forth of eternal prototypes" that Frank cites in relation to the mythic method. Moreover, Christ, as both god and man, epitomizes the conflation of the eternal and the historical, and as such he himself serves as a forerunner for the ontological double vision embodied in Joyce's depiction of Bloom as both contemporary Dubliner and figure of a mythic hero.

Joyce frequently employs Christ himself as a mythic prototype, and it is here that his use of the mythic method is at its most clearly subversive. The apostate Stephen Dedalus is consistently compared to both Christ and Satan in *A Portrait of the Artist as a Young Man*, while Bloom in *Ulysses* is a figure not only of Odysseus but also of Christ. At one point in the "Circe" chapter, Bloom momentarily becomes King of the Jews and founds the New Bloomusalem (395). But he is quickly brought low by the Romans (or at least the Roman Catholics) when Father Farley accuses him of aberrant religious beliefs (400). Bloom/Christ is then forsaken by the Jews and subjected to all manner of humiliation and disparagement, despite the fact that he performs a whole series of miracles and wears a garment that identifies him as "Jesus, the Savior of Man" (404, 406).

Bloom's travails in "Circe" quite directly anticipate those undergone by his successor HCE in *Finnegans Wake*, who is pronounced guilty of various sexual transgressions, whereupon he undergoes a series of tortures in a public spectacle reminiscent of the sufferings of both Bloom and Christ. First, he is mercilessly flogged with a variety of whips and other implements, including a pandybat left over from Stephen's punishments in *Portrait*. Then he is crucified, and his body is ceremonially eaten as in the Eucharist.

> And, hike, here's the hearse and four horses with the interprovincial crucifixioners throwing lots inside to know whose to be their

gosson and whereas to brake the news to morhor. . . . Isn't it great he is swaying above us for his good and ours. Fly your balloons, dannies and dennises! He's doorknobs dead! And Annie Delap is free! Ones more. We could ate you, par Buccas, and imbabe through you, reassuranced in the wild lac of gotliness. (*Finnegans Wake* 377.23–378.4)

Joyce's conflations of Bloom and HCE with Christ are irreverently parodic, and the punishments undergone by Joyce's two heroes carry very overt intonations of sadomasochistic sexual fascination. But the implication is not necessarily that Bloom and HCE are fallen and degraded figures relative to Christ their predecessor. Instead, Joyce's use of this motif may suggest that Christ himself exists in western culture as a figure of sadomasochistic fascination and that Christianity is fundamentally informed by sadomasochistic tendencies. In short, Joyce's use of Christ as a mythic prototype may be designed to undermine precisely the kind of Christian ideology that so centrally informs Eliot's interpretation of the mythic method.

If the similarities between Eliot's famous review of *Ulysses* and Buck Mulligan's mock Yeatsian review of Lady Gregory make *Ulysses* sound like a parody of Eliot rather than a parody of Homer, then so much the better, since Eliot embodies precisely the traditional respect for authority that Joyce seeks to subvert in his appropriation of Homer. Thus, Joyce doubly evades the trap of the past in his use of the mythic method. Not only does he refuse to accept unquestioningly the authority of past tradition, but he opposes that authority in a way that remains intensely centered in the present. Moreover, Joyce is not kicking a dead horse by parodying the activities of ancient Greeks and Hebrews like Homer and Jesus. Rather, he is using those parodies to focus his subversive energies on the continuation of ancient ideologies in a present where they are no longer useful or relevant—except as a means of perpetuating the tyranny of the past.

This dialogue between Eliot—with his privileging of the eternal—and Joyce—with his privileging of the historical—can go a long way toward delineating the very fundamental and important differences between the ideological perspectives of the two writers, differences that themselves problematize any simple characterization of the ideology of modernism. The most obvious disagreement between Joyce and Eliot is the religious one, of course, with Eliot holding to a view that organized religion is the best hope for providing a source of order and security in an uncertain world and Joyce believing that the very notion of organized religion is one of the most harmful and pernicious ideas ever to have been inflicted upon humanity.

Joyce's own private comments concerning religion—filled with references to the "Bloody Hairy Jaysus" and the like—often resembled the attitude not of Eliot but of the great antireligionist Bakunin.[6] In *Joyce's Politics*, Dominic Manganiello has demonstrated numerous affinities between the thought of Joyce and the ideas of anarchists like Bakunin and Tucker. These parallels—especially the ones between Joyce and Bakunin—not only illuminate Joyce's attitude toward religion but also emphasize the intensely political nature of Joyce's antipathy toward the Church. Ideas similar to those of Bakunin surface in Joyce's writing quite frequently, and these ideas are an important part of Joyce's aesthetics. Indeed, not only do Joyce's ideas—especially about the oppressive effects of organized religion—resemble those of Bakunin in a general way, but Joyce often expresses these ideas using images and motifs that are quite similar to those employed by Bakunin.

On the other hand, it would be as silly to read Joyce's fiction as a direct exemplification of socialist-anarchist political theories as it would be to read Joyce as an Eliotic reactionary employing art in an attempt to establish an oasis of order amid the chaos of modern life. We know that Joyce read Bakunin, so it is certainly possible that many of the parallels with Bakunin's thought in Joyce's work are intentional and that they represent cases of direct influence. But, if direct influence is often difficult to demonstrate, with Joyce it is particularly so, since he typically drew on numerous sources simultaneously in the construction of his complex, multiple-voiced texts. There are, in fact, a number of reasons why it is extremely problematic to discuss Joyce's work within the context of any conventional notion of influence.

For one thing, Joyce typically transforms his source material in dramatic and surprising ways, his brilliant and subversive reinscription of Homer being the most obvious and best-known example. This practice makes it extremely difficult, except perhaps in the case of direct quotations, to demonstrate with any certainty that a given motif was derived from a given source. In fact, even quotations can be suspect, since Joyce so often misquotes and frequently combines quotations from different sources. Thus, Bloom, giving avuncular advice to a somewhat uninterested Stephen Dedalus in the "Eumaeus" chapter of

Ulysses, proclaims the dictum, "Everyone according to his needs or everyone according to his deeds" (506). This slogan obviously refers to Marx's "From each according to his ability; to each according to his needs," and at first glance it again seems to be an example of Bloom—with his tendency to misremember quotations—merely being his flawed but lovable self. But, as with Bloom's insistent interest in the backsides of Greek statuary, this slip turns out to be extremely rich in content. As Manganiello notes, Bloom's phrase evokes both Bakunin's maxim "From each according to his deeds" and the belief held by both Bakunin and Tucker (contrary to Marx and Kropotkin) that labor ("deeds") should be paid in wages even in the ideal collective society of the future (Manganiello 111–12). Bloom's portmanteau quote thus creates a dialogic interchange between Marx and Bakunin that invites comparison of Bloom's reform program with the rich history of such programs in the nineteenth century, a history that was centrally informed by the ongoing confrontation between Marx and Bakunin (eventually won by Marx) over the direction that should be taken by socialism.

This simple example is typical of Joyce's polyphonic discourse and of the rich panorama of intertextual connections that Joyce can trigger with even the most seemingly simple gestures. And such is the nature of this method that Joyce's discourse generally includes several competing voices simultaneously with no absolute privilege given to any one of them.[7] In this example, Joyce draws from both Bakunin and Marx, and (though we know that he found Bakunin's work more congenial than Marx's) it is impossible from the text alone to tell whether Joyce (or Bloom) leans toward one or the other of these two important poles in the history of socialism.[8] Such complexities imply that it will typically be extremely difficult to determine not only whether Joyce was directly influenced by any given predecessor but even whether the influence was positive or negative. Even in cases like Joyce's career-long assaults on Irish nationalism and Catholicism, Joyce maintains a dialogic stance that has made it possible to read the implications of his work in varying ways. The self-righteousness of the languages of both of these institutions makes them rather convenient targets, but Joyce does not take the easy road of pure mockery in his treatment even of such despised foes. It is not coincidental that in *Ulysses* the most powerfully blasphemous assaults on the Church issue from Buck Mulligan (hardly an unequivocally admirable figure), and Mulligan's outrageous blasphemies (like the song "The Ballad of Joking Jesus" and the play *Everyman His Own Wife*) act both to undermine the authority of the Church and to warn against the excesses of a life with no moral values whatsoever. It is always possible that such doubleness will cause confusion, and one can easily visualize a reader who would interpret the placing of these blasphemies in the mouth of Mulligan as an attempt to undermine his subversive language and thereby to keep the authority of the Church (or at least of God) intact, despite the fact that Joyce's own personal comments and correspondence were filled with blasphemous remarks the spirit of which resembled Mulligan's closely.

However, Joyce's dialogic method makes his assault on religion not less effective but more so, since it allows him to avoid a mere repetition of the authoritarian attitudes that he seeks to subvert. On the other hand, it is certainly true that the double-voiced quality of Joyce's writing can make it difficult to decipher his own opinions, and rightly so, since one of his central projects was to undermine the conventional romantic notion of the author as originator and guarantor of meaning in his text. The resultant ambiguity greatly enriches the process of meaning generation in the reading of Joyce's texts, even as it confounds the efforts of scholars to determine the "real" meaning of those texts and the attitude taken in those texts toward the various sources upon which they draw.[9]

When Mario Vargas Llosa in *The War of the End of the World* depicts the anarchist Galileo Gall as an uncompromising fanatic, he suggests that Gall was importantly influenced by Bakunin. Indeed, at first glance Joyce's strategy of textual evenhandedness seems a far cry from the single-minded dedication of a committed revolutionary like Bakunin. But Bakunin's comments on "authorities" in *God and the State* show that Joyce's encyclopedic compilations of competing voices are highly consistent with Bakunin's thought. Bakunin suggests that he does not reject all authorities, only the idea that there can ever be a single "fixed, constant, and universal authority" (33). He grants that individual experts have special knowledge in their particular fields, and he sees nothing wrong with recognizing them as authorities in those fields. But he demands the right to challenge these authorities when he sees fit, and he suggests that the most insidious effects of authoritarianism can be avoided by recognizing a multiplicity of authorities.

> I do not content myself with consulting a single authority in any special branch; I consult several; I compare their opinions, and

choose that which seems to me the soundest. But I recognize no infallible authority, even in special questions. (32)

This privileging of multiplicity as a counter to monological authority is very much consonant with Joyce's own artistic practice of drawing on so many sources while maintaining the right to challenge those sources and to engage them in dialogue. Further, though art never played an especially central role in Bakunin's thought, his scattered comments on art often correspond quite closely to Joyce's ideas about aesthetics. Among other things, Bakunin acknowledged that art was a potentially powerful means for comprehending the world. Decrying the impersonal abstraction of Enlightenment science in a way that prefigures the work of Max Horkheimer and Theodor Adorno (or even, curiously enough, the New Critics), Bakunin argues that art, on the other hand, has the ability to deal more directly with the concrete specifics of individual lives. Thus,

> art in a certain sense individualizes the types and situations which it conceives; by means of the individualities without flesh and bone, and consequently permanent and immortal, which it has the power to create, it recalls to our minds the living, real individualities which appear and disappear under our eyes. Art, then, is as it were the return of abstraction to life. (57)

And, despite the echoes of romanticism in this apotheosis of the creative power of art, Bakunin expresses a distaste for certain romantic conceptions of the artist that rival Joyce's own antiromantic predispositions. Bakunin describes romantic literature as

> the literature of the tender, delicate, distinguished souls, aspiring to heaven, and living on earth as if in spite of themselves. It had a horror and contempt for the politics and questions of the day. . . . the dominant feature of the school of romanticism was a quasi-complete indifference to politics. (80)

This depiction of the escapist tendencies of romanticism may or may not be a fair assessment of the romantics, and it is worth keeping in mind that Bakunin's central bête noire is religion. It is thus not surprising that the evils he sees in romanticism are similar to the rejection of earthly things that is so central to western religions.[10] But what is perhaps most interesting for our current purposes is that Bakunin's critical description sounds so similar to the charges of political disengagement often leveled against the modernists, Joyce included. In particular, these romantic souls who desire so strongly an escape from earthly things are reminiscent of Joyce's Stephen Dedalus, with his intense urge to awake from the nightmare of secular history. Though Stephen himself expresses a preference for the classical over the romantic, it is clear that his own view of the artist is very similar to the one being criticized by Bakunin in connection with romanticism.[11]

Stephen, of course, is frequently given to expressing an opposition to ideas that turn out to be suspiciously similar to his own. The most famous of these, of course, is his own fierce (if highly intellectualized) rejection of Catholicism, despite the fact that Catholic modes of thought remain such an important constitutive feature of his own perceptions of the world. Even after ostensibly turning away from the Church in favor of art, Stephen still maintains a fundamentally Catholic consciousness, and when he characterizes himself late in *A Portrait of the Artist as a Young Man* as a "priest of eternal imagination" it is clear that for him (as perhaps for Matthew Arnold) poetry merely functions as a surrogate for religion. As his friend Cranly tells him, "It is a curious thing . . . how your mind is supersaturated with the religion in which you say you disbelieve" (240).

This depiction of Stephen as a thoroughgoing apostate who retains an essentially Catholic sensibility is typical of the complex doubleness that informs all of Joyce's writing. And it is important to note that Joyce's two most prominent characters are similarly limited—if Stephen is ultimately unable to break free of Catholicism, then Bloom is equally entrapped within the ideology of the bourgeoisie. Such limitations do not, of course, indicate limitations on the part of Joyce, suggesting that he lacks the imagination to envision a character who transcends the formative effects of such powerful social discourses. Likewise, the inability of any given character in Joyce to transcend certain stereotypes should not necessarily be taken as a criticism of the strength or imagination of that character. On the contrary, Joyce's continual depiction (from *Dubliners* onward) of characters who find it impossible to break free of the forces that have constituted them as subjects can be taken as a critique of the oppressive stasis of Dublin society in particular and of the power of such constitutive forces in general. And this motif is further reinforced when Joyce's readers are themselves lured into situations in which they are reminded of their own complicity with many of the same stereotypical ideas subscribed to by characters like Stephen and Bloom. For example, most readers find Bloom's kindness and sentimentality attractive, but in doing so they may be showing their own acceptance of various sentimental bourgeois myths.[12]

Joyce's theme of the futility of attempted escape from the smothering carceral oppression of turn-of-the-century Dublin resonates with Bakunin's descriptions of society in nineteenth-century Europe. Bakunin might be writing a description of the denizens of Joyce's *Dubliners* when he describes in *God and the State* the "wretched situation to which they find themselves fatally condemned by the economic organization of society." Further, Bakunin notes that the citizens of his contemporary Europe are "Reduced, intellectually and morally as well as materially, to the minimum of human existence, confined in their life like a prisoner in his prison, without horizon, without outlet," so that it is no wonder that they constantly dream of escape. For Bakunin social revolution is one valid avenue for such escape, but all too often these oppressed citizens opt for two less positive routes, "the dram-shop and the church, debauchery of the body or debauchery of the mind" (16).

For Bakunin, then, alcohol and religion join a certain vision of romantic literature as three of the most invidious strategies his contemporaries have used in an attempt to escape the unpleasantness of life in the real world. These are, of course, precisely the methods by which Joyce's Dubliners continually attempt (and fail) to break free of the bonds of Dublin. Both Joyce and Bakunin seem to realize that if miserable living conditions cause people to turn to religion as a form of escape, then it is clearly in the interest of institutional religion to keep living conditions as miserable as possible without triggering social revolution. And one of the most effective means for doing so is alcohol, which contributes to the misery of contemporary life while at the same time sapping the kinds of energies that might be turned to genuine social reform. In suggesting a certain complicity between religion and alcoholism as similar forms of "debauchery" and "licentiousness," Bakunin not only employs a typical Joycean device by turning the rhetoric of religion against itself, but he also recognizes a relationship that is frequently hinted at in Joyce's work. It is no accident, for example, that when Tom Kernan's friends come to convince him to turn to religion in "Grace" they do so while drinking stout (*Dubliners* 162).

And, when Bloom thinks of the rats that sometimes get into the vats of alcohol in breweries, his typical chain-of-association process of thinking immediately leads him to religion: "Drink themselves bloated as big as a collie floating. Dead drunk on the porter. *Drink till they puke again like Christians*" (125, my emphasis). As usual with Bloom this seemingly innocent remark carries a great deal of significance, and Joyce was certainly aware of the inherent moral contradiction in a religion that purports to provide spiritual leadership in a society in which alcoholism is a rampant and crippling problem while that religion itself includes the imbibing of alcohol in its holiest official sacrament.

Joyce's strategy here of implicating Christianity in the kinds of abject physical images (e.g., rats and vomit) from which it attempts to distance itself is one that he uses frequently.[13] And his clear understanding of Christianity as a rejection of physical life on earth strongly recalls that of Bakunin, who consistently excoriates religion for its refusal to recognize the realities of human material existence. For Bakunin, "Real humanity presents a mixture of all that is most sublime and beautiful with all that is vilest and most monstrous in the world," but Christians fail to understand this mixture, seeing humanity as a midpoint somewhere between the poles of divinity and bestiality: "They either will not or cannot understand that these three terms are really but one, and that to separate them is to destroy them" (27).

The mixture of the high and the low that Bakunin here acclaims as the essence of real humanity strongly anticipates Bakhtin's emphasis on the carnival as an image of the intermingling of the discourses of different social classes, an image of obvious relevance to the polyphonic writing of Joyce. Bakunin's acceptance of the "vile" and the "monstrous" particularly recalls Bakhtin's praise for the focus on the "material lower bodily stratum" in Rabelais.

But this same "lower bodily stratum" receives significant attention in Joyce as well, much to the chagrin of critics like Karl Radek, who have consequently found Joyce's work vulgar and disgusting. Leopold Bloom, taking an easy pleasure in almost all of the natural processes of his body, is the most vivid exemplification of the acceptance of the physical in Joyce. And it is significant that the one crucial physical activity in which Bloom cannot take pleasure is sexual intercourse and that his inability to enjoy sex—triggered by the trauma of the death of his infant son Rudy and the fear of similar results arising from Molly's subsequent pregnancies—is directly related to the unavailability of adequate techniques for birth control in Catholic Ireland. Even the down-to-earth Bloom is unable to escape torment as a result of the rejection of the physical that is so central to the prevailing ideology of his native Dublin.

The ethereal Stephen Dedalus, meanwhile, not only suffers from this ideology, but exemplifies it. Stephen, too, is unable to experience any emotionally satisfying sexual relations, but in his case the inability arises because sex and women are for him central images of the physicality and mortality that he finds so nauseating. At least Bloom can fantasize about sex, but it is clear that Stephen would much prefer that the whole dirty concept simply didn't exist. These attitudes are typical of Bloom and Stephen, with Bloom consistently trying to work within the system, as it were, and Stephen hoping to escape the system entirely. Bloom's dream of escaping the doldrums of bourgeois Dublin is itself thoroughly bourgeois—he wants to have a nice house in the country. Stephen's dream of escaping the realities of Dublin through his art— and through his flight to France—are, on the other hand, radically anti-bourgeois. But they are fundamentally religious, despite his professed apostasy, and Bakunin's comments on the ineffectiveness of religion as a means of escaping bourgeois society predict (accurately) that Stephen's project is doomed to fail.

Stephen's theory of rebellion involves a radically nonconformist rejection of all traditional symbols of authority, but his praxis involves the emulation of subversive heroes who then merely become substitute figures of authority. Interestingly, Stephen's heroes tend to resemble Bakunin's own. We find, for example, that when Stephen was at school all of his spare time "was passed in the company of subversive writers whose gibes and violence of speech set up a ferment in his brain before they passed out of it into his crude writings" (*Portrait* 78). These subversive writers sound like the kind that Bakunin might admire. Indeed, despite his distaste for romanticism, Bakunin expresses a great deal of admiration for Byron, Stephen's own favorite rebel poet.[14] But then, in the late-nineteenth and early-twentieth centuries nearly every young man with even a touch of the artist identified with Byron. For example, Byron is a favorite of Little Chandler, the would-be poetic rebel of "A Little Cloud," and ranks high on the list of role models produced by Bernard, the artist-figure in Virginia Woolf's *The Waves*: "I changed and changed; was Hamlet, was Shelley, was the hero, whose name I now forget, of a novel by Dostoevsky; was for a whole term, incredibly,

Napoleon; but was Byron chiefly" (249).[15] Even the prosaic Leopold
Bloom once identified with Byron. Molly tells us in her soliloquy that
he used to go about "trying to look like Lord Byron" (*Ulysses* 612). And
he almost fooled her, too, until she found out that there was "not an
ounce of it in his composition." Molly hopes that Stephen will prove to
be more Byronic (637).

Significantly, the most important invocation of Byron in *Portrait*
occurs in a passage in which Stephen literally enacts the role of Byronic
hero. Asked by his schoolmates Heron, Boland, and Nash to name the
"best" poet, Stephen rejects Tennyson as a "rhymester" and opts
instead for Byron, whereupon the three boys accuse Byron of heresy
and immorality and attack Stephen in an attempt to force a retraction.[16]
The retraction does not come, because this abuse only helps to
strengthen Stephen's vision of himself as Byronic hero—it has, in fact,
precisely the desired effect, the resultant suffering aiding in Stephen's
efforts at self-romanticization. This kind of glorification of suffering
and sacrifice is for Joyce one of the principal reasons why the Irish have
proved so susceptible to oppression—if it is good to suffer, then the
Irish should bear their oppression with stoic acceptance, much in the
mode of the quiescent "Shantih, shantih, shantih" with which Eliot
ends *The Waste Land*.[17] Religion is again implicated in this glorification
of suffering, with Christ himself being its principal exemplar. Thus,
when Stephen is persecuted by his schoolmates in *Portrait* for his
defense of Byron, that persecution is clearly linked to the suffering of
Christ. The boys restrain Stephen in an overt echo of the crucifixion:
"Nash pinioned his arms behind while Boland seized a long cabbage
stump which was lying in the gutter. Struggling and kicking under the
cuts of the cane and the blows of the knotty stump Stephen was borne
back against a barbed wire fence" (82).

Such Christian imagery within a context of suffering and sacrifice
occurs frequently in Joyce's work, as with the persecution of Bloom and
HCE when they become figures of Christ. Indeed, the garment that
identifies Bloom as Christ in "Circe" is inscribed "IHS," presumably
the Latin initials for Jesus Hominum Salvator, but Joyce conflates
Christ with suffering by having Molly earlier identify these initials as
meaning "I have suffered" (*Ulysses* 66). Similarly, when Gabriel Conroy
dreamily contemplates the "heroic" suffering of Michael Furey at the
end of "The Dead," he does so amid a barrage of imagery that makes it

impossible to miss the suggested parallel between the death of Furcy and the death of Christ.[18]

Links between Stephen and Christ are drawn throughout *Portrait*, like in Stephen's own repeated association of his friend Cranly with John the Baptist. In the famous pandybat episode of *Portrait*, Stephen is punished partly because Father Dolan is in a bad mood over the recent misconduct of Simon Moonan, Tusker Boyle, and their fellow smugglers. Fleming makes this association clear: "And we are all to be punished for what other fellows did?" (43). The obvious intertextual referent here is to the myth of the fall of humanity, which functions so importantly throughout Joyce's writing—we are all to be punished for the Original Sin of Adam and Eve. Stephen rejects this kind of suffering, however. This link with fallen mankind would make Stephen no different from anyone else, and it is clear that he—always wanting to be special—prefers a link to Christ, who also was "punished for what other fellows did," but in a unique way.

Joyce himself reverses Stephen's attitude by consistently rejecting Christ as an effective role model while at the same time embracing the fall of humanity as a fortunate one—the "phoenix culpum" pun proliferating throughout *Finnegans Wake* indicating that the Fall led not to death but to rebirth. Bakunin views the Fall in very much the same way, arguing that the original sin and resultant expulsion from the Garden of Eden delivered mankind from a benighted prehistory of blind obedience to divine authority and made it possible to be truly human.

> Man has emancipated himself; he has separated himself from animality and constituted himself as a man; he has begun his distinctively human history and development by an act of disobedience and science—that is, by *rebellion* and by *thought*. (12)

The echo of Nietzsche's distaste for "the crucified" is quite strong in the fierceness of Joyce's distaste for Christ as a figure of self-sacrifice, an association that Vincent Pecora recognizes: "Like Nietzsche, Joyce links a philosophical skepticism, and a belief in the primacy of individual passion, to a questioning of traditional Christian values" (237). Pecora also notes that Stephen participates in this motif as well, and, indeed, Buttigieg, within a context in which he emphasizes Joyce's affinities with Nietzsche, points out the identification of Stephen with

Christ ("*A Portrait*" 84). But, as usual, Joyce's biting satire here has both a general philosophical target (the Christian privileging of self-sacrifice) and a specific political target within the context of his contemporary Ireland. G. J. Watson notes that the Irish nationalist movement espoused a belief in the necessity of blood sacrifice for national redemption—as evidenced by the sacrificial character of Yeats's Cathleen ni Houlihan. Having its roots in ancient pagan mythology, this cult of sacrifice is able to coexist quite comfortably with Christianity, and by the time of Joyce it had become a political byword, resulting in "a conviction of the necessity for a periodic blood-sacrifice to keep alive the National Spirit" (Watson 46).[19]

Joyce's treatment of the admiration of sacrifice by both Stephen and Gabriel indicates his attitude toward this aspect of Irish politics. Stephen himself (always able to criticize others for attitudes that he himself exemplifies) makes a clear reference to this issue in his characterization of Ireland as "the old sow that eats her farrow" (*Portrait* 203). But it is in his depiction of the constant mode of betrayal that characterizes Irish politics (particularly in the case of Parnell) that Joyce makes his skepticism toward the efficacy of individual sacrifice most clear. Moreover, in linking Parnell's betrayal directly to the dominance of the Church in Irish society, Joyce recognizes (as did many of his contemporaries) a direct link between the Christian philosophy of sacrifice and the same notion in Irish nationalist politics.

Bakunin also sees a direct connection between the Christian emphasis on sacrifice and the insistent oppressiveness of the modern state. Indeed, he sees the apotheosis of sacrifice as perhaps the most pernicious of all the effects of religion.

> All religions are cruel, all founded on blood; for all rest principally on the idea of sacrifice—that is, on the perpetual immolation of humanity to the insatiable vengeance of divinity. In this bloody mystery man is always the victim, and the priest—a man also, but a man privileged by grace—is the divine executioner. (25–26)

Bakunin opposes this apotheosis of sacrifice in various ways, including the appropriation of Christ not as a figure of quiescent suffering but of bold resistance to the "representatives of the official morality and public order" (75). Bakunin even employs his own version of the mythic method by depicting his ideal of an "absolute science" (which, like Wallace Stevens's "major man," would never be achieved but merely striven for) as a new materialist Christ (34–35).

But for Bakunin the ultimate mythical figure of the revolutionary hero is Satan. Satan, he suggests, is "the eternal rebel, the first free-thinker and the emancipator of worlds," and the Satanic incitement of Adam and Eve to rebellion should be a model for us all (9–10). This simultaneous acceptance of Christ and Satan as role models for the revolutionary appears designed to undermine the consistent separation of life into opposing poles that Bakunin sees as one of the most pernicious effects of religious thinking. Joyce's Stephen also turns both to Christ and to Satan as role models. In the moment that he rejects the priest-hood, Stephen echoes the Miltonic Satan's motto of *non serviam* by noting that his "destiny was to be elusive of social or religious orders" (*Portrait* 162). In his subsequent conversation with Cranly, Stephen substantiates this identification. Asked why he will not at least feign some religious sentiment to please his mother (thus foreshadowing his fateful refusal to pray over her death bed in *Ulysses*), Stephen simply answers, "I will not serve" (239). Later, in the "Circe" chapter of *Ulysses* (where so many hidden things finally come to the surface), he is even more explicit about both this motto and his all-or-nothing attitude toward his models: "The intellectual imagination! With me all or not at all. *Non serviam!*" (475).

Stephen's choice of Satan as role model is a natural one, since Satan (especially as depicted by Milton) is a prototypical figure of the proud exile, perhaps the original Byronic hero. Marshall Grossman notes that Milton's Satan served as a forerunner of developments in the literary treatment of subjectivity over the succeeding three centuries. In particular, he notes Satan's refusal to accept the limitations that are placed upon him, a refusal that made him a hero of the romantic imagination (consider Shelley's Satanic Prometheus) and a prime figure of the romantic attempt to escape temporality.

> Milton's portrait of Satan anticipates the development of literary subjectivity over the next three centuries. As Adam and Eve's self-authorship represents the subject of the realistic novel, the self developed in conflict with a given set of historical circumstances, Satan's free-running fantasies represent the autonomy of the self achieved through the rejection of history characteristic of modernism. (Grossman 36)

Whether or not this "rejection of history" is indeed characteristic of modernism is clearly dependent upon how one defines *modernism*. And, though Grossman's suggestion that the romantics sought an escape from the temporal seems consonant with Bakunin's reading of romanticism (except for Byron), Grossman's Satan is very different from Bakunin's; for Bakunin it is the rebellion of Satan that makes history possible in the first place.

This difference between Grossman and Bakunin in their reading of Satan helps to explain how Satan can be a hero to both Bakunin and Stephen. For Stephen, Satan is indeed a figure of escape from the temporal, a figure that differs not all that much from God Himself. Stephen's characteristic "all or not at all" swings between God and Satan are partially made possible by the fact that he views them both as images of escape from the physical world and the nightmare of history. The fact that Stephen in so many cases seems to exemplify both Bakunin's position and attitudes that Bakunin would abhor can certainly be read as an indication of Stephen's own inconsistency. But it is probably more useful (and to the point) to recognize that this "inconsistency" arises from the inherent doubleness of Joyce's writing, which constantly reflects multiple and even conflicting points of view.

Despite the multiple positions reflected in Joyce's writing, it seems clear that Joyce's own attitudes are very similar to Bakunin's in many ways. In addition to the parallels discussed in this chapter, Bakunin's ideas about history and about the social constitution of the human subject also resemble Joyce's. Even the polyvocality of Joyce's writing echoes Bakunin's recommendation of an appeal to multiple authorities, despite the fact that what one might see as Joyce's ambivalence seems so different from the fierce devotion to revolution that drove Bakunin. Of course, Bakunin retains the right to be the final arbiter in his use of authorities, accepting some and rejecting others, whereas Joyce operates in a mode of all-inclusiveness that sees him refuse to accept that arbiter's role. Perhaps the fundamental difference between Bakunin and Joyce lies not in their ultimate goals as in their confidence that those goals can (or even should) be met. Bakunin works with the conviction that his program can be realized and that this realization would result in a dramatic positive benefit for mankind. Joyce, on the other hand, is far from convinced that he can topple the oppressive institutions of church and state that he so despises. And even if he could defeat these twin foes, he seems to feel that it is important to avoid setting himself up as an alternative authority, which would result in a mere repetition of the attitudes of his old enemies.

By the definition that I have employed elsewhere,[20] one might say that Bakunin's faith in the possibility of dramatic reform is a modernist one, while Joyce's relative skepticism is postmodernist, though there is an obvious danger in attempting to use a single scheme simultaneously to characterize both artists and political activists. This "modernist" Bakunin has little in common with the picture of the modernist as distant, disinterested, nail parer that has been so historically popular and can frequently be found even today. However, Eliot, who himself contributed to that picture of the modernist artist, can still easily be read as a modernist, believing that his poetry can contribute meaningfully to his conservative political project. Both Bakunin and Eliot, in short, can be read as modernists, despite their vast differences in ideology. It is, however, harder to read Joyce in this way, despite the facts that Joyce's politics resembles Bakunin's in so many ways and certain formal features of Joyce's writing resemble Eliot's. That Joyce could have been read for so long as a paradigm of the godlike, invisible, modernist artist (and that he is still often read that way) certainly tells us something about the way Joyce's polyphonic writing lends itself to multiple interpretations. Perhaps more importantly, it tells us a great deal about the history of literary criticism and about the ways in which the styles and concerns of literary critics have changed during the course of this century.

Chapter Two

Rabelais and Joyce's World: The Poetics of Inverse Transgression

Joyce, Rabelais, Bakhtin

In *Ulysses* we learn that Molly Bloom is something of a fan of soft-core pornography, examples of which (like the *Sweets of Sin* that runs as a refrain through the text) her husband often brings to her to keep her entertained. However, as she reveals in the interior monologue that ends the book, her tastes in such literature are rather pedestrian. More fantastic or literary explorations of human sexuality (like those contained in the work of François Rabelais) are not at all to her taste. She thus has no use whatsoever for "some of those books he brings me the works of Master François Somebody supposed to be a priest about a child born out of her ear because her bumgut fell out a nice word for any priest to write and her a—e as if any fool wouldn't know what that meant" (619). Molly's critique here of the story of the birth of Gargantua represents the only overt allusion to Rabelais in all of *Ulysses*. Moreover, there are no obvious allusions to Rabelais in *Dubliners* or *A Portrait of the Artist as a Young Man* and only a few passing mentions in *Finnegans Wake*. In addition, Joyce himself once claimed in a letter to Harriet Weaver never to have read Rabelais and to know Rabelais's work primarily through his reading of Sainéan's *La Langue de Rabelais*, a book that was not published until after *Ulysses* (Joyce, *Collected Letters* 255).

Nevertheless, critics have long recognized affinities between the work of Joyce (especially *Ulysses* and *Finnegans Wake*) and that of Rabelais, both in terms of the subject material and philosophical attitudes embedded in their texts and in terms of the exorbitantly heteroglossic encyclopedic styles that they use to express that material and those attitudes. Moreover, given the importance of Rabelais to Bakhtin, the affinities between Joyce and Rabelais are obviously crucial for any reading of Joyce's work within the context of Bakhtin's theories. If, for Bakhtin, the epic poet Homer serves as the emodiment of unchallenged monological authority, then it is certainly Rabelais who serves for Bakhtin as the embodiment of transgression against authority, whether through style or content. Indeed, his now-famous book on Rabelais is clearly the single work that has done most to popularize Bakhtin's ideas in the West, so much so that the ensuing widely held critical picture of Bakhtin as a thinker of carnivalesque emancipation probably represents a distortion of the real emphases of Bakhtin's career. Keeping this possibility in mind, reading Joyce through Bakhtin's reading of Rabelais suggests interpretations of Joyce's use of carnivalesque imagery that go well beyond a mere acknowledgment that Joyce's texts often flagrantly break the rules of polite society—and of conventional literature—pointing toward the real social and political significance of this rule breaking.

Of course, Rabelais has often been included on lists of previous writers cited in an attempt to characterize Joyce's complex vision. Thus, Richard Kain suggests that Joyce's

> tone is difficult to analyze: at one time it seems to partake of the carefree gusto of Rabelais or the comic *esprit* of Sterne, again of the savage indignation of Swift. . . . But frequently it has the mood of the aging Flaubert, devoting his energy to the excoriation of human falsity and stupidity. (193)

Karen Lawrence, meanwhile, places *Ulysses* in the generic tradition of the anatomy (i.e., Menippean satire) of Burton, Rabelais, and Sterne. Further, she suggests that in *Ulysses* Joyce's "nose-thumbing at convention is very much like Rabelais' in *Gargantua and Pantagruel*, both in its mélange of discourses and its exorbitant catalogues" (109).

In addition to such important stylistic and philosophical affinities, there are numerous instances of specific passages in Rabelais and Joyce that point to similarities between the two authors. Thus, Joanne Rea notes specific verbal echoes of Rabelais in passages in both *Ulysses* and *Portrait* beyond Molly's obvious allusion to Rabelais in her monologue.[1] Other parallel passages can be found as well. For example, Panurge's interpretation of the ringing of the bells of Varennes in book

3 of *Gargantua and Pantagruel* as speaking to his own condition (363) anticipates the differing interpretations of the bells of St. George by Stephen and Bloom, both of whom read the bells through their own subjective styles and concerns when they hear them in the "Ithaca" chapter of *Ulysses* (578). And this parallel, which speaks to a central concern with signification and interpretation on the part of both Rabelais and Joyce, is far from trivial. For one thing, Panurge's interpretation of the bells as urging him to wed participates in an extensive treatment of women and marriage in book 3 that has largely to do with Panurge's concern with being cuckolded should he take a wife. Panurge's general fear of being abused by women participates in an important medieval tradition, as Bakhtin notes (*Rabelais* 239–44). But it also clearly anticipates the theme of Bloom's cuckoldry in *Ulysses*, as well as the general theme of feminine abuse that is so central to Bloom's encounter with Bella Cohen in the "Circe" chapter of *Ulysses*.

Moreover, Bakhtin suggests that church bells form an important part of the carnivalesque imagery of Rabelais. Thus, we have juxtaposed in Rabelais a conventional use of such bells as images of religious authority with an opposing use of bells as images of carnivalesque celebration. For example, chapters 17–20 of book 1 of *Gargantua and Pantagruel* relate the story of Gargantua's theft of the sacred bells of the cathedral of Notre Dame in order to hang them on the harness of his giant horse, a movement that Bakhtin sees as representative of the important carnivalesque motif of ritual uncrowning (*Rabelais* 213–15). This story also involves a typical Rabelaisian clash of languages. The learned church doctor Master Janotus tries to convince Gargantua to return the bells, employing a variety of mock-scholarly arguments (mostly couched in his own particular brand of Latin), including an appeal to the authority of the Gloria Patri: "*in nomine Patris et Filii et Spiritus Sancti . . . qui vivit et regnat per omnia secula seculorum*" (Rabelais 78). On the other hand, Rabelais also provides a reminder that Master Janotus's pretentious attitude toward the bells is not the only one, supplying also the point of view of the "secular poet" Pontanus, for whom the bells are little more than noisemakers ringing out not sacred Latin but "ding-dong, bing-bang, clitter-clatter" (78).

Master Janotus's scholastic style of argumentation is somewhat reminiscent of the "applied Aquinas" intellect of Stephen Dedalus, and it is worth noting that the Gloria Patri continually runs through Stephen's Catholic-interpellated mind throughout *Ulysses*. It is not surprising, then, that when Stephen hears the bells of St. George they speak to him in Church Latin, ringing out a modified form of a standard Catholic prayer for the dying: *"Liliata rutilantium. Turma circumdet. / Iubilantium te virginum. Chorus excipiat."*[2] But for the prosaic Bloom, who here plays Pontanus to Stephen's Master Janotus, the bells ring out a much more secular message: *"Heigho, heigho. / Heigho, heigho"* (578). The contrast between the reactions of Stephen and Bloom thus constitute precisely the kind of clash of high and low discourses that Bakhtin sees as fundamental to the writing of Rabelais.

Panurge also figures for Rabelais as an image of linguistic multiplicity, as when he shifts among German, Italian, Dutch, Spanish, Danish, Hebrew, Greek, Latin, and invented nonsense languages in his initial encounter with Pantagruel in chapter 9 of book 2. In addition to providing a striking dramatization of Bakhtin's concept of heteroglossia, this encounter clearly anticipates the multilingual background of Joyce's texts, especially *Finnegans Wake*. It is no surprise, then, that Vivien Mercier, placing the *Wake* in the tradition of macaronic literature, cites Rabelais as being among Joyce's most important forerunners in this regard (32). And, though Mercier argues that Joyce's affinity with the macaronic tradition lies more in his use of archetypal figures and imagery than at a verbal level, it is clear that the linguistic experimentation of Rabelais has much in common with Joyce's method in the *Wake*.

Leo Spitzer, in a historical survey of the relationship between literature and language, notes that writers of all ages have engaged in linguistic experimentation because "the trite and petrified in language is never sufficient for the needs of expression felt by a strong personality" (15). Spitzer's discussion of the neologisms of Rabelais centers on what he calls the "autonomy of the word," on the Rabelaisian belief that words not only relate to things, but themselves *are* things, with a reality of their own (15–22). This emphasis on the materiality of language again both anticipates Bakhtin and brings to mind the intense "thingness" of the words of *Finnegans Wake*. Indeed, Strother Purdy, in a discussion of Wakean language, cites Spitzer's argument as "a basis for a demonstration of the true likeness between Joyce and Rabelais" (57).

Rosalie Colie, like Mercier, describes the work of Rabelais in terms of the macaronic tradition but places more emphasis on the verbal element.

Words are displayed, played with, used in their multiple meanings—and, when the available stock of words runs low, Rabelais
never hesitates—once more, in emulation of the divine Creator—
to create new ones. . . . The macaronic aspect of the book is one
such use of language: all the ebullience of linguistic alternative is
evoked, and with that, a critique of language itself as a means of
expressing reality. (65)

Moreover, Colie also notes the sudden changes in size and scale that
occur in *Gargantua and Pantagruel*, as well as Rabelais's knack for the
creation of multiple meaning: "Anything in the book may mean just
what it appears to mean; or it may mean something else altogether, or,
best of all, it may mean both what it appears to mean *and* something
else altogether as well" (48).

The strongest affinities between Rabelais and Joyce would appear,
then, to reside in these attitudes toward language rather than in any
specific carnivalesque or folkloric contents in their texts.[3] In particular,
Rabelais anticipates the complex signifying practice employed in
Joyce's later work, a practice that among other things places heavy
demands on the readers of both authors. Emphasizing the difficulty of
Rabelais's texts, Bakhtin describes them in terms that should seem
highly familiar to readers of Joyce.

Rabelais' work is extremely difficult. It contains a great number of
allusions, which were often understood only by his contemporaries and sometimes by his closest friends alone. The work is
encyclopedic: it contains many special terms referring to different
branches of knowledge and technology. Finally, it contains a great
number of new and difficult words which Rabelais was the first to
introduce into the French language. It is obvious that he needs
commentaries and interpretations. (*Rabelais* 110)

As Bakhtin also points out, Rabelais often acknowledges the complexity of *Gargantua and Pantagruel* within the work itself. Moreover,
these acknowledgments often parallel similar passages in Joyce. For
example, in the author's prologue at the beginning of book 2 of *Gargantua and Pantagruel*, Rabelais signals his readers that his text will repay
close and careful reading and expresses his wish that he could have

"every man put aside his proper business, take no care for his trade, and forget his own affairs, in order to devote himself entirely to this book" (167). This self-parodic acknowledgment of the effort required for readers to process the encyclopedic detail of Rabelais's book is very much in the same spirit as Joyce's famous call in *Finnegans Wake* for an "ideal reader suffering from an ideal insomnia" who can devote himself entirely to the study of the text (120.13–4).

Bakhtin's readings of Rabelais call attention to a number of aspects of Rabelais's writing that resemble Joyce's. In particular, Bakhtin argues that Rabelais's work, through the power of laughter and an emphasis on the physical realities of life, undermines the rejection of physical life that underlies the rigid, hierarchical, authoritarian structure of medieval Catholicism (and, by extension, of Stalinism). Bakhtin's use of the Catholic Church as an image of oppression is already suggestive of Joyce's Irish-Catholic context, of course, but what is particularly crucial is the clear way Bakhtin uses the breakup of the medieval worldview at the beginning of the Renaissance as an image of the kind of cultural crisis that he sees in modern Russia and that so many modernist writers have seen in the modern world as a whole. For Bakhtin, Rabelais's work clearly grows out of this crisis, though Bakhtin at different times emphasizes rather different aspects of this relationship. In "Forms of Time and Chronotope in the Novel," for example, Bakhtin sees Rabelais as a recuperative writer attempting to pick up the pieces of a shattered medieval world and working through his encyclopedic constructions "to gather together on a new material base a world that, due to the dissolution of the medieval world view, is disintegrating" (*Dialogic Imagination* 205). In *Rabelais and His World*, on the other hand, Bakhtin treats Rabelais much more as a transgressive writer who is attempting through his revolutionary texts to bring down a medieval power structure that is still in place, though faltering. The carnival on which Bakhtin focuses in this book is purely emancipatory and anti-authoritarian, representing a "temporary liberation from the prevailing truth and from the established order; it marked the suspension of all hierarchical rank, privileges, norms, and prohibitions" (10). Among other things, these changing emphases may merely mean that Bakhtin's interests and ideas varied at different times in his career. But the combination of these two readings of Rabelais also serves to suggest that Bakhtin was never the kind of wildly defiant opponent of all forms of order and authority that he is sometimes seen to be in western appropriations of his work.[4]

In addition, Bakhtin's somewhat contradictory readings of Rabelais are entirely appropriate given Bakhtin's own emphasis on the complex and contradictory nature of the Renaissance itself as a time informed by violent clashes among radically different worldviews. It is the ability to reflect these clashes that gives Rabelais's work much of its dialogic character, just as one might see the intense dialogism of Joyce's texts as growing out of the profound social and cultural contradictions of the modern world. For Bakhtin, of course, it is at such fundamental levels that the informing characteristics of genres arise, so it is perhaps no surprise that the most important similarities between Joyce and Rabelais are broad generic ones rather than parallels in specific passages or motifs.

The doubleness of Bakhtin's readings of Rabelais is also highly appropriate given Bakhtin's own emphasis on double-voiced writing. But this doubleness also serves as a reminder that any literary motif (especially extreme motifs such as one finds in Rabelais or Joyce) can be read in varying ways. Reading Joyce through Bakhtin's Rabelais suggests that Joycean motifs like the use of scatological imagery or of radical mixtures of different discourses serve as transgressive assaults on official authority and as joyous carnivalesque celebrations of life. But the carnival itself can be read in various ways. For example, numerous critics of Bakhtin have pointed out that the medieval carnival was fully sanctioned by the Church, which presumably saw the carnival as an opportunity for the harmless release of potentially subversive energies that might have been building beneath the oppressive weight of Church authority in the Middle Ages.[5] In addition, carnival motifs such as ritual uncrowning often involved a considerable amount of violence, which was typically directed at precisely the marginal social groups that Bakhtin sees as being liberated by carnivalesque transgression.[6]

It is also important to note that critics have become more and more aware in the past decade or so that Bakhtin's study of Rabelais is importantly informed not only by considerations of Rabelais in his historical context but by Bakhtin's historical context as well. In particular, the book can be read at least partially as a disguised polemic against Stalinism.[7] *Rabelais and His World* is informed by a powerful faith in the revolutionary potential of the carnival, and especially in the revolutionary potential of carnivalesque literature as an enemy of official authority. But, as Michael Holquist has pointed out (in "Bakhtin"), the authority in question may be as much Stalinism as medieval Catholicism, and Bakhtin's emphasis on revolution can be read as an attempt to salvage the Russian Revolution from the perversion of Stalinism. On the other hand, to dismiss Bakhtin's book merely as a diatribe against Stalin is inappropriate as well. This is essentially the approach taken by Richard Berrong, who concludes that *Rabelais and His World* "is an allegorical work of political criticism and theory" that shows admirable courage in its assault on Stalin, but that the book has no "real value as historical criticism" in its account of Rabelais (109). Samuel Kinser, on the other hand, finds Berrong's own figuration of Rabelais's historical context inadequate and concludes that Bakhtin's book is in fact inspiring as a study of Rabelais, even if its status as a contemporary political polemic requires that some of its specific descriptions of Rabelais and his context are inaccurate.[8]

Kinser also argues that Bakhtin's real theme in *Rabelais and His World* concerns not Rabelais's use of the folkloric tradition as a weapon against authority so much as Rabelais's signifying practice, which involves a complex "systematization of images" and an "encouragement of oblique readings of text" (257). In particular, Kinser argues that Bakhtin's reading of Rabelais reveals a subversive potential of literature that lies not in populist content but in literary style. Bakhtin thus shows "fiction's capacity—and hence also criticism's capacity, in dealing with such fiction—for bewildering recursive communication (who is the author? where is the reader?) and bitingly ambivalent polysemy (how does a text refer, coordinate, mean?)" (258). The "oblique" method of reading that Kinser sees as being endorsed by Bakhtin has clear applications to Joyce's texts and might prove especially useful for reading Joyce's relation to his literary predecessors. For Kinser, Bakhtin uses Rabelais to make points not only about both Rabelais and Stalinism but also about the relationship between written texts and historical contexts in general.

Lukács, Joyce, and the Pathology of Modernism

Kinser's interpretation of the Rabelais book essentially supports the contention of Morson and Emerson that Bakhtin's reputation as an apostle of wildly antinomian rule breaking has been greatly exaggerated. Such revisionary readings of the revolutionary potential of carnivalesque imagery also speak to the criticisms of Georg Lukács, who saw the elements of Joyce's work that one might label as Rabelaisian as symptomatic of a decadence that Lukács felt to be characteristic of the modernist project. Lukács's comments on Joyce and on modernism in general are worth reviewing in some detail because they remain highly influential even among Marxist critics who seem in many ways to have reversed Lukács and to have found a powerful political potential in Joyce's writing. In essence, Lukács sees in the dazzling verbal constructions of modernist writers a tendency toward the kind of reification that he finds rampant in modern capitalist society. He criticizes Joyce and other modernists for making technique an end in itself, without regard to the human realities that technique is supposed to convey. But for Lukács this "negation of outward reality" is not a failure of Joyce's writing. On the contrary, it is a complete success, in that for Lukács Joyce's ideological intention is to effect just this divorce from reality and thereby to disengage his texts from reality. And this disengagement is in direct complicity with the main cultural thrust of bourgeois society. Modernist texts are thus for Lukács not dynamic documents, interacting with history in a positive and productive way. Instead, they are sterile artifacts, divorced from history and totally caught up in the inexorable drive of capitalist society to convert all it touches into mere commodities.

Much of Lukács's criticism of Joyce and other modernist writers has to do with his belief that their formal fragmentation participates in a process of reification that is itself central to the fragmentation of social life under capitalism. This critique is thus related to a tendency toward totalization that inheres in all orthodox forms of Marxism, a tendency that is clearly implicated (whether he intended it or not) in Bakhtin's criticisms of monological and centripetal thought of all kinds.[9] On the other hand, many of Lukács's comments on modernism are not necessarily central to Marxist thought, as the opposing views of Marxists like Brecht, Benjamin, and Adorno illustrate. In fact, Lukács's views often smack of a rather traditional humanism and even of a revulsion at the depiction of sexual and excremental processes in many modernist texts. In his important essay "The Ideology of Modernism," Lukács grants that modernist texts can contain a great deal of naturalistic detail, a suggestion with which any reader of *Ulysses* would have to agree. But the problem with modernism for Lukács is that these details are intended not as a representation of typical elements of reality; instead, they are mere allegorical stand-ins for abstract ideas: "Modernist literature thus replaces concrete typicality with abstract particularity" (*Realism* 43). The consistently allegorical quality of modernist literature implies that, despite the importation of abundant and vivid details from Dublin life into Joyce's texts, those texts are not "about" Dublin at all but about some generalized abstract city with no genuine relevance to the concrete specifics of human life on the streets of any real city: "Joyce uses Dublin, Kafka and Musil the Hapsburg Monarchy, as the locus of their masterpieces. But the locus they lovingly depict is little more than a backcloth; it is not basic to their artistic intention" (21).[10]

Lukács does not clearly explain how it is that we can detect this intention in modernist art, and his only concrete example of the failure of modernist art to address the "typicalities" of the human condition concerns what he sees as an "obsession with the pathological," which he compares to a similar fascination in Freudian psychoanalysis (*Realism* 30). Lukács offers Robert Musil's Moosbrugger—"a mentally-retarded sexual pervert with homicidal tendencies"—as his principal example of this obsession, but he hints that Joyce's focus on the streams of consciousness of his individual characters bespeaks a similar fascination with the aberrant. Of course, it is far from clear whether this charge has any relevance to Joyce—sex and excrement may make some squeamish readers uncomfortable, but one could make an excellent argument that it is this discomfort itself (and not the sexual and excremental imagery that triggers it) that is pathological. On the other hand, Lukács's critique of modernist texts like Musil's *The Man Without Qualities* raises issues that are worth examining in some detail.

Much of the tension of Musil's book arises from a dialogic interaction between the title character (the utterly rational Ulrich) and the sinister psychopath Christian Moosbrugger. One might view this dialogue as a clash between the Apollonian and the Dionysian as described by Nietzsche, and indeed a resurrection of Dionysian energies has been seen as central to the modernist project.[11] But Moosbrugger's lurid crimes go far beyond any philosophical representation of the irrational as an alternative to the Enlightenment tradition. Musil's text describes at least one of these crimes in graphic detail.

> Moosbrugger had killed a street-woman, a prostitute of the lowest type, in a horrifying manner. The reporters had described in detail a throat-wound extending from the larynx to the back of the neck, as well as the two stab-wounds in the breast, which had pierced the heart, the two others on the left side of the back, and the cutting off of the breasts, which could almost be detached from the body.

They had expressed their abhorrence of it, but they did not leave off until they had counted thirty-five stabs in the abdomen and described the long slash from the navel to the sacrum, which continued up the back in a multitude of smaller slashes, while the throat showed the marks of throttling. (75)

The implied suggestion here that newspaper reports of the crime showed a prurient fascination with it does not disguise the fact that the text itself seems to show the same fascination, and it is no wonder that Lukács singles out Musil's text as an example of the pathological focus of modernism. And Musil is by no means an isolated instance. A certain strain of modern literature—especially the French tradition running from Sade through Lautréamont to Genet, Artaud, Bataille, and others—derives important energies from abject descriptions of cruelty, violence, and perversion. But it is also worth remembering that such images appear frequently in the "mainstream" texts of modernism, including not only the crimes of Musil's Moosbrugger but such other instances as the suicide of Virginia Woolf's Septimus Smith, the crimes (and subsequent death) of William Faulkner's Joe Christmas, and the execution-slaying of Franz Kafka's Joseph K.

Critics have often focused on the crystalline formal perfection of modernist texts, seeing this intense emphasis on structure and form as an attempt to escape from the messiness of historical reality. But, in point of fact, modernist texts are often messy, indeed, importing the most abject and horrific details from the external world into the texts themselves. However, as Musil's dialogue with the newspaper indicates, there is nothing so perverse and pathological in modernist texts that it cannot also be found in real life. Perhaps Lukács's charges of a focus on the pathological in modernist writing should therefore not be casually dismissed, if only as a counter to the tendency to see modernist texts as inhabiting some ideal aesthetic realm where "pathological" events simply have no place. Lukács, of course, sees the abjection of modernist texts as a turning away from the world, with individual artists focusing on the personal miseries of pathological individuals to the exclusion of any interest in public social issues. Yet Musil's depiction of Moosbrugger resonates with his evocation of a widespread sense of historical crisis in the waning days of the Austro-Hungarian Empire; the ordeal of Kafka's K. participates in this same crisis and in the feeling of helplessness in the face of massive inhuman institutions that is so much a part of the experience of modernity; Woolf's description of the postwar trauma of Septimus Smith is part of an antiwar motif that informs almost all of her work as well as a specific criticism of the treatment of World War I veterans by British society; and the travails of Faulkner's Christmas constitute a devastating exposure of the brutality and stupidity of racism.

The experiences of unusual, even pathological individuals can have widespread social significance. Moreover, times change, and in the case of Joyce many elements that originally seemed pathological to some now seem rather tame. Few readers are shocked by now that in *Ulysses* Bloom defecates, urinates, and masturbates; that Molly copulates and menstruates; or that Stephen picks his nose. These are, after all, normal (rather than pathological) human activities, even if in 1922 it was not so normal to depict them in fiction. And after Bakhtin's work on Rabelais we can even see how to argue that the depiction of such normal activities of the "lower bodily stratum" carries a positive, transgressive, political potential through its carnivalesque leveling of the kinds of hierarchies upon which oppressive political systems are built. Indeed, Joyce typically treats such material with a Rabelaisian exuberance that bears little resemblance to the kind of loathing suggested by Lukács. On the other hand, it is also true that, in addition to the typical physical activities of everyday life, Joyce's writing contains scenes of far less ordinary subject matter, including abject scenes of violence and perversion that can rival Musil or even Bataille.

His reputation as the "great man of modern literature" notwithstanding, Joyce's writing (especially in *Finnegans Wake*) is often downright strange, and any attempt to recuperate his texts within the purely rational confines of Enlightenment reason is doomed to failure—or at least to an impoverishment of his radical texts. Despite his acceptance by the literary establishment in recent decades, Joyce shares much with the company of such marginalized figures as the "mad poets" Hölderlin, Nerval, Nietzsche, Artaud, and Roussel. And, despite the meticulous Apollonian care Joyce put into the construction of his texts, his experimental writing strategies clearly participate in the Dionysian, antirational, avant-garde movement praised by Theodor Adorno as a mode of resistance to the Enlightenment ideology of domination. Indeed, the Horkheimer/Adorno critique of reason as domination suggests that the images of cruelty and perversion that occur in the work of Joyce and others might act not as an apotheosis of irrational violence against authority but as a critique of the ostensibly rational violence by which authority is established and maintained.

Any number of modern thinkers—from Foucault's explorations of madness, to Adorno's attacks on reason, to Bakhtin's privileging of excremental imagery, to Bataille's emphasis on the subversive energies of sexuality—have suggested a powerful subversive potential in the literary depiction of material that would normally be deemed shocking or unacceptable by polite society. And it may indeed be that this kind of "direct" transgression—in which literature drags back into glaring view images and ideas that have been repressed by the powers that be—can make a genuine political statement. But within the confines of a modern bourgeois society in which transgression itself is a central defining paradigm of the status quo, the subversive power of "transgression for the sake of transgression" is open to question.[12] And the arguments of Lukács and others that such emphases on shocking transgressive images take attention away from more important social and political issues are still worth considering.

Allon White is probably entirely correct when he warns against a "false essentializing of transgression" in the works of a family of writers that includes Sade, Baudelaire, Lautréamont, Nietzsche, Bataille, Artaud, Burroughs, Pynchon, and others, in addition to Joyce ("Pigs" 60). One does not mount an effective political program merely by conducting extreme formal experiments or by filling one's work with material that is offensive to bourgeois taste. White suggests that "The question of the political dimensions of sexual and aesthetic transgression can only be answered historically" (60). Unfortunately, he never elaborates on this point, but I think what he basically means is that effective transgression requires the specification of a social dimension to this transgression. Indeed, White indicates a very Lukácsian concern that modern transgressive literature has a tendency to focus on the internal concerns and problems of isolated individuals rather than on social issues. White notes that

> It is precisely because transgression becomes subjectivized in romanticism that modern theory has the utmost difficulty in reconstituting its public domain. . . . The traditional carnival attack on social oppression gives way to a subjectivized attack on individual repression. (69)

In point of fact, for Joyce the individual *is* a public, social phenomenon. But even without that stipulation, White's argument does not provide support for those who would see Joyce as disengaged from social and political issues. Indeed, White himself exempts Joyce from some of his most telling criticisms. He argues (again echoing Lukács) that in modern transgressive literature the exuberant carnivalesque spirit valorized by Bakhtin for its political energies has been lost, both through a shift from public to private perspectives and through an emphasis on crime and violence that leads to a shift from a tone of joy and celebration to one of terror and abjection. Thus, "The whole dimension of social pleasure (the belly laugh, the amusement, the frank and shared enjoyment of communal festivity and bodily functions) is largely lost *(except perhaps in Joyce)*" ("Pigs" 61, my emphasis). Similarly, noting the prevalence of scenes of erotic violence in modern transgressive literature from Sade to Pynchon, White claims that *"with the exception of James Joyce*, the 'great transgressors' of modernism seem haunted by this need for cruelty" (65, my emphasis).[13]

And White's absolution of Joyce is highly appropriate, as Joyce quite diligently "reconstitutes" his images of transgression in the "public domain," as White advocates. Joyce's transgressions might be described as being of an "inverse" kind; they seek not to valorize violence and depravity so much as to reveal (and to condemn) the violence and depravity that lie at the heart of certain specific social and political institutions and practices in modern society. This motif of inverse transgression can be seen in many aspects of Joyce's work, not the least of which is stylistic, as his almost constant mode of parody allows him to speak with the voice of those he is seeking to condemn. Joyce also employs such issues as madness, cannibalism, and transgressive sexuality (including sadomasochism) to good inverse effect, consistently associating such imagery not with resistance to the powers that be but with the ways official power is itself established and maintained.

Madness and Religion in Joyce and Flaubert

The valorization of madness as transgression in the work of certain modern writers (and critics) may represent the clearest example of the kind of subjectivized carnival that draws White's censure. Bakhtin himself expressed doubts about the effectiveness of madness as a transgressive motif in modern texts. Invoking the energies of the medieval carnival as a metaphor for transgression, Bakhtin concludes that the modern carnivalesque is a degraded form that has lost most of its subversive force. Joyce also refuses to valorize madness, though elements of madness frequently intrude into his texts, and his work certainly participates in the widespread modern suspicion of reason as a potentially totalitarian force. But Joyce implies that the forces of reason and rationality often themselves go to insane lengths. Similarly, Joyce frequently employs abject subject matter—like cannibalism and sadomasochism—but nowhere does he propose such images as alternatives to existing society. Instead, he suggests that the structures of power in modern society are already informed by such forces.

None of Joyce's major characters are overtly mad, but it is certainly true that Joyce's writing itself does not necessarily conform to rational expectations. For example, the generation of meaning in Joyce's texts has much in common with processes like condensation and displacement through which meaning, according to Freud, is generated in dreams. Accordingly, many readers have appealed to dreams in their attempts to interpret Joyce, the most notable example probably being the tendency (after Campbell and Robinson) to try to recuperate the entire text of the *Wake* as the dream of a single sleeper.[14] Probably the best-known example of ostensibly mad writing in Joyce occurs in the "Circe" chapter of *Ulysses*, in which a series of bizarre events and transformations seem to evoke the seething irrationality of the unconscious mind. Indeed, many of the wild events of "Circe" closely parallel the fantasies of real psychotic patients, as can be seen from a comparison of Bloom's experiences in the chapter with those reported by Daniel Paul Schreber in his memoirs. Bloom's dramatic reversals of fortune in "Circe" are reminiscent of the procession from feelings of persecution to illusions of grandeur that Freud remarked, in "Psycho-Analytic Notes," in his reading of Schreber as being characteristic of paranoid patients. Even bizarre events like Bloom's gender transformation and his giving birth to numerous children recall the fantasies of Schreber, who felt that he was being "unmanned," turned into a woman so that he could become the wife of God and give birth to a new race of humans.[15]

In keeping with Schreber's swings between paranoia and megalomania, this "unmanning" does not always lend itself to such grand purposes. Initially, Schreber feels that he is being transformed into a woman so that he can be sexually abused and used for "lewd purposes" by his doctor and others, recalling the treatment of Bloom by Bella Cohen in "Circe." Indeed, Bella/Bello announces Bloom's transformation into a female by proclaiming that "you are *unmanned* and mine in earnest, a thing under yoke" (*Ulysses* 436, my emphasis). The obvious referent here is *The Odyssey*, in which the transformation of Odysseus's men into swine is described as an unmanning. By using the same phrase to indicate a gender change, Joyce subtly critiques the way the masculine has long been considered the human norm in western society, a loss of manliness thus being equated with a loss of humanity. And Bloom's gender transformation is described in great physical detail, as when Bello "bares his arm and plunges it elbowdeep in Bloom's vulva" (440). Schreber describes the details of his own unmanning in similar detail, including the "almost complete dissolution" of his penis (*Memoirs* 132) and the growth of a "pretty well-developed female bosom" (207). And, if Bloom has Ulysses as a mythic prototype, Schreber has one as well, one that links him even more closely to Bloom. His forerunner is the "Eternal Jew," who, in order to renew mankind as God's wife, "had to be *unmanned* . . . to be able to bear children" (73).

In addition to such specific parallels, Schreber's memoirs constitute among other things an extended meditation on language with highly Joycean resonances. Schreber can comment upon language from an oddly detached perspective—he lives in a world of disembodied language, a world in which he (like Beckett's Unnamable) hears himself speak words that he is convinced are not his own. Octave Mannoni notes, however, that this motif of speaking the words of others bears some striking resemblances to the literary tradition of indirect discourse (46). Joyce was a master of this technique, and his view of himself as a "scissors and paste man" represents very much an understanding that his texts were assembled from the language of others.

Schreber goes on to describe certain characteristics of the language used by the various voices he hears. He notes a tendency toward "an empty babel of ever recurring monotonous phrases in tiresome repetition" (*Memoirs* 139). When he hears birds speaking to him he notes that these birds "do not understand the *meaning* of the words they speak; but apparently they have a natural sensitivity for *similarity of sounds*" (168). And these voices regard language in an extremely literal way, seeking to convince Schreber that he need only speak something to make it so (183). The language described here by Schreber is quite typical of that which has been observed in psychotic patients, particularly those diagnosed as schizophrenic. For example, Silvano Arieti describes certain similar tendencies:

> Schizophrenics, as well as some aboriginal people, often confuse the word for the thing that it symbolizes ... the phonetic sound of the word often acquires a value that is connected with the sound itself. Moreover, in some cases this particular value of the sound is added to the usual meaning of the word. ... Schizophrenic patients often associate words not according to their meanings but to their phonetic quality, a process called "clang association." (79)

Repetition, homophonic logic, words treated as things—all characteristics of the speech of schizophrenics but also central features of the writing of Joyce, especially in his later work. In addition, Jean-François Rabain has performed a rhetorical analysis of Schreber's memoirs, concluding that the most common figure employed by Schreber is oxymoron, also a central feature of Joyce's work.

Such parallels obviously do not indicate that Joyce (or Bloom) shared Schreber's psychosis. Indeed, Philippe Sollers has suggested that Joyce might be seen as a sort of anti-Schreber who moves from the castration anxiety of Schreber's male paranoia toward a female paranoia that he then transcends in his writing (118–19). There is also no evidence that Joyce was intentionally alluding in "Circe" to Schreber or to Freud's reading of Schreber, though he certainly might have been, especially given the dialogue with psychoanalysis implied by Joyce's depiction of Buck Mulligan as a psychiatrist in the chapter. But Joyce's text exhibits many of the traits of madness, and these traits contribute to the way the text resists the mastery of rational analysis and interpretation. Indeed, from Jung to Lacan, numerous observers (perhaps sensing a hint of madness in the margins of Joyce's text) have suggested ways in which Joyce's work bears a certain relation to madness.[16] And many other modern writers (Woolf is a good example) have provoked similar diagnoses. No doubt such links between writing and madness owe much to the way Freud saw the creation of art as a sublimation of unconscious impulses, leading to a view of the artist as one who, like the psychotic, has an unusual kind of communication with her unconscious self. Freud's own ideas on art were clearly influenced by the romantic notion of the Coleridgean mad poet with flashing eyes and floating hair, but the notion that artistic creativity is somehow associated with madness is as old as western civilization itself. E. R. Curtius traces these links back at least as far as Plato:

> The theory of the poet's divine frenzy is, of course, set forth in Plato's *Phaedrus* (which the Middle Ages did not know), but in diluted form it was to be found throughout late Antiquity and it passed to the Middle Ages as a commonplace. (474)[17]

Dodds, in fact, notes that the notion of an inspired, "frenzied" poet goes back to Democritus (before Plato), and suggests it to be a "by-product of the Dionysiac movement with its emphasis on the value of abnormal mental states" (82).

"Mad" writing like that found in the "Circe" chapter of *Ulysses* clearly participates in a long cultural tradition, and as such "Circe" has many specific predecessors—though as usual Joyce's dialogue with his predecessors is quite complex. Among other things, "Circe" can be read as a parody of the romantic notion of art as a form of irrational inspiration. One of the most important texts that "Circe" parodies is Flaubert's *The Temptation of St. Antony*, allowing Joyce to suggest that it is not art that is mad but religion.[18] Flaubert's text, written (like Joyce's) in play format, presents a pageant of bizarre apparitions presented to tempt the ascetic St. Antony away from his meditations on God, in the tradition of the depiction of these events in Bosch's fantastic painting of the same title. Flaubert's *Temptation* and Joyce's "Circe" contain many of the same elements: fantastic transformations, transgressions of the boundary between human and beast, a confusion of ontological levels between reality and hallucination, a powerful atmosphere of forbidden sexuality. There are also many of the same elements of sadomasochistic fascination, as when St. Antony vigorously lashes himself as penance for being tempted (82). Antony screams with agony, and yet (like Bloom or Sacer-Masoch's Severin) he finds a certain pleasure in the pain: "Ah! It's not so bad! One gets used to it. . . . Such agony! Such bliss! It's like being kissed. I'm melting to the marrow!" (82–83). That Antony's religious pleasure in pain reflects such clearly sadomasochistic tendencies would doubtless not be lost on Joyce, who consistently satirizes the sexual core of the religious ascetic tradition. Thus, in keeping with his inverse mode of transgression, Joyce identifies such "aberrant" sexual energies not with transgressors against the Church but with the Church itself. A mad text like "Circe" thus seems to show Joyce himself adopting characteristics he wants to attribute to his political enemies. But Joyce is a master parodist, and in point of fact he writes considerably more often in the voice of his foes than of his allies.

The relationship between "Circe" and *The Temptation* and other predecessors helps to illuminate the strategy by which Joyce subtly suggests a complicity between madness and reason. Indeed, one cannot appreciate the significance of "Circe" without understanding the way it was meticulously constructed from a patchwork of allusions to various sources, including Homer, Virgil, Goethe, Ovid, Dante, and others in addition to Flaubert. This pattern of allusions shows that, even in this bizarre chapter, Joyce was not acting as a divinely inspired mad poet. Instead, "Circe" was constructed by a careful "scissors and paste man," sedulously forging his text through a meticulous process of assembly of intertextual fragments. Flaubert's text is especially important in this light not only because it anticipates "Circe" in both form and content but because it was constructed by a similar technique of bricolage. As Michel Foucault has emphasized, Flaubert's book is most of all a book about other books, and as such it stands as an important predecessor not only of Flaubert's own *Bouvard and Pecuchet* but of a whole movement in modern literature: "Flaubert produced the first literary work whose exclusive domain is that of books: following Flaubert, Mallarmé is able to write *Le Livre* and modern literature is activated—Joyce, Roussel, Kafka, Pound, Borges. The library is on fire" (*Language* 92).

Flaubert's *The Temptation* is, by standards of everyday life, a mad text. Yet it was constructed by an impeccably rational procedure, deriving its material from a wide range of literary and scholarly sources and reproducing that material faithfully within its own bizarre context: "*The Temptation* is not the product of dreams and rapture, but a monument to meticulous erudition" (Foucault, *Language* 89). The same might be said of Joyce's "Circe," though Joyce's own book itself becomes central among the texts being refigured in the chapter. But, if ostensibly mad texts can turn out to be such careful literary constructions, then surely the line between madness and reason is not so clear and absolute as the Enlightenment tradition would have us believe. Foucault has noted that madness frequently seems informed by entirely rigorous structures of logic (*Madness* 95–96). For Foucault madness and reason are thus perhaps not so different as we would like to believe, and the continuing existence of madness, even in the Age of Reason, reminded the Enlightenment of "the precariousness of a reason that can at any moment be compromised, and definitively, by madness" (211). Himself operating in a mode of inverse transgression, Foucault suggests not that madness be considered as an alternative to the rational, but that rationality itself may already be insane. And, if the rejection of madness as irreducibly alien to rational experience is, as Foucault suggests, a central means by which rationality defines itself, then the suggestion that rationality and madness are not easily distinguished undermines one of the principal foundations of official modern western civilization.

This highly subversive possibility has clear implications for discourses of rational mastery like science and philosophy, but it particularly suggests itself when madness is juxtaposed with religion, as it is in both *The Temptation* and "Circe." Religion, after all, is the one discourse of truth that shares most with madness, and in point of fact a great number of the most cherished religious beliefs would be indistinguishable from madness were they not sanctioned by the authority of tradition and by the institutional power of the Church. It is no accident that the delusions of madness are so often—as with Schreber—religious in nature or that so many madmen come to believe that they are Christ or other religious figures.

Foucault notes in his history of madness the long-standing recognition of a certain complicity between religion and madness, with religion traditionally being cited as both a cause of and a potential cure for madness. In particular, there is a French tradition (which Flaubert inherits), dating back to the anti-Catholic humanism of the Revolution, which associates Catholicism with madness in an especially direct way. According to this view the Catholic emphasis on miracles and iconography frequently leads believers into madness, and indeed it was observed that French insane asylums around the beginning of the nineteenth century contained an inordinate number of priests and monks (*Madness* 255).

Madness thus seems an ideal thematic weapon for use in Joyce's all-out assault on Catholicism, and one might recall that Joyce begins his writing career in "The Sisters" with the story of a priest who may be mad. Indeed, White notes the prevalence of the sacred as a focus for the transgressive energies of writers like Joyce, Kristeva, Bataille, and Foucault. But White wonders whether, in a century following the death of god, such continual focus on religion does not amount to kicking a dead horse, perhaps even paradoxically bringing it back to life in new form.

In this respect transgression seems not merely to have missed its moment but to have reversed, at least in part, the original libertine sacrilege of Sade's night carnival. Transgression easily becomes a displaced religion in the very vehemence of its blasphemies. . . . The metaphysics of revolt, the celebration of the carnivalesque body, can all too easily be pressed into the service of transcendence. ("Pigs" 64)

Of course, as Joyce's work emphasizes, the horse of religion is far from dead in Dublin, continuing to trudge onward like the never-to-be-forgotten Johnny, entrapping Dubliners within the institutional power of the Church even when genuine faith is gone. But White's point is worth pondering carefully. The danger that revolutionary programs eventually will simply repeat the structures of power they seek to replace is very real, as history has shown. Foucault, recognizing this danger, has maintained a resolutely critical perspective, refusing to adumbrate detailed alternative programs because "We know very well that, even with the best intentions, those programs become a tool, an instrument of oppression" (Martin, "Truth" 10). Or, as he puts it elsewhere, "I think that to imagine another system is to extend our participation in the present system" (*Language* 230). As such, Foucault participates in a modern tradition of radically oppositional thinking that has Nietzsche as its most notable forebear. Joyce to a certain extent partakes of this tradition as well, refusing to adopt specific political programs that might lead him into a repetition of the dogmatic authoritarianism of British imperialism, Irish nationalism, or the Catholic Church.

Joyce, Cannibalism, and the Rabelaisian Feast

Joyce clearly does not propose transgression as an alternative religion, because he consistently identifies transgression with authority not with the opponents of authority. This movement of inverse transgression can be seen in Joyce's numerous references to cannibalism. Cannibalism represents a serious breach of acceptable conduct in any "civilized" society, so images of cannibalism presumably contain considerable potential as shocking examples of transgression. However, Joyce does not celebrate cannibalism, even metaphorically; he does not use cannibalism as a trope for rule breaking. Instead, he uses it as a trope for rules, and for the way individuals are devoured by the structures of power in modern (particularly Irish) society. For Joyce cannibalism embodies the ultimate lack of respect for the Other and the ultimate effacement of difference; it therefore functions as the ideal metaphor for the treatment of the Irish people by such forces as the Catholic Church, the British Empire, and Irish nationalism.

Joyce's references to cannibalism can often be usefully illuminated through reference to Bakhtin's reading of Rabelais, especially as eating and feasts in general are so central to that reading. For example, the dinner party hosted by the Misses Morkan in "The Dead" is clearly related to the Twelfth Night celebration, which has its roots in the carnivalesque festivities of the Roman Saturnalia. Bakhtin notes the carnivalesque background of the related feast of the Epiphany, suggesting that this feast shares with all "popular festive forms" the characteristic of being "related to time, which is the true hero of every feast, uncrowning the old and crowning the new" (*Rabelais* 219). Thus, Geoffrey Hartman invokes Bakhtin's reading of Rabelais to argue that in Shakespeare's *Twelfth Night* "there are crownings and uncrownings at every level" (40).

As the Morkans' party is so clearly related to the traditions of Twelfth Night and the feast of the Epiphany, one might expect to find openly carnivalesque elements in "The Dead" as well.[19] However, the ritual uncrowning and crowning associated with the folk traditions of such festivals is related to myths of death and rebirth, but Joyce's Dubliners, who, like Gretta Conroy, are "perished alive," constitute a group of the walking dead for whom no rebirth has come (*Dubliners* 177). The very absence of an overt spirit of carnival in the story thus serves an important thematic function. In this sense, "The Dead" also offers a vivid illustration of Bakhtin's belief that in modern society the carnival has been deprived of much of its subversive force.

> A major concern of Bakhtin, one that often colors his views of the past, is what he saw as the drastic diminution of a carnivalesque component in modern social life and the concomitant restriction of carnivalization to literature where it often turned bitter or involuted for want of a sustaining social and cultural setting. (LaCapra 306)

The contrast between the spiritless dinner at the Morkans' party and the riotous revels of Rabelais's *banqueteurs* is made all the more striking by a recognition of the fact that so many elements of the Rabelaisian revel are present in Joyce's story stripped of their carnivalesque exuberance. One of the more striking instances (and one of Bakhtin's favorite examples) of carnivalesque banqueting in Rabelais occurs in the fifth chapter of book 1 of *Gargantua and Pantagruel*, titled "Les Propos des Beuveurs," literally "The Discourse of the Drinkers," emphasizing the importance of talk and language in the chapter. In Rabelais, the riotous talk of the drinkers can serve a genuine subversive function, but in Joyce's Dublin the function of such talk has been reduced to one of men showering girls with "palaver" for "what they can get out of you"—as the servant girl Lily so bitterly remarks (*Dubliners* 178).[20] Similarly, the larger-than-life roisterous drunkards of Rabelais's chapter have shrunk to the debased dimensions of Joyce's Freddy Malins and Mr. Browne, snickering secretively over dirty stories that no doubt could never measure up to the kind that any good Rabelaisian celebrant would declaim at the top of his lungs. And, finally, "The Dead" also includes images of madness, an important motif in the carnivalesque tradition. In "The Dead" it is Michael Furey who is the "marker of madness" (Kershner, *Joyce, Bakhtin* 150), and Bakhtin might almost have Michael in mind when he links the modern debased carnival to the romantic grotesque, noting that here "madness acquires a somber, tragic aspect of individual isolation" (*Rabelais* 39).

Perhaps the difference between the Rabelaisian feast and the Morkans' feast in "The Dead" is best summed up in the multilingual punning of one of Rabelais's revelers.

> *Respice personam*, respect the person; *pone pro duos*, pour for two! You marvel that I say *duos* for *duobus*, that I, an erudite man, make such an error? Let me tell you that *bus* is obsolete. *Je bus* means I *have* drunk, in the *past*; while our drinking is forever conjugated in the present tense. (*Gargantua*, Le Clerq translation 18–19)

Like the novel for Bakhtin, Rabelais's drinkers are thoroughly contemporary. In contrast, it is forever the fate of Joyce's drinkers to be conjugated in the past tense. However, the heavy reliance on wordplay in Rabelais suggests a way Joyce's work points to a remedy for the paralysis of Dublin through the medium of language itself.

Bakhtin, in his discussion of Rabelais's "Palaver" chapter, notes the plays on *tripes*, which may refer either to the guest's own bowels or to the bowels of the ox being consumed by the guest. This confusion blurs the distinction between inside and outside and calls into question the traditional dichotomy that would draw a strict line between that which is the body and that which is the world external to the body. "The dividing line between man's consuming body and the consumed animal's body is . . . erased" (*Rabelais* 225). Rabelais's guest apparently renders this pun intentionally. However, in "The Dead" Joyce produces the same effect in a more subtle way through the naming of his central character. As Thomas Dilworth points out, the name Conroy has often been taken as a reference to royalty via the French, but in Irish it actually means "hound of the plain" (163). In addition, Dilworth notes that a Gabriel hound is, in fact, a goose (168). Thus, the consumption of the goose at the Morkans' dinner is subtly linked with the motif of cannibalism, a link that becomes stronger if one recalls that Gabriel's name may derive from Bret Harte's novel *Gabriel Conroy*, which is based partly on the experiences of the Donner Party, a group of pioneer settlers trapped by winter weather in the Sierra Nevada in 1846–47 and forced to resort to cannibalism to survive. The resultant identification of Gabriel Conroy with the goose that he himself carves is one of many motifs in "The Dead" that serve to undermine Gabriel. But cannibalism hardly functions here as an overt challenge to authority, both because the motif is so subtle and because it works against the figuration of the protagonist as a heroic individual.

Joyce's use of cannibalism as a motif is most prominent in *Ulysses*. In the early "Proteus" chapter, for example, Stephen Dedalus walks on the beach musing on the fact that the French journalist Drumont had referred to England's Queen Victoria as an "Old hag with yellow teeth," in an apparent reference to the folkloric belief that cannibalism yellows the teeth of its practitioners (36). This extremely subtle metaphoric suggestion of the cannibalistic tendencies of the British Empire is especially important given the historical importance of cannibalism as an image of the savagery of colonized peoples—and thus as a justification for European colonial domination.[21] This suggestion is followed a few pages later by an even more subtle reference to cannibalism as Stephen imagines the corpse of a recently drowned man, his genitals being devoured by fish: "A quiver of minnows, fat of a spongy titbit, flash through the slits of his buttoned trouserfly" (41). This image is then immediately followed by a protean series of associations: "God

becomes man becomes fish becomes barnacle goose becomes featherbed mountain" (41–42). This famous chain may be, as Stuart Gilbert
suggests, "a variant of the kabalistic axiom of metempsychosis" (128),
but it is also a sort of food chain that illustrates the monotonous
sequence of devourers and devourees that make up life in Dublin—
much in the mode of Wallace Stevens's poem about the mind-sapping
dreariness of the quotidian, "Frogs Eat Butterflies, Snakes Eat Frogs,
Hogs Eat Snakes, Men Eat Hogs."

But this particular chain of associations does far more than suggest
the tedious dog-eat-dog nature of life in Dublin. The chain, after all, is
triggered by the image of a fish eating a man. Meanwhile, the progression God becomes man (indicating the Incarnation of Christ) becomes
fish (indicating the symbolic use of Christ by the early Church) provides a link between the initial image of the drowned man and Catholicism, suggesting that the Church is feeding on the people of Ireland. In
particular, this connection indicates that the Church is feeding on the
genitals of the Irish people, in keeping with Joyce's insistent argument
that the most oppressive effect of the Church has to do with its repression of sexuality. The continuing chain might thus suggest the complicity of the Irish people in their own subjugation, with the barnacle goose
that eats the fish being an image of the Irish people who eat Christ in
the Eucharist and who also continue to turn to the Church for moral
sustenance despite its negative impact on their lives. The featherbed
mountain (an actual mountain just south of Dublin) might then represent Dublin itself, in particular the rigid nature of Dublin society,
which, as unmovable as a mountain, keeps the Irish people fixed in the
grip of a social and spiritual paralysis.

Certainly one could argue that Stephen's association of cannibalism with both British imperialism and Catholicism is merely a reflection of the lurid preoccupations of his own morbid mind. But these
associations in fact ripple throughout the text of *Ulysses*, even when
Stephen is not present. Stephen's ruminations on cannibalism in the
"Proteus" chapter are followed soon after by Bloom's more down-to-
earth associations. Thus, in the "Aeolus" chapter Bloom produces his
own rendition of Stephen's series of transformations from "Proteus,"
this time leaving no doubt of the link to both religion and cannibalism.
Thinking of the efforts of his now-deceased father to interpret the symbols in his Jewish "hagadah" book, Bloom free associates from his
memory of a phrase in the book.

And then the lamb and the cat and the dog and the stick and the water and the butcher. And then the angel of death kills the butcher and he kills the ox and the dog kills the cat. Sounds a bit silly till you come to look into it well. Justice it means, *but it's everybody eating everybody else*. (101, my emphasis)

Bloom here is beginning to show a weariness with life on this discouraging day, and he will reach his lowest point of the day amid the frequent cannibalism images of the next chapter. Significantly, the Homeric equivalent of that next chapter is the episode of the Lestrygonians, the cannibals who devour most of Odysseus's men in book 10 of *The Odyssey*. Bloom's worst moment (corresponding with that of Odysseus) occurs in this chapter, when he summarizes life in the world of Dublin in the most abject of terms: "Eat or be eaten. Kill! Kill!" (139).

But we are dealing here not with Bloom's personal despondency so much as with social commentary. Bloom's mind is not so supersaturated with Catholicism as Stephen's, so his musings on cannibalism tend to refer less to the Church and more to the dynamic of domination and cruelty that informs Dublin life in general. But it is in fact Bloom whose thoughts most clearly indicate the link between cannibalism and the Catholic sacrament of the Eucharist. As he visits the All Hallows Church, Bloom observes the sacrament in progress, and (as usual) he is able to get right to the heart of the matter, free of the abstractions that tend to clutter Stephen's thinking: "*Corpus*: body. Corpse. Good idea the Latin. Stupefies them first. Hospice for the dying. They don't seem to chew it: only swallow it down. Rum idea: eating bits of a corpse. Why the cannibals cotton to it" (66). And when, during his visit to Glasnevin Cemetery, Bloom contemplates the eating of corpses by rats, the thought links up not only with his earlier meditations on the Eucharist but also to a consistent pattern of images linking rats to the Church that runs throughout Joyce's work.[22]

As Joyce's allusive use of the Lestrygonians episode indicates, the cannibalism motif in *Ulysses* provides one of the richest connections between Joyce and Homer. As an epic *The Odyssey* seeks to establish an image of ideal community for the Greek people. To this end, the poem consistently privileges hospitality, courtesy, and community, employing the sharing of food in public feasts as an especially prominent image of communal sharing. Likewise, images of cannibalism—as in the Lestrygonians or the Cyclops—function as a dark travesty of hospitality and of communal feasting. It is, after all, rather rude to devour rather than to feed one's guests. In relating cannibalism particularly to the practices of the Catholic Church, Joyce thus plays on the irony of the fact that the sacrament of the Eucharist, supposedly a central communal moment in the Church (it is, after all, also referred to as Communion), is based precisely on cannibalism, regardless of how sublimated.[23] The point seems to be that the Church, far from providing the inspiration for a positive and healthy community, instead undermines any hope of establishing such a community in Ireland, thus assuring that the Irish people will not be able to work together to throw off their oppressors. Meanwhile, Joyce stands *The Odyssey* on its head as well, using Homer's text—itself not only an established literary "classic" but also a blatant apology for official cultural and political power—as a weapon for criticizing official power.

Joyce also uses the cannibalism motif to attack political targets other than the Church. Homer's central example of lack of community in *The Odyssey* involves the radically individualistic (and cannibalistic) Cyclops, so perhaps it comes as no surprise that one of Joyce's central images of lack of community in *Ulysses* occurs in the "Cyclops" chapter, in which he shows how the ideology of exclusion that informs Irish nationalism (here figured as anti-Semitism) leads the Irish to work against rather than with their fellow citizens. The Homeric equivalent here suggests a metaphoric element of cannibalism in the Irish nationalist rejection of difference, echoing Stephen's characterization of Ireland in *Portrait* as the "old sow that eats her farrow." Meanwhile, Joyce's most horrific image of cannibalism is aimed at the British and at the Irish who act in complicity with the them. In the "Circe" chapter of *Ulysses* the "croppy boy"—hero of an Irish folk song about rebellion against the British—is brutally hanged, then mutilated and cannibalized by a fellow Irishman, showing the way the Irish tend to feed on their own fallen heroes.

> The assistants leap at the victim's legs and drag him downward, grunting. The croppy boy's tongue protrudes violently. . . . He gives up the ghost. A violent erection of the hanged sends gouts of sperm spouting through his deathclothes on to the cobblestone. . . . [Rumbold] undoes the noose . . . he plunges his head into the gap-

ing belly of the hanged and draws out his head again clotted with coiled and smoking entrails. (485)

Sexual Violence in Joyce and Bataille

As with Stephen's thoughts on the beach, the cannibalism in the croppy boy episode is of a particularly sexual variety, and indeed the consistent focus on sexuality in Joyce's work might at first seem to support the charges of Lukács and others that Joyce was overly concerned with individual subjective experience—especially of a perverse kind. But for Joyce sexuality is a matter not of private preferences and perversions so much as important public issues. Richard Brown notes the centrality of sexuality to Joyce's writing, paralleling Joyce's art to that of the mythical Daedalus, who started out as a maker of sex aids, creating a wooden cow by means of which Pasiphaë was able to perform sexual acts with a bull. Of Joyce's art, Brown notes: "No less than that of Daedalus, it is based on sexual transgression and, like that of Daedalus, its work develops as a labyrinthine concealment more than as an explicit statement of that transgression" (153). This concealment can at least partially be attributed to the fact that Joyce was an intensely public writer who (unlike, say, Sade) wrote specifically for publication. Joyce was forced to consider practical requirements like being able to get the work that he produced by the censors in Ireland and elsewhere. Thus, in an early work like *Dubliners*, originally intended specifically for Irish publication, there is no explicit depiction of sexual scenes whatsoever, no genuinely "foul" language, and no mention of any kind of perversion. And, if it is sacrilege to suggest that a "great artist" would modify his writing to suit the available market, it is also a testament to Joyce's great skill as a purveyor of smut that he managed in his first book to get across a full range of intensely sexual matter in ways that would eventually elude the proscriptions of most censors, though certainly not without difficulties along the way.

Most readers of "The Sisters" suspect that Father Flynn's death is caused by syphilis, and that there was a certain illicit sexual desire, enacted or not, in Flynn's relationship with the boy narrator of the story. Yet neither syphilis nor pedophilia is ever mentioned in the story. Few readers miss the hints of sexual perversion in Joyce's depiction of the "queer old josser" in "An Encounter," yet one would be hard pressed to find any specific statements made by the old man that might not have been made in certain moods by the local parish priest.[24] And most readers agree that sexuality is a key element of "Araby," though nothing explicitly sexual is mentioned in the entire story. *Dubliners* is a masterpiece of double entendre and sly innuendo, which in itself is a commentary on the system of censorship in Ireland, suggesting that the repression of sexuality in Ireland veils a deep-seated obsession with all things sexual. One must already have a dirty mind to realize that *Dubliners* is dirty, a fact to which the innocent readings of bright-eyed undergraduates often testify. But Joyce is not simply suggesting that Dubliners are dirty minded, and the transgressive sexuality implied in his work is far from gratuitous. His transgressions are very specifically engaged with history, as White recommends. In particular, by investing his works with an insistent sexuality Joyce conducts an ongoing guerrilla campaign against the Irish Catholic Church, whose conscription of sexuality Joyce saw as a major evil afflicting Irish society. As Joyce points out in *Finnegans Wake*, "there's no plagues like rome" (465.34).

Joyce's work emphasizes that the oppressive policies of the Church make it almost impossible for the people of Dublin to have rewarding sex lives, whether those policies involve an emphasis on sin that laces virtually all sexual experiences with guilt or a ban on contraception that invests any "normal" sexual activity with a threat of pregnancy. Joyce is particularly critical of the attempts by the Church to legislate exactly what normal and acceptable sexual activity entails, and he makes it clear in *Ulysses* that the Blooms' marriage has been crippled by the Catholic proscription of anything other than "complete carnal intercourse, with ejaculation of semen within the natural female organ" (605).

Such suggestions of the repressive power of the Church in its attempts to control the sexual energies of its constituents have a special relevance in Catholic Ireland, and Joyce's mere use of sexual motifs beyond the control of the Church potentially works against this repression. Joyce thus often employs images of "aberrant" sexual behavior that the Church would no doubt condemn.[25] But (in keeping with his strategy of inverse transgression) Joyce attempts to undermine the Church not only through the use of sexuality as a locus of antirepressive energies but also through specific suggestions that the Church is itself motivated by fundamentally sexual drives. The Church is implicated in some of Joyce's most transgressive sexual imagery, and it is no accident that the one direct mention of Rabelais in *Ulysses* contains the reminder that the transgressive Rabelais was himself a priest. For example, Joyce parodies the strict Catholic definition of intercourse by having Bloom own an erotic photograph showing the "anal violation by male religious . . . of female religious" (593), an image that links up with the earlier blasphemous (though subtle) suggestion that Joseph and Mary may have had anal intercourse ("Joseph's sovereign thievery") in order to maintain her technical status as a virgin (533).[26] Similarly, it is no accident that the hints of perversion in "The Sisters" involve a priest or that sexually charged language continually invades the meditations of Stephen Dedalus during his highly autoerotic attempts to mortify his flesh after his "conversion" at the Catholic retreat in *Portrait*. Indeed, Stephen's turn to religion constitutes a clear sublimation of sexual energies, and his experience is a prime example of the way the Church attempts to harness sexual energies and to use them for its own purposes. Anticipating Foucault's commentary on the explosion of discourses regarding sexuality in the nineteenth century, Joyce suggests that, far from seeking to exterminate sexuality, the Church feeds on it and depends on it for its very existence.

Joyce depicts an especially strong connection between Catholicism and sadomasochism, as when both HCE and Bloom undergo various torments while playing the roles of Christ figures. The patriarchal authoritarian figure of Shaun the Post is exemplary of the links in *Finnegans Wake* among politics, patriarchy, religion, and sexuality, standing as he does as a figure of both religious and political oppression. And his production (in his guise as Jaun) of a list of words of advice for his sister Issy concerning proper behavior for young girls is a virtual manifesto for male domination of women. Jaun, the "killingest ladykiller" (430.32–33), begins this list as a revision of the Ten Commandments, but it soon degenerates (in typical Shaun fashion) into a dirty-minded exposition on underwear and urinary functions.

> First thou shalt not smile. Twice thou shalt not love. Lust, thou shalt not commix idolatry. Hip confiners help compunction. Never park your brief stays in the men's convenience. Never clean your buttoncups with your dirty pair of sassers. Never ask his first person where's your quickest cut to our last place. Never let the primising hand usemake free of your oncemaid sacral. . . . Where you truss be circumspicious and look before your leak, dears. (433.22–34)

Then he warns his sister of the danger of disobedience: "if you've got some brainy notion to raise cancan and rouse commotion I'll be apt to flail that tail for you till it's borning" (436.35–437.1). The conflation of Shaun's authoritarian attitude with religious language and sadistic threat suggests that authoritarianism and religion are often both implicated in a sadistic drive for domination, especially of women by men.

Some of the clearest examples of Joyce's association of Catholicism with sadomasochism occur in *Portrait*, in which the Catholic Church is a consistent locus of sadomasochistic tendencies. For example, when Stephen's friends Heron and Wallis demand that he admit his fascination with the girl E—C— (echoing the old josser from "An Encounter"), Stephen begins to recite the Confiteor in a parody of the sacrament of Confession (78).[27] And, when he is persecuted by his schoolmates for his loyalty to the heretic Byron, that persecution is clearly linked, like that of HCE, to the suffering of Christ. In *Portrait*, Stephen's unjust pandying is carried out by a clearly sadistic Father Dolan, and *Portrait* clearly implies that priests like Dolan do not seek to extirpate activities like "smugging"; rather they feed on such activities, which provide them with opportunities to exercise their sadistic power. Later in the book, Stephen, laden with guilt over his precocious sexual encounters with Dublin's prostitutes, attends a Catholic retreat, and here the sadomasochistic impulse underlying the Church's emphasis on the punishment of sin becomes quite clear. The preacher at this retreat describes with obvious glee and graphic detail the sufferings of the sinners in hell, demonstrating the strong tendency toward sadomasochism that is characteristic of priests everywhere in Joyce's work. Some of these descriptions would do Sade proud.

> Imagine some foul and putrid corpse that has lain rotting and decomposing in the grave, a jellylike mass of liquid corruption. Imagine such a corpse a prey to flames, devoured by the fire of the burning brimstone and giving off dense choking fumes of nauseous loathsome decomposition. And then imagine this sickening stench, multiplied a millionfold and a millionfold again from the millions upon millions of fetid carcasses massed together in the reeking darkness, a huge and rotting human fungus. (*Portrait* 120)

Even without the highly Joycean puns on *mass* and *prey* in this passage, the critique of priestly delight in pain seems clear. But Joyce is not simply suggesting that some priests are perverts. Rather, the implication is that the Church as a whole is pleased that sin exists because the continuing existence of sin allows it to maintain its institutional power through ongoing threats of retribution.[28]

Stephen's reaction shows the effectiveness of this policy; he is thoroughly terrorized by such detailed depictions of his future suffering. Repentant, he rushes to a chapel to confess his sexual sins—precisely supporting Foucault's claim that the power of the Church in the nineteenth century was largely oriented toward provoking just such confessions. Stephen then sets forth on a highly masochistic program of mortification of the senses and purification through suffering. Stopping short of the self-flagellation so central to the ascetic tradition, he nevertheless finds numerous inventive (and comical) ways to make himself suffer.

> He never consciously changed his position in bed, sat in the most uncomfortable positions, suffered patiently every itch and pain, kept away from the fire, remained on his knees all through mass except at the gospels, left parts of his neck and face undried so that air might sting them and, whenever he was not saying his beads, carried his arms stiffly at his sides like a runner and never in his pockets or clasped behind him. (*Portrait* 151)[29]

Sadomasochistic scenes of domination and submission also occur in *Ulysses*, especially in the bizarre "Circe" chapter. Here, depictions of explicit sexual violence combine with scenes of military and political oppression within a powerfully antirealist textual matrix that radically undercuts any attempts by the reader to master the text through rational interpretation. Some of these episodes are highly graphic, but Joyce consistently manages to invest them with a specific political orientation. The best-known instances of sexual domination in "Circe" involve the travails of Bloom, who early in the chapter is placed on trial and accused of all manner of perversions, particularly of a penchant for masochism. Bloom's sexual predilections are explicitly linked to those of his namesake Sacher-Masoch, as a Mrs. Bellingham testifies that Bloom "addressed me in several handwritings with fulsome compliments as a Venus in furs" (380). Indeed, a number of female witnesses charge Bloom with behavior echoing that of Sacher-Masoch's Severin in quite direct ways, and he is pronounced guilty, then sentenced to be hanged, anticipating the fate of the croppy boy later in the chapter.

Bloom, though, undergoes a change of fortune and becomes temporarily ascendent, being pronounced "emperor-president and king-chairman" of Dublin (393). The reformer Bloom then announces an ambitious political program, dispenses a few bits of sage advice to his constituents, and declares his support for a variety of radical social policies. All this, though, is too much for the Catholic clergy, who (as usual) stand in the way of meaningful political change in Ireland. So a Father Farley denounces Bloom as "an episcopalian, an agnostic, an anythingarian seeking to overthrow our holy faith" (400).

Bloom, like Parnell before him, is unable to weather the censure of the clergy, and the tone once again shifts to one of denunciation for his many sexual sins, including the use of condoms (401), a highly political issue in an Ireland dominated by Church-inspired strictures against contraception.[30] Meanwhile, true to Foucault's analyses of the complicity between psychoanalysis and institutions like the Church in defining and circumscribing aberrant sexual behavior, Buck Mulligan (now transmogrified into a famous "sex specialist") then supports the priests by diagnosing Bloom as "bisexually abnormal" (402). These hints of Bloom's uncertain gender then intensify as Dr. Dixon declares him not only to be "a finished example of the new womanly man" but to be pregnant as well (403).

Actually, Bloom greets this latest news joyfully (he promptly proceeds to give birth to eight male metallic children, all of whom quickly rise to prominence in society), but the abuse from the crowd continues, now taking an anti-Semitic turn. Eventually a bag of gunpowder is placed around his neck and he is burned for his sins, after which he goes away with the English prostitute Zoe to pay a visit (along with Stephen and Lynch) to Bella Cohen's brothel, where he will undergo an intensive regimen of sexual humiliation. Bella, "a massive whoremistress" with "a sprouting moustache" (429), is a dominating figure, and Bloom at once submits to her power: "Exuberant female. Enormously I desire your domination" (430). He then proceeds to get his wish, as Bella becomes Bello, Bloom becomes female, and the domination proceeds in graphic terms that often parallel Severin's treatment by Wanda in Sacher-Masoch's *Venus in Furs* quite closely. Bloom undergoes a variety of abuses, including being forced to recount various earlier sexual peccadillos (like voyeurism and wearing Molly's underwear) in an apparent parody of the Confession that resonates with Foucault's claim that Christianity made "sex into that which, above all else, had to be confessed" (*History* 35).[31] Bloom and Bella eventually recover their original genders, and the action proceeds to other levels, including an encounter with some bullying British soldiers, which brings imperialism into the fray. But this brief and partial summary of the contents of "Circe" already indicates the centrality of themes of domination and submission to the chapter, as well as the prevalence of depictions of sex, death, and abject violence in portraying these themes. Importantly, though, Joyce does not celebrate this violence but rejects it by associating it with his political enemies.

The difference between Joyce's project of inverse transgression and that of "direct" transgressors like Bataille can perhaps best be seen in a specific example. In the climactic scene of Bataille's *Story of the Eye*, Simone, Sir Edmond, and the narrator break into a Spanish church. Simone enacts Foucault's analysis of the sexual orientation of the Confession by confessing her sexual sins to the priest, then confessing that she has been masturbating during her confession and even exposing herself in the act before the priest's eyes. Following this parodic confession, the three principals engage in a series of extreme blasphemies that culminate in the rape and murder of the priest—with suggestions that the cleric may be enjoying his chance at martyrdom. As with Joyce, the target of Bataille's transgressions is clearly identified as the Catholic Church, in particular the sacraments of Confession and the Eucharist and the tradition of asceticism and sacrifice. But transgression itself does seem to be elevated almost to the status of an alternative religion in Bataille's scene, though it is difficult to see how a religion based on rape and murder would be preferable to Catholicism itself.

Bataille's scene in the Spanish church recalls Joyce's depiction of the hanging of the croppy boy in "Circe" in a number of ways. Based on the conventional premise that "men who are hanged or garrotted have such stiff cocks the instant their respiration is cut off, that they ejaculate," the final rape of the priest is conducted by strangling him, causing an erection that allows Simone to mount him, and he does indeed ejaculate at the moment of his death, sending her into ecstasy (79–81). Sir Edmond then mutilates the body of the dead priest by removing its eye, which Simone inserts into her vagina, whence it stares out at the narrator as the scene comes to a close.

Strong material indeed, and with a tone far darker than the Rabelaisian carnival evoked by Bakhtin.[32] But the content of Bataille's scene is no more graphic or excessive than Joyce's scene of the hanging of the croppy boy. However, the orientations of these scenes are drastically different. In Bataille, the "heroes" seem to be those who perform sexual violence on the priest, and the apparent valorization of the atrocity seems to have no valid position from which to critique the atrocities historically committed by the Catholic Church. In Joyce, on the other hand, the hero is the victim, and the call is for an end to the cycles of violence that have informed Irish history. Violence in Joyce's work is carried out not *against* priests, but *by* priests, which seems a much more effective criticism of the stifling effect of Catholic power in Ireland— and of official power in general.

In Joyce, motifs like sex, crime, madness, and violence are used critically to suggest a complicity between such elements and structures of power that would seek to present themselves as natural representatives of law, order, morality, and decency. As such, his work hardly shows the fascination with the pathological for which Lukács criticizes it. Lukács is right that one strain of modern literature shows such a fascination, and I think he is also right in concluding that this fascination does not necessarily serve a positive political purpose. But he makes a mistake in categorization when he includes Joyce among such writers, and it is a mistake highly indicative of critical treatments of Joyce's work throughout the century.

Such categorical mistakes are, in fact, the central danger embodied in the very notion that literary history can be divided into periods or movements, a notion that sometimes obscures the fact that contemporary writers can be involved in very different projects indeed. For example, the apotheosis of Joyce by the literary establishment as part of the general institutionalization of modernism tends to efface the differences between his work and that of very different writers like Pound and Eliot. At the same time, the establishment of Joyce at the center of a canon of authorized works that all "educated" people should read and know tends (in contrast to Lukács) to make Joyce's work seem overly prim and proper. The fact is that Joyce's work *does* contain numerous abject and pathological elements, but he uses such elements as part of a subversive project to indicate the pathological nature of the structures of power in his contemporary Ireland and, by extension, in western society as a whole. Indeed, that Joyce is now an officially "approved" writer of the canon may potentially make the offensive elements of his work all the more powerful by allowing them to disrupt expectations of proper textual conduct from within an "authorized" text.

Bakhtin argues that Rabelais's use of images from the "material bodily lower stratum" serves a positive celebratory function that contests the high seriousness of official Catholic medieval culture. At the same time, he claims that these images in Rabelais are not intended to shock but to demonstrate that sex, excrement, and other Rabelaisian topics are not really shocking. Bakhtin's emphasis on the positive aspects of various outrageous Rabelaisian motifs is instructive, both for our understanding of Rabelais and for our reading of similar motifs in Joyce. At the same time, there is an element of abjection in Joyce's specific use of motifs like madness, castration, and cannibalism that readings of his work as a carnivalesque celebration of physicality and marginality threaten to conceal. Any attempt to gloss over the occurrence of motifs like madness, cannibalism, and sexual violence in Joyce's work as some sort of purely celebratory or purely aesthetic device threatens to deprive his work of its subversive force. Joyce's work can, in fact, be disgusting, but only because Joyce seeks to reveal aspects of official authority in the modern world that are especially vile.

Chapter Three

The Historicity of Language and Literature: Joyce, Dante, and the Poetics of Appropriation

Dante Alighieri is another monumental figure from the literary past whose relationship to Joyce has received extensive critical attention. Marilyn French, for example, suggests that Dante's *Commedia* is a more important structural model for *Ulysses* than is the *Odyssey*, arguing that the reader of *Ulysses* undergoes a journey of enlightenment similar to that undergone by Dante in the *Commedia* (4). In any case, it is certainly true that Joyce's work bears many more formal similarities to Dante's than to Homer's and that Dante's medieval Catholic world is far more a part of Joyce's intellectual background than is the world of ancient Greece. Joyce also specifically alludes to Dante far more than to Homer. In *Joyce and Dante* Mary Reynolds has performed the most exhaustive study of Dante-Joyce parallels, beginning with the assertion that

> In all of Joyce's work Dante is a massive presence, judged, evaluated, and measured in every dimension. Joyce was probably engaged with Dante more broadly and deeply than he was with any other author except Shakespeare and Homer. To read Joyce by this theory is to discover, among other things, a poetics of Dante. (3)[1]

Of course, Reynolds's remark also implies that to read Dante is to discover a poetics of Joyce. Indeed, both Dante and Joyce include their poetic theories as integral parts of their art. Works like the *Commedia*, and like *Ulysses* and *Finnegans Wake*, are not only important works of literature but also important statements of literary theory. Reynolds proceeds to compile a useful catalog of parallels between Dante and Joyce in terms of specific Dantean allusions in Joyce's work and of analogous moments and techniques in the works of the two writers. However, the significance of many of the important parallels between the poetics of the two writers can be further illuminated, especially if one reads the relationship between Joyce and Dante through the optic of Bakhtin. Bakhtin's work also supplies important insights into the major ideological differences that separate Dante from Joyce, despite their many formal similarities.

One of the most obvious parallels between Joyce and Dante is that both writers produce extremely complex texts that generate richly multiple meanings. In a process that one might call sliding signification, Joyce's language creates any number of meanings simultaneously.[2] Because of the complex mixture of styles and voices, because of the denial of Aristotelian logic, because of the understanding of the fundamentally polysemic nature of language in Joyce's texts, meaning is generated on many levels and in many directions at once. Readers tend, in an effort to achieve coherence, to focus at a given time on one level and one direction of meaning, but this focus tends to be highly unstable, and meaning frequently changes direction or slides from one level to another. This sliding signification often occurs at the level of individual words, as in Joyce's frequent utilization of the multiple signification of puns, but it also inheres in virtually every aspect of Joyce's signifying practice. Thus, Leopold Bloom may recall sometimes Faust and sometimes Mephistopheles, sometimes Dante and sometimes Virgil. He may at once be an ordinary Dubliner in 1904, a reminder of Charles Stewart Parnell, a reinscription of the mythical Ulysses, a figure of Christ, and a universal figure of Everyman, with the complexity of such multiple meanings being further complicated by the ironic and self-parodic presentation of each. This sliding signification is overtly represented in the "Circe" chapter, as Bloom freely and liquidly undergoes a number of transformations and role changes. Similarly, Stephen Dedalus can be both Telemachus and Hamlet—in addition to a variety of other figures (like Christ, Satan, Icarus, and Byron), while Molly can be both Penelope and Calypso, Penelope's antithesis—in addition to Gea Tellus and other figures. And there are times when Stephen corresponds to Odysseus (who, after all, has a dead mother and fallen father), even as Bloom corresponds at times to Hamlet.

The radical collapse of linguistic hierarchies and boundaries in *Finnegans Wake* is Joyce's most vivid enactment of sliding signification.

If the changing styles of *Ulysses* indicate the mutliplicity of style, then the *Wake*, in which various styles are superimposed simultaneously, makes this point even more strongly. The swirling "chaosmos" of the *Wake*—with its "changeably meaning vocable scriptsigns"—creates a richly polysemic linguistic texture in which a virtually unlimited number of meanings can be generated for any given passage or even any given word. Indeed, in the *Wake* Joyce himself places a curse on any reader who would try to reduce the violent plurality of his writing: "every word will be bound over to carry three score and ten toptypsical readings throughout the book of Doublends Jined (may his forehead be darkened with mud who would sunder!)" (20.14–17).

In some ways, the *Wake* thus stands as the ultimate example of the complex modernist linguistic artifact. On the other hand, the polysemic language of the *Wake* has numerous historical precedents dating all the way back to the hieroglyphic puns of the ancient Egyptians.[3] Dante is one of Joyce's most important predecessors in this respect. Indeed, the inherent multiplicity of language is one of the main subjects of the *Commedia*. For example, when Dante and Virgil encounter the Medusa in Canto IX of *Inferno*, Dante warns the reader to look carefully at this episode for hidden messages that go beyond the meaning of the surface narrative.

> O you possessed of sturdy intellects,
> Observe the teaching that is hidden here
> beneath the veil of verses so obscure.
>
> (l. 61–63)

In particular, the danger that Dante and Virgil will be turned physically to stone serves here as a metaphor for the intellectual and spiritual petrification of literal and univocal interpretation. In this episode, as John Freccero notes, "petrification can mean the inability to see the light of truth in an interpretive glance. Thus, the threat of the Medusa may in a sense be a danger to be averted by the reader as well as the pilgrim" (121).[4] To avoid this danger, the reader must remain open to the dynamic generation of multiple meanings not only in this episode but throughout the text. Indeed, the Medusa episode links up with numerous other allegories of reading and its dangers that run throughout *Inferno* from the famous story of Paulo and Francesca in Canto V to the story of Count Ugolino and his sons in Canto XXXIII.[5]

The most obvious source of the multiple meanings throughout the *Commedia* is Dante's use of a complex multilayered allegorical structure apparently based on the medieval Catholic tradition of the fourfold exegesis of Scripture. According to this method of allegorical reading, Biblical texts generate meaning simultaneously on four different levels: literal, historical meaning; allegorical meaning, in which the significance of facts or deeds is increased by their relationship to other facts or deeds; moral meaning; and anagogical meaning, which relates this world to God's and thus reveals a divine pattern in the universal history of humankind.[6] As Hollander points out, Dante's use of the fourfold exegesis technique makes the *Commedia* stand apart from most other literary works of its time, which typically contained no literal, historical element. Indeed, only Chaucer's *Canterbury Tales* employed such an element in the major works written between the time of Virgil and the sixteenth century (Hollander, *Allegory* 53).

Echoing Dante's warning against literal interpretation, Joyce identifies the tendency to be locked into literality as one of the symptoms of the paralysis that he attributes to his fellow Dubliners. We are told in the opening sentence of "The Dead" that "Lily, the caretaker's daughter, was literally run off her feet" (175). As Hugh Kenner has pointed out, this construction seems odd because Lily is clearly not *literally*, but *figuratively*, run off her feet. But the figure is a banal one such as Lily herself might employ (*Voices* 15). To Kenner this is a mistake that any caretaker's daughter might make and is therefore entirely appropriate. However, it may be that Lily's confusion between the literal and the figurative is symptomatic of something much larger. In Dublin, metaphors have lost the spark of "semantic impertinence" (in Paul Ricoeur's felicitous phrase) that is generative of meaning and have thus descended into the petrification of literalness. Joyce's appreciation of this phenomenon shows an understanding of language that not only recalls Dante but is reminiscent of Friedrich Nietzsche, who argues that all literal uses of language are in fact simply dead metaphors that we have forgotten are metaphors.

> Truths are illusions which we have forgotten are illusions; they are metaphors that have become worn out and have been drained of sensuous force, coins that have lost their embossing and are now considered as metal and no longer as coins. ("On Truth" 84)

This hardening of illusion into "truth" is always for Nietzsche insidious and indicates the need for the perpetual and continual "coining" of fresh metaphors.

Joyce's radical texts clearly participate in this attempt to renew language. Like Dante's, Joyce's work generates meaning on multiple levels, including the realistic one.[7] One might see this multiplicity as symptomatic of the "unprecedented" modernist difficulty of Joyce's texts, but Dante's use of fourfold allegory is in fact a quite important precedent for Joyce's technique. Thus Umberto Eco (discussing Joyce's general debt to medieval models) relates the multiple meanings of *Ulysses* to a medieval allegorical practice that sounds highly Dantean: "The types and characters in Dublin life constitute only the *literal* dimension of a much vaster *allegorical* and *anagogical* system" (33). Similarly, Philippe Sollers has suggested that "Like Dante, Joyce uses a dispositif of four superimposed layers of sense" (116).[8]

Joyce and Dante often achieve the level of textual complexity required to support this intricate allegorical structure in similar ways. For example, one of the most obvious similarities between Dante and Joyce concerns the way both authors import such a wide variety of materials from such diverse sources into their texts. Literature is perhaps the most obvious of these sources, and both authors employ a spectacularly impressive array of literary allusions. But both Joyce and Dante also draw upon an encyclopedic variety of extraliterary discourses, encompassing the full range of the historical, social, cultural, and political moments in which they work. This aspect of Joyce's technique has often been cited by critics, though (as usual) Joyce himself provides what is perhaps the best description of the resultant heteroglossic nature of his texts in the catalog of the contents of the lair of the *Wake*'s author figure, Shem the Penman.

> The warped flooring of the lair and soundconducting walls thereof, to say nothing of the uprights and imposts, were persianly literatured with burst loveletters, telltale stories, stickyback snaps, doubtful eggsheels, bouchers, flints, borers, puffers, amygdaloid almonds, rindless raisins, alphybettyformed verbage, vivlical viasses, ompiter dictas, visus umbique, ahems and ahahs, imeffable tries at speech unasyllabled, you owe mes, eyoldhyms, fluefoul smut, fallen lucifers, vestas which had served, showered ornaments, borrowed brogues, reversible jackets, blackeye lenses, family jars, falsehair shirts, Godforsaken scapulars, neverworn breeches, cutthroat ties, counterfeit franks, best intentions, curried notes, upset latten tintacks, unused mill and stumpling stones, twisted quills, painful digests, magnifying wineglasses, solid

objects cast at goblins, once current puns, quashed quotatoes, messes of mottage, unquestionable issue papers, seedy ejaculations, limerick damns, crocodile tears, spilt ink, blasphematory spits . . . (183.8–24)[9]

Joyce's use of bits and pieces of other texts to construct his own texts, especially *Ulysses* and *Finnegans Wake,* has impressed critics from the very beginning. Valery Larbaud (in a famous early article begun while *Ulysses* was still in the draft stage) notes that *Ulysses* "is a genuine example of the art of mosaic." And, describing Joyce's compilation of bits of information on note sheets for gradual incorporation in the text, Larbaud suggests that these note sheets are highly reminiscent of "the boxes of little coloured cubes of the mosaic workers" (102). A little more than a decade later Frank Budgen suggested that "If there is a correspondence for Joyce's writing in the pictorial arts it is the mosaic artists of Rome and Ravenna who would supply it" (174). Indeed, Joyce himself referred to the corrected galleys of *Ulysses* as "mosaics" (*Collected Letters* 172).[10] And, in a reference to this mosaic technique, he elsewhere declared that he was "quite content to go down to posterity as a scissors and paste man for that seems to me a harsh but not unjust description" (*Collected Letters* 297).

Of course, Joyce here participates in a quite broad movement in modern art. One recalls, for example, Theodor Adorno's declaration, in *Aesthetic Theory,* that "all modern art may be considered montage" (223). Similarly, Gregory Ulmer has suggested that "collage is the single most revolutionary formal innovation in artistic representation to occur in our century" (86). And, though collage is not as much a twentieth-century innovation as Ulmer here indicates (he himself admits that it has ancient roots), his point concerning its importance in modern art is well taken.[11] In addition, descriptions of Joyce's process of composition as an art of mosaics clearly anticipate Julia Kristeva's famous suggestion (based on an insight that she attributes to Bakhtin) that "any text is constructed as a mosaic of quotations; any text is the absorption and transformation of another. The notion of *intertextuality* replaces the notion of intersubjectivity" (*Desire* 66, Kristeva's emphasis). In particular, Kristeva's comment suggests that Joyce's texts are unusual not in their use of preexisting materials but in the way they make explicit what is in fact an implicit property of all texts. Joyce's practice here also anticipates a number of other recent structuralist and poststructuralist meditations on intertextuality. For example, this practice seems to have much in common with the process referred to by Claude Lévi-Strauss as bricolage, where the *bricoleur* is a sort of junk man who randomly collects odd bits and scraps without any particular plan, and then uses those diverse materials as the need arises. The concept of bricolage has gained considerable prominence in recent critical discourse. For example, Jacques Derrida sometimes relates his own methods to those of the *bricoleur*, and even suggests that, due to the "necessity of borrowing one's concepts from the text of a heritage which is more or less coherent or ruined, it must be said that every discourse is *bricoleur*" ("Structure" 255). As Gayatri Spivak puts it, echoing Kristeva's reminder of the inescapability of intertextuality, Derrida's views on the limitations of knowledge imply that "The reason for *bricolage* is that there can be nothing else" (xix).

Joyce's recognition of the inherited nature of his literary materials, including language itself, is clearly foregrounded in his last two novels and provides much of the drive for the daring literary experiments involved therein. Through this recognition, Joyce enters into a complex dialogue with the romantic notion that the greatest art arises, new and unprecedented, from the mind of the inspired artist. Dante, on the other hand, does not have to deal with the myth of the romantic artist. Indeed, as A. C. Spearing notes, medieval poets "assume that the poet's role will not be that of a creator or inventor. He will begin with a pre-existing *materia*, and his task will be to re-present and reinterpret that *materia* for the benefit of his audience. . . . poetry is less a matter of inspiration than of craftsmanship" (74). Dante's relationship to his literary predecessors thus differs fundamentally from Joyce's in that Dante writes in an epoch when little positive aesthetic value was placed on originality and innovation.

Dante signals that he is taking his place in a long poetic tradition when Homer, Horace, Ovid, Lucan, and Virgil invite the pilgrim to join their ranks in *Inferno* IV. On the other hand, Dante makes it clear that he believes his *Commedia* to have a unique status, noting in *Paradiso*, for example, that "The waves I take were never sailed before" (Canto II, l. 7).[12] And later, in Canto XIX, he emphasizes his newness.

And what I now must tell has never been
reported by a voice, inscribed by ink,
never conceived by the imagination.

(l. 7–9)

However, Dante's claim here that his poem is without precedent should not be taken as a romantic boast of his inspiration as an artist. The inspiration of which he speaks is religious, not aesthetic, and his poem supposedly arises not simply from his own mind but from God's inspiration. Meanwhile, Dante makes it clear that his highly allusive poem is unprecedented not because it breaks free of the literary tradition but because it conscripts that tradition in the interest of its own pious project. Dante constructs his story of a journey never before traveled principally through the deft manipulation of prefabricated material. *Inferno* in particular (but to some extent all of the *Commedia*) can be accurately described as a mosaic of preexisting stories from literature, myth, and history.

Joyce's work parallels Dante's not only in the frequency of allusions to other texts, but in the way those allusions are employed as part of a complex network of interrelationships that greatly contributes to the generation of meaning. The various Homeric parallels in *Ulysses* do far more than simply initiate dialogues between Joyce and Homer, no matter how interesting those dialogues might be. For example, Ulysses is also a prominent character in *Inferno*, so that Joyce's use of the Ulysses story potentially opens a complex three-way conversation among Homer, Dante, and Joyce. Indeed, Dante's own use of Ulysses in *Inferno* XXVI provides a striking example of the kind of creative appropriation of preexisting materials that is central to Joyce's artistic technique. Dante did not know Homer's text directly, but the fact that Dante's Ulysses comes to a completely different end than does Homer's cannot be attributed to simple misinformation on Dante's part. Rather, Dante builds on the neoplatonist interpretation of the voyage of Ulysses as an allegory of the flight of the soul to transcendent truth, then "sabotages" that voyage to demonstrate that such transcendence cannot be achieved by human and secular means alone. Freccero notes that "Dante's Ulysses ends up a shipwreck rather than in the arms of some paradisiac Penelope in order to indicate what Dante thought of such purely philosophical excursions" (15). Moreover, the flight of Daedalus was interpreted by the neoplatonists as a movement toward this same transcendence, providing another link to Joyce, in whose texts the Daedalus myth is constantly present.[13]

Joyce's direct allusions to Dante can be especially rich. In the "Telemachus" chapter of *Ulysses*, for example, Stephen Dedalus, about to leave the Martello Tower for the day, contemplates giving the key to the tower to his roommate Buck Mulligan. "It is mine," Stephen thinks. "I paid the rent. *Now I eat his salt bread.* Give him the key too. All. He will ask for it" (17, my emphasis). As Reynolds and others have pointed out, the italicized phrase is easily recognizable as a reference to Cacciaguida's prophecy of Dante's exile from Florence in *Paradiso* XVII. Clearly, the allusion nicely illustrates the status of Stephen as exile, a theme that is synonymous with his appearance in Joyce's fiction. However, the above lines barely begin to demonstrate the richness of the allusion. In Dante's poem, Cacciaguida continues as follows:

> And what will be most hard for you to bear
> will be the scheming, senseless company
> that is to share your fall into this valley;
>   against you they will be insane, completely
> ungrateful and profane; and yet, soon after,
> not you but they will have their brows bloodred.
>
> (l. 61–66)

Thus, with the appropriation of a single Dantean phrase, Joyce manages to evoke not only the fact that Stephen is in the position of an exile, but to indicate Stephen's bitterness over this position and to include an opprobrium of and a vow of revenge against his tormentors. Among other things, this motif clearly links Stephen's quotation from Dante (whom he greatly admires as a poet) with his youthful fascination with *The Count of Monte Cristo* in *A Portrait of the Artist as a Young Man*.[14] Stephen's allusion to Dante thus opens up a dialogue between the "high" culture of Dante and the popular culture of Dumas's adventure novel, challenging in the process the traditional high/low hierarchical distinctions that have informed western culture for the last two centuries.

Similarly, Joyce gets a tremendous amount of mileage out of his passing allusions late in *Ulysses* to the problem of squaring the circle. It seems that some years before the action in the novel a youthful Leopold Bloom had tried his hand at the problem of squaring the circle in response to a contest. Lipoti Virag, the apparition of Bloom's deceased grandfather who appears in the "Circe" episode, chides Bloom accordingly: "You intended to devote an entire year to the study of the religious problem and the summer months of 1886 to square the circle and win that million. Pomegranite! From the sublime to the ridiculous is but a step" (419). Just a step, indeed, for the long-unsolved problem of squaring the circle is here transposed from its position at the very sublime ending of Dante's *Paradiso* to the often ridiculous amateur scientific investigations of Leopold Bloom, alias Professor Luitpold Blumenduft. The result is a dialogic confrontation between science and religion—two powerful discourses of authority that lie behind the worldviews of imperial England and Roman Catholicism, the two foreign masters that dominate the culture and politics of the Ireland of Stephen and Bloom.

That Joyce's references to the squaring of the circle may in fact indicate an allusion to Dante is further indicated when this motif reappears in the "Ithaca" chapter as an emblem of human limitation. Here, we find that Bloom had been forced to abandon the project for the very practical (and highly Bloomian) reason that the calculations involved would probably require too much paper (574). Dante, in his more ethereal mode, also uses the problem of the squaring of the circle as a symbol of human limitation, and particularly of his own inability to understand the mystery of God.

> As the geometer intently seeks
> to square the circle, but he cannot reach,
> through thought on thought, the principle he needs,
> so I searched that strange sight.
>
> (*Paradiso* XXXIII, l. 133–36).

Importantly, Dante immediately follows with a second metaphor for his inability, "and my own wings were far too weak for that" (l. 139). The image of one whose wings limit the height of his flight of course suggests Icarus, the mythical figure with whom Stephen, son of Simon Dedalus, is to be more or less identified throughout Joyce's work.[15] Thus Bloom's squaring of the circle leads through Dante to Stephen's association with Icarus, establishing through the sort of intertextual serendipity that often occurs in Joyce's texts another link in the subtle chain of associations between Bloom and Stephen. And the use of such subtleties is far more than simply a case of literary (or interpretive) preciosity. The point is precisely that such links between people often *are* subtle and difficult to discern, but nevertheless they are there. Intertextuality does indeed become a figure of intersubjectivity, as Kristeva suggests.

Joyce's allusions to Dante often create dialogic energy through specific challenges to the ideology of Catholic idealism that Dante represents. Thus Joyce's attitude toward Dante and his religious ideology is often highly irreverent, as when the authoritarian Shaun the Post in *Finnegans Wake* endorses the reading (or at least skimming) of "*Through Hell with the Papes* (mostly boys) by the divine comic Denti Alligator" (440.5–6). Perhaps the most obvious instance of this kind occurs near the end of *Portrait* when Stephen rejects Dante's sublimation of his feelings for Beatrice from the physical into the spiritual realm, referring to this aspect of Dante's project as "the spiritual-heroic refrigerating apparatus, invented and patented in all countries by Dante Alighieri" (252). There is, of course, a great irony here in that Stephen himself is often given to similar attempts to escape physical reality through flights into the ideal realm of poetry. Meanwhile, as I have argued elsewhere, one can read an especially powerful challenge to Dantean idealism in Joyce's use of a complex network of parallels to the *Commedia* in the "Circe" chapter of *Ulysses*, parallels that place the whoremistress Bella Cohen in the role of the ethereal Beatrice, with considerable parodic effect.

> Thus Joyce, in typical dialogic fashion, manages to conflate the myth of woman-as-angel with the equally invidious myth of woman-as-threat, showing that each in fact implies the other and using each to parody and undermine the other. Joyce's depiction of Bella Cohen, like everything in Joyce, is susceptible to a number of interpretations. But at least one of the effects of this depiction is a powerful questioning of the idealistic tradition of woman-as-angel of which Beatrice is a central instance. (Booker, "From the Sublime" 366)

Aside from such direct encounters with Dante, Joyce's practice of enriching his texts with complex polyphonic intertextual dialogues mirrors Dante's own use of the literary tradition. For example, in the *Commedia* Dante often draws upon both Virgil and Augustine in ways that set up confrontations between those two crucial predecessors. This dual appropriation takes on a special significance due to the fact that Augustine had earlier appropriated (and rejected) Virgil in the *Confessions*. Dante imports the tension of this previous dialogue into his own text, giving it renewed energy by virtue of having been recast in a new context. Indeed, Dante's appropriations of Virgil are often filtered through Augustine, while his appropriations of Augustine are frequently filtered through Virgil. For example, if the reading of Francesca and Paulo in *Inferno* V clearly echoes (yet inverts) the reading experience of Augustine as he undergoes his conversion in book 8 of the *Confessions*, it also inevitably echoes Augustine's earlier rejection of his reading of the *Aeneid* in book I. That rejected reading involved the episode of Dido, and in *Inferno* V we are told that Francesca and Paulo come to Dante "from the ranks where Dido suffers" (l. 85).

Beyond the institution of such complex, multivoiced dialogues, both Dante and Joyce use a variety of techniques for intertextual generation of meaning. For example, both authors frequently employ misquotations to call attention to their encounters with other texts. By making subtle alterations to well-known quotations and clichés, Joyce generates ironic perspectives on those quotations that not only call attention to their status as clichés but also potentially renew them through defamiliarization. The fabric of *Finnegans Wake* is constructed largely of such warped and fractured discourse ("quashed quotatoes"), including examples from such memorable sources as Shakespeare ("My fault, his fault, a kingship through a fault! [193.31–32]) and Keats ("A king off duty and a jaw for ever!" [162.35]). Joyce also takes on everyday clichés with constructions such as "look before you leak" (433.34) and "there's no plagues like rome" (465.34–35).[16] Popular culture is a favorite source of Joyce's discourse, such as his remaking of a well-known nursery rhyme: "Lonedom's breach lay foulend up" (239.34–35). Finally, he also uses his own discourse as a source for such misappropriations, including fractured versions of the opening of *Portrait* like "Once upon a drunk and a fairly good drunk it was" (453.20).

Dante, too, gets considerable mileage from misappropriation of literary and linguistic materials. In fact, misquotation becomes a fundamental structural principle of Dante's hell, that land of misreading and lack of understanding: "Textually, the governing principle of the *Inferno* is misuse, which is objectified into a series of misquotations operating at all levels of textual activity" (Barolini 4). Thus, as Dante proceeds along his journey the quotations given in the text tend to become more and more accurate, demonstrating the increased clarity of vision that accrues in the course of his progress.

The story of Statius related by Dante in the *Purgatorio* provides another good example of his misappropriation of historical and literary materials. It is in Dante's thematic and narrative interest to have a

Christian predecessor and to have Virgil serve as a guide toward Christianity for that predecessor. Therefore, he creates the story of Statius having been a closet Christian, led to conversion through the reading of Virgil's texts. Certainly, the "Christianization" of classical poets was not unusual in Dante's time, but there is no obvious source for this story other than the fact that it serves Dante's purposes. This depiction of Statius as a "strong misreader" of Virgil makes an obvious comment on the nature of interpretation and the mutability of literary tradition. It is instructive to note, however, the suggestion by Barolini that Statius was chosen for this role as a pure matter of practical convenience, Statius being the only member of Dante's standard "canon" of classical authors for whom the role would have been at all credible (259). The *bricoleur* uses whatever material happens to be at hand in whatever way he can.[17] Moreover, the literary *bricoleur* updates those materials, making them contemporary. If Dante's anachronistic Christian readings of classical poets participates in a widespread medieval tradition, it also anticipates the rereading of writers like Joyce, Shakespeare, and Dante himself by later generations of writers and literary critics.

Dante's manipulation of the story of Statius parallels in many ways the famous "Shakespeare theory" put forth by Stephen Dedalus in the "Scylla and Charybdis" episode of *Ulysses*. Here, Stephen appropriates information from a variety of studies (such as those separately published by George Brandes, Frank Harris, and Sidney Lee around the turn of the century) to construct a detailed fictional account of the life and career of Shakespeare. He intentionally falsifies his materials (as he himself admits in a series of "asides" to the reader) to suit his purposes, which are apparently to reform Shakespeare's career into a sort of forerunner of his own—just as Dante makes the conversion of Statius under the leadership of Virgil prefigure his own experience.

Joyce's play with clichés contributes to the general assault on mechanical language use that centrally informs all of his work, especially *Finnegans Wake*.[18] In this sense, Joyce's practice especially recalls the characterization of the avant-garde by Renato Poggioli, who saw the project of the avant-garde as a sort of defamiliarization and renewal of language itself. For Poggioli, avant-garde linguistic experiment was a "necessary reaction to the flat, opaque and prosaic nature of our public speech" and thus countered "the degeneration afflicting common language through conventional habits" (37). This description of the avant-garde project directly echoes William Carlos Williams's charac-

terization of *Finnegans Wake*. Williams, defending Joyce's radical linguistic experimentation, suggests a similar process of defamiliarization.

> Joyce maims words. Why? Because meanings have been dulled,
> then lost, then perverted by their connotations (which have grown
> over them) until their effect on the mind is no longer what it was
> when they were fresh. . . . Joyce has not changed words beyond
> recognition. They remain to a quick eye the same. But many of the
> stultifying associations of the brutalized mind (brutalized by mod-
> ern futility) have been lost in the process. (184–85)

Indeed, the clearest example of Joyce's own recognition of the
inevitability of bricolage occurs in the *Wake*, where he literally constructs his very *words* by a sort of bricolage. Margot Norris notes that
the bricolage technique in the *Wake* "is most striking at the level of
words themselves, where it consists of breaking up words and phrases
and reassembling them as they come to hand, without regard to their
original functions" (138). But Dante, too, constructs neologisms from
the building blocks of the language he is given. In *Paradiso* IX, when the
pilgrim first encounters Folco, he expresses his desire to know this new
spirit better, saying:

> Già non attendere' io tua dimanda,
> s'io m'intuassi, come tu t'inmii.
>
> (l. 80–81)

Mandelbaum adequately translates these lines as "I would not
have to wait for your request / if I could enter you as you do me."
However, it is important to note that the phrase "s'io m'intuassi, come
tu t'inmii" is a neologistic construction literally meaning "if I me-in-
you'd as you you-in me'd."[19] Dante here forces the words *me* and *you*
literally to interpenetrate one another as he seeks to do with Folco.
Reynolds, in fact, argues for a major parallel between Joyce's linguistic
experimentation in the *Wake* and Dante's innovative use of language in
the *Commedia*.

> What compelled Joyce's interest was, however, nothing so simple
> as word coinage or the fracturing of syntax; it was a concern with

the ultimate reality of language, with its most fundamental and most general principles. (*Joyce and Dante* 202)

One of the "general principles" that most concerns both Dante and Joyce is the inevitable historicity of language, a favorite theme of Bakhtin's as well. Both Dante and Joyce recognize that linguistic and literary change is unavoidable and that to be successful their texts must be capable of gaining new life with new generations of readers. Thus Dante notes in the *Commedia* that his approach must be bold so that he will not "lose my life among / those who will call this present, ancient times" (*Paradiso* XVII. 119–20). In *De vulgari eloquentia* Dante proposes a historical model of language, suggesting that the original Adamic speech was Hebrew and that this original vernacular remained the universal language until the building of the Tower of Babel, whereupon the punishment levied by God led to a proliferation of different languages, which themselves were historically changeable:

> since man is a most unstable and changeable animal, his language cannot be lasting or constant, but must vary according to times and places as do other human things such as manners and customs, I do not think there should be any doubt that language varies with time, but rather that this should be retained as certain; for if we examine our other works, we see much more discrepancy between ourselves and our ancient fellow-citizens than between ourselves and our distant contemporaries. (24–25)[20]

It is this very awareness of the changeability of the vernacular that leads to the medieval emphasis on the use of Latin, with its fixed and well-defined structure, as a language of authority. But, as Eugene Vance notes,

> what is particular to Dante is his insistence, despite the universality of Latin, upon the "nobility" of the vernacular: it is only through the vernacular, he argues that the individual may gain access to Latin. (263)

Indeed, Hollander asserts that Dante "insists upon the stylistic equivalence of Italian and Latin and the theological equivalence of Italian and the first vernacular spoken in Eden" ("Babytalk" 128–29). It is, in short,

Dante's awareness of the historicity of language that leads to his decision to write the *Commedia* in the vernacular. This connection is made even more clear in *Paradiso* XXVI, where Adam relates to Dante the "true" history of language, updating Dante's earlier view in *De vulgari*.

> The tongue I spoke was all extinct before
> the men of Nimrod set their minds upon
> the unaccomplishable task; for never
>   has any thing produced by human reason
> been everlasting—following the heavens
> men seek the new, they shift their predilections.
>   That man should speak at all is nature's act,
> but how you speak—in this tongue or that—
> she leaves to you and to your preference.

(l. 124–32)

Here Adam reveals that the historicity and conventionality of human language derives directly from the results of the Fall, in fact predating the Tower of Babel. As such, this linguistic condition is a fundamental property of mankind's being in the world. It is God's will that language be this way, and Dante, trusting that God's will is good, complies by writing his poem in the vernacular. Stated otherwise, if the Incarnation renders the Fall a fortunate one, then it must render the arbitrariness and mutability of vernacular language fortunate as well. Dante takes advantage of this good fortune to construct a poem the richness of which is made possible by the very polysemy of vernacular language.

Dante's understanding of the historicity and conventionality of language bears obvious similarities to many twentieth-century developments in the study of semiotics. And perhaps the modern author who has best exemplified those developments is Joyce. Early in *Finnegans Wake*, for example, Joyce presents a detailed allegory of the historical development of language, leading from its origin in a mistaken belief that thunder was the voice of God, through the development of the alphabet, and finally through the development of the printing press and the movement to typographical culture. But perhaps Joyce's clearest statement concerning the historicity of language occurs in the "Oxen of the Sun" chapter of *Ulysses*. Here, Joyce constructs a collage of prose styles that roughly trace the historical development of English prose from its early Anglo-Saxon origins through the early twentieth century. This chapter thus nicely illustrates Joyce's appropriation of the styles and languages of others for his own purposes. Moreover, by casting the series of styles in terms of a historical progression, Joyce demonstrates his profound understanding of the historicity of style. The styles of "Oxen" are scrupulous imitations of the manners of Malory, Bunyan, Swift, Sterne, Dickens, and others; they are not exaggerations. And yet most of the styles, taken from their original contexts and defamiliarized by their new surroundings in *Ulysses*, appear to be highly extreme and artificial. The style that is "normal" in one era, the chapter clearly shows, will not be so in another.

Joyce's detailed treatment of both literature and language as historical progressions serves as a reminder that his own work exists as a part of those progressions. In fact, his work calls attention to the way that it has been literally generated by the tradition in which it takes its place. However, this generation is far from simple. Texts like *Ulysses* or *Finnegans Wake* may derive largely from the literary tradition, but they also modify that tradition, which in turn further modifies *them*, and so on. Among other things, this movement means that each subsequent Joyce text encounters a tradition that has been modified by the participation of Joyce's previous texts in that tradition. Indeed, central among the literary predecessors of each of Joyce's texts are Joyce's own previous texts. As David Hayman notes,

> Details, characters, events, effects, and techniques from one work carry over into the next much as the image or event occurring in one chapter will turn up in later episodes as a symbol or an echo. Like a thrifty housewife, Joyce used the stock and ingredients from yesterday's soup to flavor today's casserole. (*"Ulysses": The Mechanics* 15)

This "casserole" effect is particularly striking in *Finnegans Wake*, which carries on a highly ironic dialogue with all of Joyce's previous works. "Quashed quotatoes" such as the one cited above from *Portrait* appear time and again in the *Wake*, and a number of specific comments on previous texts appear as well. *Ulysses*, for example, is referred to as the "usylessly unreadable Blue Book of Eccles" (179.26–27), and most of its chapters are catalogued in a later passage:

> Ukalepe. Loathers leave. Had days. Nemo in Patria. The Luncher Out. Skilly and Carubdish. A Wondering Wreck. From

the Mermaids' Tavern. Bullyfamous. Naughtsycalves. Mother of
Misery. Walpurgas Nackt [Calypso. Lotus Eaters. Hades. Aeolus.
Lestrygonians. Scylla and Charybdis. The Wondering Rocks.
Sirens. Cyclops. Nausicaa. Oxen of the Sun. Circe (my "transla-
tion")]. (229.13–16)[21]

Joyce's autocitations in the *Wake* also include numerous references to
himself as an individual. For example, Joyce himself is clearly the
"Jack" to which the various repetitions of "the house that Jack built"
refer. Brian McHale discusses the strong biographical presence of Joyce
in the *Wake*, noting that Joyce "is not merely distributed among the
characters but disseminated among the *words* of the text; like Shem the
Penman, he is the substance of the text" (209, McHale's emphasis).

Such a powerful personal presence of the author in his text is a far
cry from Stephen Dedalus's early nail-paring invisible God, but it is not
so far from the way Dante's own biography informs the *Commedia*.
Dante also precedes Joyce in making extensive use of allusions to his
own earlier works. Indeed, a great deal of Dante scholarship has gone
into the analysis of the dynamic interplay between the *Commedia* and
Dante's earlier works. Of particular interest is the frequent use of palinodes, in which Dante appears to retract positions taken in his earlier
works, most notably the *Convivio*, signifying a turning away from philosophy. Jeremy Tambling discusses the frequent use of palinodes in
Dante, noting in particular their dialogic nature. "These palinodes suggest re-writing, rather than development, discontinuity rather than
consistency, and qualify unitary truths with the sense of lability, doubleness, and difference" (132). Moreover, Tambling argues that there is a
strong element of technique (as opposed to sincerity) involved in
Dante's palinodes. Barolini presents a detailed discussion of the importance of autocitation in Dante within the framework of his technique of
appropriation in general: "In a text that functions largely through a
dialectical process of revision and appropriation, the moments in
which the poet looks to his own poetic past, through autocitation,
acquire a peculiar significance" (3). She goes on to note that Dante's
citations of his own poems create a sense of the progression of Dante's
career toward a culmination in the writing of the *Commedia*, suggesting
that "it seems not unlikely that he chose these poems precisely for the
archaeological resonance they afford" (31).

Perhaps the most powerful use that both Dante and Joyce make of autocitation, however, is the way a text often cites itself rather than previous texts by the same author. Thus each text operates within a historical dynamic of intratextual as well as intertextual dialogue. Joyce's texts constantly revise and update themselves as they go. The theme of repetition runs throughout both *Ulysses* and *Finnegans Wake,* and both works are filled with repeated phrases, though typically those phrases are repeated in somewhat altered form (or at least in altered context) with each use. In *Ulysses,* the effect is particularly marked in the "Circe" episode, where all of the previous events of the book (including a great number of actual phrases) are recapitulated within the defamiliarizing context of a surrealistic Nighttown. In *Finnegans Wake* this technique is generally more purely linguistic, though it can be noted that most of the major themes of the book appear on the first two pages, the remaining six hundred plus pages being constructed of repetition and elaboration. Joyce's repetition of refrains from within the same work functions as a sort of leitmotiv approach, allowing recurrent themes to be triggered in the text by phrases that the reader learns to recognize.[22] One of the best examples of such leitmotivs in the *Wake* derives from "the house that Jack built," which becomes a sort of ironic self-reflexive commentary that resounds throughout the *Wake* in such reformulations as "the hoax that joke bilked" (511.34).

Indeed, by the time of *Ulysses* and *Finnegans Wake* such repetitions provide a major structural principle, though repetition is important in Joyce's texts even as early as *Dubliners,* where images and motifs that appear in one story frequently reappear in the changed context of later stories, not only allowing the earlier story to echo in the first but also allowing the later story to retrospectively amend the meaning of the earlier one. For example, the book opens as the boy narrator of "The Sisters" looks for signs of death candles outside the window of Father Flynn. Candles, this sentence tells us, have great symbolic significance, especially in Catholic Dublin. As a result, the reader of *Dubliners* is alerted to be on the lookout for candles as symbols, and indeed candles appear at crucial points many times in the book, ranging from the almost preposterously Freudian scene in which Bob Doran uses his phallic candle to light the fire of loosely clad Polly Mooney (67), to the rejection of ceremonial candles as popish mumbo jumbo ("magic-lantern business") by former Protestant Tom Kernan (171), to Gabriel Conroy's rejection of the hotel candle so that he may seduce his wife in near darkness—the lighting, apparently, in which she looks best now that her aging face is "no longer the face for which Michael Furey had braved death" (216, 222).[23] And these links are far from gratuitous. Each subsequent reactivation of the candle motif serves to build and reinforce the complex symbolic mutual involvement among sexuality, death, and religion that forms one of the central themes of both *Dubliners* and Joyce's entire project.[24]

Similarly, the "process of revision" noted by Barolini as central to the technique of the *Commedia* occurs as various motifs are repeated in the course of a journey but repeated with a difference that suggests the nature of Dante's progress. An obvious example of this technique includes the way Dante takes waves that were never sailed before in *Paradiso* II, repeating, with the difference of faith, the journey of Ulysses described in *Inferno* XXVI. Similarly, the counterfeiter Master Adam from *Inferno* XXX is repeated by the original Adam in *Paradiso* XXVI, the difference being that this Adam has learned to reject the transgression of signs that so marked the project of Master Adam. These sorts of obvious repetitions can be found throughout the *Commedia*. Moreover, Dante also employs far more subtle techniques such as the repetition of specific words and phrases in new contexts. The use of these techniques leads to a highly complex structure, which can only be appreciated by a careful process of cross-indexing and movement back and forth through the text. R. A. Shoaf has emphasized the value of reading the poem vertically rather than horizontally, suggesting, for example, that a reading of the three cantos XXVI can be used to map Dante's exploration of the historicity and temporality of language, while the three cantos XXX map his strategy for the recovery of speculation and reflection in art and life (*Dante* 22).

The *Commedia* can thus be read in several directions at once: not only can it be pursued either vertically or horizontally within its own pages, but it also triggers numerous interpretive voyages outside those pages through its heavy use of allusions and other intertextual devices. This kind of complex, multidirectional reading is also clearly indicated by Joyce's texts, especially *Finnegans Wake*. Thus John Bishop, describing his own process of reading the *Wake*, notes that this procedure obviates any notion of linear reading and

> has licensed me to lift quotations from all over the book, ripping single words out of context and attributing to the *Wake*'s sleeping

hero phrases that ostensibly bear on other characters; . . . this kind of reading has required a flagrant abandonment of sequential progression along the printed line and instead has cultivated sense by a broad-ranging and digressive association. (305)

The complex networks of intratextual connections that make such processes of reading possible (and even necessary) for both the *Wake* and the *Commedia* recall the "spatialization" of form noted by Joseph Frank in connection with modernist literature. Frank's highly influential analysis begins with a brief review of Lessing's suggestion that form in the plastic arts is necessarily spatial because of their visual nature and that literature is primarily temporal because it is composed of language that must be read in a sequence proceeding through time. Following Wilhelm Worringer's work on the history of art, Frank then suggests that time and space are the two extremes describing the limits of literature and the plastic arts and that the evolution of art forms can be traced by their oscillations between these two poles. He presents Eliot, Pound, Proust, Joyce, and Djuna Barnes as exemplars of the modern trend toward "spatial form" in literature, since "All these writers ideally intend the reader to apprehend their work spatially, in a moment of time, rather than as a sequence" (9). According to Frank, what these writers attempted in their major works was "to undermine the inherent consecutiveness of language, frustrating the reader's normal expectation of a sequence and forcing him to perceive the elements of the poems as juxtaposed in space rather than unrolling in time" (10). Frank cites *Ulysses* as a prime example of spatial form, noting that

the reader is forced to read *Ulysses* in exactly the same manner as he reads modern poetry, that is, by continually fitting fragments together and keeping allusions in mind until, by reflexive reference, he can link them together to their complements. . . . Joyce cannot be read—he can only be reread. (18, 19)

The complexity of *Ulysses* (not to mention *Finnegans Wake*) is indisputable. However, Frank's suggestion that this complexity leads to "spatialization" and to a loss of any sense of sequentiality is highly debatable. Meanwhile, for Frank this movement toward spatialization is part of an overall modernist flight from history, and, though Frank himself does not appear to find this movement troubling, numerous critics have seen this presumed flight as evidence of political conservatism or irresponsibility among modernist writers. Such conservatism in Pound and Eliot is easily demonstrable, but in Joyce it is not, and it makes little sense to conclude that Pound, Eliot, and Joyce share similar ideologies simply because they use some of the same formal methods of composition.

In the same way, many of the formal similarities between Joyce and Dante threaten to obscure crucial ideological differences between the two writers. Umberto Eco presents an extensive and enlightening discussion of the affinities between the work of Joyce and various medieval thinkers, suggesting in a passage that especially recalls the formal similarities between the texts of Dante and Joyce that the medieval view of the world as a chain of relationships

> generates the grid of allusions in *Ulysses* and the system of puns in *Finnegans Wake*. Every word embodies every other because language is a self-reflecting world. . . . If you take away the transcendent God from the symbolic world of the Middle Ages, you have the world of Joyce. (7)

More colorfully, Eco calls Joyce "the last of the medieval monks" (81). Indeed, the medieval Catholic world greatly contributed to the formation of Joyce's intellectual and literary style. In many ways Joyce, like Shem the Penman in *Finnegans Wake*, is "middayevil down to his vegetable soul" (423.28).

But Eco puts his finger on the major difference between Dante and Joyce when he suggests that Joyce's vision lacks the "transcendent God" of the Middle Ages. This large and significant lack radically redefines the implications of almost all of the medieval techniques that Joyce employs, especially as the religious difference between Dante and Joyce goes well beyond Joyce's personal rejection of Catholicism. It is not simply Joyce, but the world in which he lives, that lacks a transcendent God, at least in the way that such a God was a living presence for Dante. The respective presence and absence of this transcendent God in the texts of Dante and Joyce is of crucial importance. In particular, the absence of a divine underpinning in Joyce's texts removes the basis of Dante's entire theory of language and signification.

As Bishop notes, the complex nonlinear reading practice he recommends for *Finnegans Wake* is much like the ancient practice of *sortes Virgilianae*, a process of serendipitous intertextuality through which a reader would open his Virgil at random and begin reading to find guidance for the conduct of his personal affairs (305). This is precisely the mode of reading that Augustine rejects in *Confessions* 4. Here the young Augustine, struggling for guidance on his road to salvation, is warned by a learned doctor against false methods of enlightenment.

> He said that people sometimes opened a book of poetry at random, and although the poet had been thinking, as he wrote, of some quite different matter, it often happened that the reader placed his finger on a verse which had remarkable bearing on his problem. (74)

But, adds the doctor, any relevance found in the passages so located is a matter of pure chance and has no real meaning. Augustine fully accepts this interpretation, concluding that this advice must have come indirectly from God Himself.

This passage takes on special significance later, near the end of book 8, when Augustine is finally able to complete his conversion to Christianity. In this key scene Augustine hears a child's voice crying "Take it and read," which he interprets as a divine command to "open my book of Scripture and read the first passage on which my eyes should fall" (177). He does so, and the verse so found turns out to be Romans 13:13, 14:

> Not in revelling and drunkenness, not in lust and wantonness, not in quarrels and rivalries. Rather, arm yourselves with the Lord Jesus Christ; spend no more thought on nature and nature's appetites. (Qtd. in Augustine 178)[25]

A more apt command to turn away from his former life could never be found, and so Augustine turns away from his sinful past and is saved.

At first glance, this crucial reading experience seems to involve precisely the element of chance that had led Augustine earlier to reject *sortes Virgilianae*. The crucial difference, of course, is that in the latter case Augustine finds the appropriate passage not through chance but through the guidance of God. Similarly, the polysemous dissemination of meaning that runs through Dante's *Commedia* operates fully under

Divine control and authority. As Charles Singleton first pointed out, Dante's multilayered and polyvocal text is anything but an anti-authoritarian gesture. Instead, it is Dante's great innovation to attempt to apply biblical modes of composition and interpretation like fourfold allegory to the writing of a non-Scriptural text.

> The poet chose his model well. That model was nothing less than God's way of writing. The poet's way will imitate that Divine polysemous way, whereby an event such as Exodus can signify both our Redemption through Christ and the conversion of the soul. (112)

The multiple levels of meaning in Joyce's writing are also reminiscent of the literal, allegorical, moral, and anagogical levels of medieval biblical exegesis. But in the sliding signification of Joyce the generation of multiple meaning is not under the ultimate control of a monological deity. For medieval Catholics the levels of biblical allegory were clearly distinguished, and the proper interpretation of the various levels could be assured by seeking assistance from God. Thus, if Dante appears audacious in attempting to write in the manner of God, it is only because he feels that his inspiration comes from God and that his readers will be able to count on similar divine guidance in their attempts to unravel his multivocal text. In the thoroughly secular world of Joyce, however, no such guidance is available, and Joyce employs his complex mode of allegory not because he sees himself as a godlike creator but because he recognizes that words and things are so thoroughly divorced that multiple meanings are inevitable. Anything in Joyce can be simultaneously part of a relatively realistic story, a commentary on Dublin society, a commentary on human societies in general, and a commentary on certain universal facts of human life. But these levels exist within an overarching reflexive commentary on language that tends to ironize them all, even as Joyce's sliding signs make any neat separation between levels of meaning impossible.

Similarly, Dante's intertextual method in constructing his poem can be compared to the modern concept of bricolage, but it is more appropriate to evince here Shoaf's concept of juxtology, a practice by which diverse materials and concepts are linked together in medieval texts. In particular, Shoaf suggests that the principle of such linkages is primarily a linguistic one, that it is based on the notion that language itself is "in charge" and that "words yoke themselves together, and together with things, in the most unpredictable ways" ("Play" 45). Elsewhere, Shoaf describes juxtology in even more striking terms.

> Juxtology emerges from the ancient epistemology of knowledge by contraries and pursues, by comparisons—be they of thinkers and their ideas or of the minutest items of a text, syllables and even individual letters—the aleatory juxtapositions of minds or of sounds that produce the phenomena of meanings. ("Medieval Studies" 23)

Shoaf here could almost be describing the work of Joyce, and indeed Jonathan Culler, discussing Shoaf's work, has called Joyce the "supreme juxtologist" (9).

But the ideological basis of Dante's juxtological method of composition differs dramatically from that of Joyce's technique. Dante can rely heavily on previous sources because as a human poet he cannot be expected to create anything truly new: for Dante true creation is the province of God. Joyce's bricolage methods, however, arise not because he cedes creativity to God but because he recognizes that any author must work with an inherited language that has been used before in other contexts and that traces of these contexts remain even when the words are reused in new contexts that are radically different from the former ones. Dante the juxtologist clearly believes that language can be given its head in his work because at a fundamental level God is always in charge, making sure that the seemingly chance juxtapositions resulting from Dante's combination of diverse materials will work out for the best and that organic unity will be preserved through the offices of that ultimate unity, God. As Shoaf puts it, medieval juxtologists operate in a mode authorized by Scripture in John 3:8: "the Spirit blows where it will, and you hear its voice, but you do not know whence it comes or where it goes" ("Play" 45).

To medieval poets language may be in charge (as Shoaf suggests), but God is in charge of language, and any sliding signification that occurs will do so under divine guidance. But for modern writers like Joyce the divine link between signifier and signified has long been shattered; language is certainly still in charge in modernist texts, but there is no transcendent center that authorizes and guides language. The difference between Dante and Joyce here can be illuminated by the historical model of language put forth by Michel Foucault in *The Order of Things*. Foucault suggests that, during the rule of the medieval epistemé, words and things were connected in the direct, mystical way suggested by the Word of God. He argues that western thinkers from the Stoics to the sixteenth century accepted a ternary model of the sign in which signifier and signified were held together by a third element, or "conjuncture," which effected a connection between words and things based on resemblance (42). Even this medieval conception of language—coming after the punishment inflicted at Babel—lacks the absolute connection between words and things of Adamic language, though Foucault does suggest that modern Hebrew still "contains, as if in the form of fragments, the marks of the original name-giving" (36). For Foucault the change to a classical epistemé then involves a further shift from the Adamic language, a change (in the seventeenth century) to a binary conception of signification in which words and things are divorced and language represents—but is not mystically connected to—reality. The modern epistemé, then, involves a nineteenth-century shift from representation to signification in which language takes on a life of its own apart from its representative functions.[26]

Foucault resembles Bakhtin in his view of modern language as the product of a complex social context of intersecting and competing discourses that destroys any notion of monological control of the generation of meaning. Indeed, Bakhtin's theories of language, and particularly his discussions of Dante, provide an extremely useful framework within which to view the ideological gap between Dante and Joyce. For example, Bakhtin's comments on encyclopedism in the novel are also particularly useful for understanding the difference between the bricolage of Joyce and the juxtology of Dante. For Bakhtin the novel, especially what he calls the "Second Line" novel, strives for "generic, encyclopedic comprehensiveness," including the heavy use of inserted genres, which "serve the basic purpose of introducing heteroglossia *into* the novel, of introducing an era's many and diverse languages." It embodies the view that "the novel must be a full and comprehensive reflection of its era . . . the novel must represent all the social and ideological voices of its era, that is, all the era's languages that have any claim to being significant; the novel must be a microcosm of heteroglossia" (*Dialogic Imagination* 410–11). However, true dialogism requires not just that material be imported into the pages of the novel but that it be engaged in an active and ongoing dialogue. For Bakhtin the largely monological "First Line" novel also incorporates "a multitude of different semiliterary genres drawn from everyday life." However, rather than engaging these genres in a dialogue that calls attention to the heteroglossia that informs them, the First Line novel seeks to subjugate these foreign genres in the interest of its own ideology, "to eliminate their brute heteroglossia, replacing it everywhere with a single-imaged, 'ennobled' language" (410).

In the *Commedia* Dante employs a highly poetic and tightly controlled language and structure in the interest of an extremely monological religious project. The various colorful sinners, with their multifarious points of view encountered by the pilgrim Dante on his journey through hell are there not to contest Dante's Catholic ideology but to reinforce it. There is never any question whose position is superior, never any doubt that the sinners are in the wrong and that Dante's Catholic God is in the right. Dante, then, brings opposing voices into his text in order to defeat them and to demonstrate the superiority of his own position, precisely as Bakhtin describes in relation to the First Line novel. Joyce, on the other hand, never supplies an authoritative viewpoint from which the multiplicity of social voices sounding in his texts can be judged. Instead, he allows opposing voices to sound on their own terms, never interceding in the ensuing clash of disourses and ideologies to assure the ultimate outcome of these battles in favor of any given perspective. Joyce, then, would seem in this respect to epitomize the embracing of heteroglossia Bakhtin's Second Line novel.

Reading the relationship between Joyce and Dante through Bakhtin thus helps to identify the ideological implications of the differences between Joyce and Dante in their use of appropriated materials in their texts. In particular, it helps to illuminate Joyce's relationship to the Catholic ideology that forms such an important part of his intellectual background. The radical difference between Joyce and Dante in their attitudes toward the heteroglossic materials imported into their texts can be read as an indication of their fundamental difference in religious attitudes and in their attitudes toward authority in general. In addition, the radically opposed religious perspectives of Dante and Joyce are reflected in very different attitudes toward history. Both authors demonstrate a central concern with historicity, but Dante appears to reject secular history in favor of the eternal perfection of paradise, while Joyce opts to embrace the temporal world and to reject religious idealism.

The texts of both Joyce and Dante have a dynamic character as different scenes and motifs constantly reappear in new contexts that revise and update their meaning. However, in Dante this process is not endless. At the end of the poem, all contradictions and ironies are resolved, as the pilgrim reaches God, the ultimate image of unity and self-identity. "Journey's end, the vision of the Incarnation, is at the same time the incarnation of the story, when pilgrim and author, being and knowing, become one" (Freccero 120). This textual movement toward the fixed and final goal of God closely parallels the Christian apocalyptic model of teleological history. Joyce's texts, on the other hand, achieve no such final closure but remain ever open. Even the circular structure of *Finnegans Wake* is radically open: the end of the text points back to the beginning, but the textual mechanics of the *Wake* are such that any subsequent reading will differ dramatically from previous ones.

The movement of Dante's text epitomizes the kind of utopian history that Bakhtin consistently rejects, while Joyce's open texts illustrate Bakhtin's view of history as a process with no "last word." Bakhtin himself calls attention to Dante's attempt to escape from history as an ongoing process. In his essay "Forms of Time and Chronotope in the Novel" (*Dialogic Imagination*), Bakhtin traces the history of attitudes toward time and space in the novel roughly from the ancient Greeks to Rabelais, supplemented by a few remarks on later writers like Goethe. Rabelais (and to a lesser extent Goethe) figures in this essay as the exemplar of the kind of connection with the flow of history that Bakhtin identifies as a crowning achievement of the novel as a genre. Dante's work, on the other hand, figures in Bakhtin's essay as a sort of last ditch effort to resist the historicization of literature that marked the transition from the medieval to the Renaissance world.

Bakhtin notes the purely spatial structure of the multilevel world of Dante's *Commedia*:

> The temporal logic of this vertical world consists in the sheer simultaneity of all that occurs (or "coexistence of everything in eternity"). Everything that on earth is divided by time, here, in this verticality, coalesces into eternity, into pure simultaneous coexistence. (*Dialogic Imagination* 157).

This spatial structure is clearly related to the religious ideology that Dante seeks to impose on his poem. However, for Bakhtin it is never possible for literary works fully to avoid showing traces of the historical context in which they are produced. Thus Dante, writing at a time of impending cultural crisis, when the medieval Catholic worldview is already beginning to crumble, is unable fully to eliminate the echoes of that crisis in his poem. In particular, "the human beings who fill (populate) this vertical world are profoundly historical, they bear the distinctive marks of time; on all of them, the traces of the epoch are imprinted" (*Dialogic Imagination* 157). For Bakhtin, it is in fact the tension between Dante's quest for spatial form and these insistent reminders of temporality that give the *Commedia* its most vital energies.

Clearly, Bakhtin's reading of Dante as a poet seeking to use poetry as a momentary stay against the confusion of a historical crisis has much in common with many conventional descriptions (like Frank's work on spatialization) of modernist writers. It particularly recalls modernist works like Eliot's *The Waste Land*, which (perhaps not coincidentally) uses Dante's *Commedia* as a prime source. Reading Joyce against Dante (much like reading Joyce against Homer) thus simultaneously contrasts the historical engagement of Joyce's work with conventional visions of a modernist flight from history. Moreover, a careful analysis of the similarities between Dante and Joyce in terms of writing practice (while at the same time maintaining an awareness of their ideological differences) can go a long way toward illuminating the way different modernist writers often use very similar formal techniques toward very different ideological ends.

Chapter Four

The Unfinalizability of Literature and History: Joyce, Goethe, and the Poetics of the Prosaic

Compared to other great literary figures like Homer, Dante, and Shakespeare, Johann Wolfgang von Goethe appears to play a relatively small role in Joyce's work. While there are passing references to Goethe in Joyce's fiction and private correspondence, none of Goethe's specific works seem to have served as important models or inspirations for any of Joyce's, and little of Joyce's technique as a writer seems especially similar to Goethe's. On the other hand, reading Joyce in the light of Bakhtin's emphasis on the chronotope of prosaic development that informs Goethe's use of the bildungsroman genre usefully illuminates aspects of Joyce's work that might otherwise remain obscure. In particular, this focus not only clarifies the treatment of time and history in Joyce's work but also points toward additional sources of dialogic complexity in that work.

Joyce's most overt indication of having been favorably impressed by Goethe's work was his suggestion to his brother Stanislaus that *Ulysses* (then in the planning stages) would depict an "Irish Faust" (Ellmann, *James Joyce* 265). However, a decade or so later, when he was well into writing *Ulysses,* Joyce proclaimed to Frank Budgen that Faust was an inadequate model for his new hero: "Far from being a complete man, he isn't a man at all. Is he an old man or a young man? Where are his home and family? We don't know. And he can't be complete because he's never alone. Mephistopheles is always hanging round him at his side or heels" (Budgen 15–17). In the meantime Joyce seems to have rejected Goethe himself as a figure of bourgeois conformity, calling the German poet/politician/scientist "a boring civil servant" (Ell-

111

mann, *James Joyce* 394). Indeed, perhaps the most direct literary encounter between Joyce and Goethe occurred when Eugene Jolas, ever the modernist, decided in 1932 to publish a special issue of his avant-garde journal *transition* as an homage to Joyce. In particular, Jolas wanted to counter the widespread apotheosis of Goethe during that year (the centenary of his death) by offering Joyce as an example of the superiority of the modern over the traditional. Joyce himself agreed to this strategy but only on the condition that Jolas also print articles that were critical of Joyce (Ellmann, *James Joyce* 642).

There are, nevertheless, echoes of Goethe sprinkled throughout Joyce's work. Thus, while noting the tenuousness of some of the apparent parallels between Goethe and Joyce, Harold Jantz concludes that the link is still demonstrable.

> Nevertheless, there is something to be said for a direct Goethe-Joyce connection. There are signs all along the way that Joyce knew and read Goethe, from the splendid passage on creativity in his early *Portrait of the Artist as a Young Man* to the last years of his life when his constant companion was a volume containing Goethe's conversations with Eckermann. (37)

Meanwhile, numerous critics from Stuart Gilbert onward have noted the numerous similarities in atmosphere and magical motifs between the "Circe" chapter of *Ulysses* and the two Walpurgisnacht episodes of *Faust* 1 and *Faust* 2.[1] But in general Joyce critics have paid relatively little attention to Goethe as a possible source of illumination of Joyce's work. Ellmann's exploration of the implications of the contents of Joyce's Trieste library in *The Consciousness of Joyce*, published in 1977, has changed many of our ideas about Joyce's sources, however, and Goethe (along with political thinkers like Bakunin) is one of the main beneficiaries of Ellmann's study. Ellmann (who rather plays down the importance of Goethe to Joyce in his influential biography) concludes in the later book that Goethe was in fact a crucial influence on Joyce.[2] Tracing several Goethean motifs in *Ulysses*, Ellmann concludes that the "connections with Goethe are less overt than the connections with Homer. They are, however, deeply ingrained" (22).

Melvin Friedman identifies the focus on Goethe in *The Consciousness of Joyce* as one of Ellmann's important contributions to Joyce scholarship, but Ellmann's revelation has hardly led to a barrage of comparative studies of Joyce and Goethe (Friedman 135). Indeed, about the only subsequent study to concentrate on Joyce and Goethe is a 1989 article by Brian Shaffer, who points to Ellmann's study in a not entirely convincing exploration of the "ubiquitous presence" of Goethe's novel *Elective Affinities* in Joyce's play *Exiles* (199). Shaffer's study is based more on structural and thematic parallels than on specific allusions, and one can certainly identify numerous such parallels between Goethe and Joyce. Faust's encyclopedic learning, for example, resembles the encyclopedism of Joycean texts like *Ulysses* and *Finnegans Wake*. Moreover, Faust's feeling that facts alone are insufficient to comprehend reality anticipates motifs like the parody of scientific learning in the "Ithaca" chapter of *Ulysses*, which seems designed to illustrate the inadequacy of pure information to convey the intricacies of human experience. And there are Faustian echoes in the parallel that Joyce draws in *Finnegans Wake* between writing and alchemy as he depicts Shem the Penman converting through some mysterious alchemical procedure his own waste material into ink and his skin into paper as part of the process of writing, especially as Joyce himself elsewhere reminds us of the young Goethe's interest in alchemy (*Critical Writings* 99).

Interestingly, however, it is Faust's assistant, Wagner, rather than Faust himself, who ultimately seems to resemble Shem—or even Joyce. Faust, who is displeased with his assistant's dogged devotion to the rational principles of secular Enlightenment science, anticipates Joyce the "scissors and paste man" when he castigates Wagner for his attempts to conscript the knowledge of others in the interest of his researches: "Well, well, keep at it: ply the shears and paste, / Concoct from feasts of other men your hashes, / . . . But what is uttered from your heart alone / Will win the hearts of others to your own" (*Faust* 1 49). Goethe's lifelong admiration for the culture of ancient Greece shows that he himself was far from accepting this romantic viewpoint on creativity in any simple way, of course.[3] Indeed, what Goethe shares most with Joyce as an artist is his consistent reliance on literary works of the past as *materia poetica* for his own compositions. Thus Kenneth Weisinger, whose thoroughly modern reading of Goethe's "classical" works is often highly suggestive of possible parallels between Goethe and Joyce, emphasizes that

most of Goethe's greatest literary achievement is directly derived
from literary works of the past. . . . This borrowing of earlier material to fashion new was by no means a naive borrowing; all of these
works depend for their very sophisticated effect on our awareness
of their status *as* appropriation and reworking of earlier material.
(20)

In his more romantic moments, then, Faust significantly deviates
from the practice of Goethe, just as the aesthetics of Stephen Dedalus
deviate dramatically from those of Joyce. Indeed, the romantic Faust
often seems to have more in common with Stephen than with Joyce,
especially in his quest to transcend the mortal and the physical in his
researches. In particular, Faust often anticipates Stephen in his use of
images of flight to express this longing for escape from the bounds of
the human. In his warning to Wagner against excessive pride in the
capabilities of mortal science, Faust even describes himself as a sort of
Icarus figure:

> I, God's own image, who have seemed, forsooth,
> Near to the mirror of eternal truth,
> Compassed the power to shed the mortal clay
> And revel in the self's celestial day,
> I, who presumed in puissance to out-soar
> The cherubim, to flow in Nature's veins,
> With god-like joy in my creative pains,
> I rode too high, and deep must I deplore:
> One thunder-word has robbed me of my reins.
>
> (*Faust* 1 51)[4]

Such parallels in no way indicate a direct influence of Goethe on
Joyce, though they do demonstrate certain parallels in interests and
artistic practice between the two writers. These parallels can be used to
establish dialogic confrontations between the two authors, confrontations that can not only illuminate Joyce's work through reference to
Goethe (as Joyce scholars have typically done) but that can also illuminate Goethe's work through reference to Joyce. Thus, the Goethe
scholar Jantz notes the presence of Goethe in Joyce's work but (Jantz's
interest being what it is) asks not what Goethe can tell us about Joyce
but what Joyce can tell us about Goethe. And, while Jantz is extremely

cautious about jumping to anachronistic conclusions, he does conclude
that reading Goethe through Joyce usefully illuminates aspects of
Goethe's work that might otherwise remain obscure. In particular, this
reading highlights Goethe as a forerunner of modern movements such
as surrealism.

There are identifiable allusions to Goethe in all of Joyce's major
works, though many of these are incidental at best. In *Dubliners*, for
example, the clearest link to Goethe occurs when Mary Jane, the niece
of the Misses Morkan in "The Dead," tries to steer the dinner conversation toward her recent attendance at Ambroise Thomas's opera
Mignon, which is loosely based on a motif from *Wilhelm Meister's
Apprenticeship* (*Dubliners* 199).[5] More significantly, in *A Portrait of the
Artist as a Young Man*, Stephen's schoolmate Donovan identifies Goethe
(along with Lessing) as an important forerunner of Stephen (and Joyce)
in the figuration of an opposition between romantic and classical
schools of art, though it is also true that Donovan's understanding of
Goethe's aesthetic philosophy is vague at best (*Portrait* 211). In addition
to the clear parallels between the "Circe" chapter of *Ulysses* and
Goethe's Walpurgisnacht, *Ulysses* includes several allusions to
Goethe's work.[6] Finally, *Finnegans Wake* refers to Goethe several times,
including a memorable (but irreverent) listing of Goethe, Dante, and
Shakespeare as a sort of composite figure of the "great European poet":
"that primed favourite continental poet, Daunty, Gouty and Shop-
keeper, A. G., whom the generality admoyers in this that is and that this
is to come" (539.5–8).[7]

One of the most important direct allusions to Goethe in Joyce's
work occurs in the opening of the "Scylla and Charybdis" chapter of
Ulysses, as the librarian Thomas William Lyster reminds a group of
literati gathered at the Irish National Library that *Wilhelm Meister's
Apprenticeship* contains a historically important discussion of *Hamlet*:
"And we have, have we not, those priceless pages of *Wilhelm Meister*. A
great poet on a great brother poet" (151).[8] The bulk of this chapter is
then concerned with Stephen's own reading of *Hamlet*, placing him
clearly in a position parallel to that of Goethe's Wilhelm. Both Stephen
and Wilhelm present detailed (but rather eccentric) explications of
Hamlet; reading these explications side by side thus initiates a dialogue
between Joyce and Goethe that potentially illuminates the work of both
authors.

Wilhelm's disquisitions on *Hamlet*, given in book 4 of *Wilhelm*

Meister's Apprenticeship, occupy an extremely influential place in the history of Shakespeare criticism. Thus, James Marchand (who figures Goethe here as a forerunner of modern psychoanalytic criticism) describes the *Hamlet* discussion in *Wilhelm Meister* as a "milestone" in criticism of the play. Indeed, Arthur Eastman calls this discussion of *Hamlet* "probably the most famous of all remarks made about a Shakespearean character" (80). Wilhelm's Hamlet is a soul too sensitive to bear the weight of the worldly responsibilities thrust upon him in the light of political realities in Denmark after his father's death and his mother's subsequent marriage. For Wilhelm the crux of *Hamlet* is Shakespeare's representation of

> a great action laid upon a soul unfit for the performance of it. In this view the whole play seems to me composed. There is an oak-tree planted in a costly jar, which should have borne only pleasant flowers in its bosom: the roots expand, the jar is shivered.
>
> A lovely, pure, noble, and most moral nature, without the strength of nerve which forms a hero, sinks beneath a burden it cannot bear and must not cast away. (*Wilhelm Meister* 234)

This reading of the play, influential as it might have been, has also been widely rejected, most importantly by A. C. Bradley in his seminal *Shakespearean Tragedy*.[9] T. S. Eliot, in his own famous discussion of *Hamlet*, identifies the nature of Wilhelm's reading, grouping Goethe with critics who have projected their own personalities into their interpretation of Hamlet's character and arguing that Goethe "made of Hamlet a Werther," just as "Coleridge made of Hamlet a Coleridge" ("Hamlet" 95). Indeed, Wilhelm's reading of *Hamlet* may be historically important less for its specific view of Hamlet as a sensitive youth inadequate to the political realities he faces than for its subjective style. The notion that Hamlet as a character is interesting precisely because he invites such readings is now well established.[10] Arthur Davis, for example, calls Hamlet "the mirror in which each man may see himself" (2), while Norman Holland points to *Hamlet* as an exemplification of his psychoanalytically oriented theory that readers in general project their own concerns and preoccupations into the texts they read. *Hamlet*, for Holland, is especially rich because it has no fixed content or meaning, but responds to different readings like "a magician's cocktail shaker from which one can pour at will martinis, daiquiris, coca-cola, and vanilla milkshakes" (420).

Wilhelm's reading of *Hamlet* can be taken as the prototype of such subjective approaches to the play. It also serves as one of the most vivid examples of the way the play has been radically revisioned (and thus revised) by numerous critics over the centuries. One might, for example, contrast the ruthless and violent Hamlet envisioned by Mallarmé.[11] The majority of critics have, like Eliot and Joyce's Lyster, routinely considered Wilhelm's interpretation of *Hamlet* to be Goethe's own, despite the complex irony that often informs the relationship between Goethe and Wilhelm. Marchand, for example, dismisses arguments that Wilhelm's *Hamlet* theory is spoken by a fictional character, not by Goethe, claiming that the question is a vain one because "all the views held by Meister are inventions of Goethe" (144). And, though this rather sanguine identification between author and character seems naive, Marchand is careful to point out that Goethe's own recorded comments on *Hamlet* do, in fact, accord rather well with the views expressed by Wilhelm.[12]

This tendency to equate the views of Wilhelm with those of Goethe is strikingly reminiscent of the critical tradition (still extant in some circles) of equating Joyce's views on art and other matters with those of Stephen Dedalus. Indeed, one of the most obvious things that Goethe and Joyce have in common as artists is their tendency to draw upon autobiographical materials in their writings. Much in the depiction of Werther, Wilhelm, and Stephen derives from the youthful experiences and attitudes of their creators—to the extent that critics have interpreted the works of both Goethe and Joyce in sometimes naively autobiographical ways, despite the irony with which both Goethe and Joyce typically transform their experiences when using them as *materia poetica*. But Goethe the mature writer is not Wilhelm, and he is certainly not Werther, just as the mature Joyce is most assuredly not Stephen. Especially beginning with the pioneering work of Hugh Kenner in works like *Dublin's Joyce*, Joyce critics in the last few decades have come more and more to focus on the differences between Stephen and Joyce. Such critics point out that, while Stephen's attitudes toward art and literature are demonstrably similar to those of the young Joyce, they are not those of the older Joyce, who reflects back on his own youthful naïveté in a highly critical and ironic manner. Similarly, the Wilhelm who dis-

courses on *Hamlet* in *Wilhelm Meister's Apprenticeship* is a youthful figure who still has much to learn, a fact that is paramount to the movement of Goethe's entire text.

In this sense, it is significant that both Goethe and Joyce aban-
doned the original texts in which they presented Wilhelm and Stephen,
respectively. A comparison of *Wilhelm Meister's Apprenticeship* with
Wilhelm Meister's Theatrical Mission (its initial version) shows a major
increase in the ironic distance between Goethe and Wilhelm, just as
Joyce makes far more clear his difference from Stephen in *Portrait* than
he did in *Stephen Hero*. The textual histories of these bildungsromans
thus curiously trace the development and maturation of Goethe and
Joyce as artists, even as the texts themselves trace the development of
Wilhelm and Stephen. For Marchand, a major point in favor of seeing
Wilhelm's reading of *Hamlet* as Goethe's own is that this reading is carried over almost verbatim from *Wilhelm Meister's Theatrical Mission* to
Wilhelm Meister's Apprenticeship. Thus, the composition of this theory
occurred in the midst of Goethe's own youthful "Hamlet-mania," and
(for Marchand) the fact that Goethe did not modify it later indicates
that he continued to believe it (143). But this argument assumes that
any changes in Goethe between the writing of the two texts would be
reflected in Wilhelm himself, whereas it may simply be that Wilhelm
stayed the same while Goethe's attitude toward Wilhelm changed.

In point of fact, Wilhelm's projection of his own preoccupations
into his interpretation of *Hamlet* has a decidedly immature ring to it. In
particular, as William Diamond pointed out long ago, Wilhelm's view
of Hamlet "resembles more strikingly Wilhelm Meister himself than
Shakespeare's Prince of Denmark" (92). But there is more at stake in
Wilhelm's reading than a mere confirmation of Holland's notion that
we all project our own identities into the texts we read, or, for that matter, of Bakhtin's emphasis on the constitutive role of the reader of literary texts. Wilhelm conscripts *Hamlet* with a specific project in mind,
willfully doing a great deal of interpretive violence to Shakespeare's
play as he seeks to find "an external confirmation of what Wilhelm
wants to believe" (Blackall 120).[13] According to Blackall, it is not Hamlet but Wilhelm who feels inadequate to deal with practical reality, and
by projecting that inadequacy onto Hamlet Wilhelm presumably finds
a certain solace. This motif becomes especially obvious when Wilhelm
produces an adaptation of *Hamlet* for use by Serlo's acting company,
with Wilhelm himself (of course) playing the leading role. In this adap-

tation Wilhelm shows little respect for the integrity of Shakespeare's text, despite his expressed admiration for it. In particular, he freely excises from the play any passages that seem to show Hamlet taking decisive action, passages that are inconsistent with Wilhelm's vision of Hamlet as a fragile flower. Wilhelm, in short, is obviously interested not in understanding Shakespeare's play but in using it to soothe his own conscience, and much of the point to Goethe's depiction of Wilhelm's engagement with *Hamlet* is lost if one simply attributes Wilhelm's reading of the play to Goethe himself.

If one accepts the ironic distance between Joyce and Stephen, then approaching Wilhelm's reading of *Hamlet* through Joyce tends to support the views of critics like Blackall and Diamond, who see Wilhelm's reading as the product of a fictional character whose attitudes do not necessarily accord with those of Goethe, as opposed to the views of critics like Marchand or Gerlach, who see Wilhelm's reading of *Hamlet* as Goethe's own. Clearly, then, the *Hamlet* theory presented by Stephen Dedalus in the "Scylla and Charybdis" chapter of *Ulysses* can affect the way one reads the discussion of *Hamlet* in *Wilhelm Meister's Apprenticeship*. Lyster's introduction sets up Wilhelm's reading as a predecessor of the detailed discussion of *Hamlet* that will be delivered by Stephen in the course of the chapter, though there is certainly an irony in the fact that Lyster (something of a Goethe scholar in his own right) seems to respect Goethe more than Stephen does.[14] Indeed, at first glance the details of Stephen's interpretation of *Hamlet* seem to have very little in common with those of Wilhelm's. Stephen's Hamlet (and, for that matter, his Shakespeare) is ruthless, tough minded, and bent on revenge, a far cry from the sensitive figure depicted by Wilhelm. In this sense, one could see Stephen's reading as a refutation of Wilhelm's. However, Stephen in fact follows quite closely in the footsteps of his German predecessor in the way he projects his own subjective concerns into his vision of the play. It is, however, significant that Wilhelm projects his own paralysis onto Hamlet, while Stephen raises his sights and identifies not only with Hamlet but with Shakespeare himself as the image of the dedicated artist that Stephen wishes to be.

Stephen's identification with Hamlet, of course, has been carefully prepared for in the book's opening chapters, in which the melancholy, black-clad Stephen serves so clearly as a figure of the Danish prince. It comes as no surprise, then, that Stephen's discourse on *Hamlet* evolves into an extended meditation on his own private concerns. In the process, Stephen presents nothing less than a general theory of the nature of artistic creation, figured particularly in the trope of paternity. All artists, according to Stephen, create by projecting their own images into their works: "His own image to a man with that queer thing genius is the standard of all experience" (*Ulysses* 161). Here Stephen echoes Oscar Wilde's *The Picture of Dorian Gray*, in which the artist Hallward declares that "every portrait that is painted with feeling is a portrait of the artist" (144).[15] As John Paul Riquelme puts it, "For Stephen, in every act of artistic creation, the artist reproduces himself" (207). Moreover, Riquelme adds that Stephen depicts a Shakespeare who has "fulfilled Stephen's own highest expectation" as an artist (207).

Stephen's reading of Shakespeare as an autobiographical artist who doggedly converts his own life experiences into the stuff of poetry clearly echoes Stephen's own procedure in constructing his *Hamlet* theory; it also echoes the use of autobiographical materials by both Joyce and Goethe, though perhaps without acknowledging the irony with which such artists transform those materials.[16] Moreover, Stephen uses his interpretation of *Hamlet* to justify his own egocentrism, just as Wilhelm produces a Hamlet who helps him to live with his own inaction. Where Stephen and Wilhelm part company, however, is in Stephen's increased self-consciousness, a self-consciousness that itself can be immobilizing but that at least keeps Stephen very much aware of the way he is distorting both *Hamlet* and the biographical facts of Shakespeare's life in using them as grist for his mill in producing his theory of artistic creation.

As Stephen delivers his exposition to his listeners in the library, his accompanying interior monologue continually subverts his own authority with a series of Elizabethan-style asides—only one of the ways Joyce's text (which at one point shifts to iambic pentameter) mimics Shakespeare's own. At one point, Stephen reminds himself to put in convincing details in order to involve his listeners in the performance: "Local colour. Work in all you know. Make them accomplices" (*Ulysses* 154). At another point he alludes to *Hamlet* to indicate the spurious nature of his own discourse: "They list. And in the porches of their ears I pour" (161). Later, he congratulates himself on the success of his concocted theory: "I think you're getting on very nicely. Just mix up a mixture of theolologicophilological. *Mingo, minxi, mictum, mingere*" (168).[17] And he is perfectly willing to embellish his depiction of Shakespeare's greatness by mentioning a supernova that appeared in the heavens at

Shakespeare's birth, despite the fact that this event (which caused considerable speculation in Elizabethan England as a possible announcement of the second coming of Christ) occurred in 1572–74, while Shakespeare was born in 1564. Stephen, of course, is quite aware of this distortion, as he points out in a subsequent aside, "Don't tell them he was nine years old" (173). These and other interior comments are topped off at the end of Stephen's presentation when he admits to his audience that he doesn't believe his own theory (175).

Among other things, the self-canceling nature of Stephen's discourse on *Hamlet* illustrates the palinodic movement that informs Joyce's texts in general, a movement that clearly identifies Joyce as a predecessor of writers like Samuel Beckett who have made central use of this device.[18] It is significant that Stephen, in the discussion in the library, clearly separates himself from those around him, presenting a bogus theory to his listeners while accompanying that theory with "true" comments that are reserved for himself alone. It is this self-conscious inward focus that principally separates Stephen from Wilhelm as characters in the bildungsroman tradition. Breon Mitchell grants that in many ways *Portrait* is a "surprisingly conventional" representative of the bildungsroman genre (63). However, he notes that works in this genre traditionally end in a resolution between the hero and society, while *Portrait* ends with the hero going away from his society into exile. This significant difference, says Mitchell, shows that "Part of Joyce's particular genius was the ability to draw upon the literary past and deliver it to the future in an enriched form" (74). It also shows that Stephen's movement is toward interiorization and separation from his society rather than toward accommodation with it. Quintessential bildungsroman protagonist that he is, Wilhelm gradually moves toward integration with the society around him. Stephen's development, on the other hand, is primarily inward; if anything, he grows more and more alienated from his surroundings as he grows older.

Bakhtin's comments on the bildungsroman greatly illuminate the significance of this movement; they also provide an extremely useful framework within which to compare the use of this genre by Goethe and Joyce. As Michael Hulse notes, Joyce's transformation in *Finnegans Wake* of "Goethe" into "Gouty" finds "the very word to express an Anglo-Saxon conception of Goethe which is based on the writer's patrician old age, a conception which sees him as huffy and puffy and pompous" (19). This image suggests that Joyce might have considered

Goethe as a traditional figure of authority, though it is also true that Goethe has sometimes been seen (by Byron and Shelley, among others) as a literary rebel. Joyce employs this same image earlier in the *Wake* when he refers to *"Gouty Ghibeline"* in HCE's listing of the abusive names he has been called in the course of his travails (71.26). Interestingly, this appellation seems to enlist Goethe in the ranks of the Ghibelines, the faction opposed to Dante and his Guelphs in the Florentine political schism that plays such a major role in the *Commedia*. Joyce thus suggests Goethe as a figure of potential contrast to Dante, which is precisely the way Bakhtin depicts Goethe in "Forms of Time and Chronotope in the Novel." For Bakhtin, in contrast to Dante's attempted flight from history into eternity, Goethe's work is the epitome of engagement with temporality.

Indeed, if the exact importance of Goethe to Joyce remains unclear, the importance of Goethe to Bakhtin does not. Goethe stands with Rabelais and Dostoevsky as the central literary influences on Bakhtin's career and seems in particular to have been the major figure in Bakhtin's book-length study *The Novel of Education and Its Significance in the History of Realism.* However, the complete nature of Bakhtin's engagement with Goethe in this work remains unclear because the manuscript, already in the hands of the publisher, was destroyed or lost when the publishing house Soviet Writer was blown up during the World War II German invasion of the Soviet Union. Bakhtin himself, meanwhile, seems to have used most of his own copy of the manuscript for tobacco paper during the shortages of the war, thus ironically repeating Goethe's presumed destruction of the manuscript of *Wilhelm Meister's Theatrical Mission* in about 1785 and Joyce's attempted burning of the manuscript of *Stephen Hero* in 1908. Fortunately for literary historians, however, portions of all three manuscripts remained, enough to indicate that Goethe's and Joyce's books were both bildungsromans and that Bakhtin's was a study of that genre using *Wilhelm Meister's Apprenticeship* as his principal exemplar.

The remaining fragment of Bakhtin's lost study of the bildungsroman is now available in English translation as "The *Bildungsroman* and Its Significance in the History of Realism," published in his *Speech Genres and Other Late Essays.* Among other things, this essay serves as a companion piece to the important chronotope essay. In particular, the bildungsroman fragment presents Goethe, especially in *Wilhelm Meister*, as an exemplar of "chronotopicity."[19] Goethe, according to Bakhtin, has a uniquely intense sense of place and time. Of all authors, in fact, it is Goethe who has the most profound sense of history and of the mutual involvement of time and space in human events.

> Everything—from an abstract idea to a piece of rock on the bank of a stream—bears the stamp of time, is saturated with time, and assumes its form and meaning in time. Therefore, everything is intensive in Goethe's world; it contains no inanimate, immobile, petrified places, no immutable background that does not partici- pate in action and emergence (in events), no decorations or sets. On the other hand, this time, in all its essential aspects, is localized in concrete space, imprinted on it. In Goethe's world there are no events, plots, or temporal motifs that are not related in an essential way to the particular spatial place of their occurrence. (*Speech* 42)

This intense sense of situatedness in place and time is also a char- acteristic of Joyce's work, especially *Ulysses*, where the narrated actions occur in very well delineated places (usually real locations in Dublin) and at clearly defined times. Meanwhile, Morson and Emerson note that Bakhtin's figuration of Goethe's sense of place and time shows Goethe to be the model for Bakhtin's notion of the prosaic, of the impor- tance of the accumulated small details of everyday life in the large process of history (419). Again, this description might also be applied to the work of Joyce, in which the mundane plays such a major role and seemingly insignificant items or events can turn out to be of crucial importance. For example, the recurrence of motifs in Joyce's texts often results in a sort of *Nachträglichkeit* effect in which events that initially seemed unimportant turn out to have been highly significant as they link up with subsequent moments in the text. After the funeral of Paddy Dignam in the "Hades" chapter of *Ulysses*, Bloom politely points out to the lawyer John Henry Menton that his "hat is a little crushed." Menton takes off and straightens the hat, thanking Bloom rather per- functorily (95). But small things like hats can have great importance in Joyce's work. Bloom's encounter with Menton and his hat already echoes Bloom's focus on his own "high grade ha," but we do not learn for more than four hundred pages that this incident echoes in Bloom's mind what was perhaps his proudest moment—once, when Charles Stewart Parnell's silk hat was inadvertently knocked off in a crowd, Bloom picked it up and restored it to him. Parnell, unlike Menton, had offered his thanks quite elegantly: "*Thank you, sir*, though in a very different tone of voice from the ornament of the legal profession whose headgear Bloom also set to rights earlier in the day, history repeating itself with a difference" (535, Joyce's emphasis). Meanwhile, after Stephen is knocked down by Private Carr, Bloom is careful to save first Stephen's hat, then Stephen, reiterating Bloom's consistently solicitous attitude toward headgear as well as repeating the frequent Joycean link between Stephen and Parnell (491). These instances of *Nachträglichkeit* demand a mode of reading in which not even the tiniest element of the text can be ignored. Moreover, they suggest the importance of small events in the flow of history, indicating that even the most insignificant people or events might be able to influence the outcome of the great events of history.

This *Nachträglichkeit* effect also contributes to the dynamic unfinalizability of meaning in Joyce's texts by preventing the reader from reaching final conclusions along the way. This unfinalizability derives directly from historical continuity and from a sense that events are not simply "over" as they occur but instead contribute to an ongoing development. This sense accords very well with that attributed by Bakhtin to Goethe. Paraphrasing Bakhtin's discussion of unfinalizability in Dostoevsky, Morson and Emerson conclude that Bakhtin might have summarized Goethe's historical vision as follows.

> For nothing absolutely conclusive has yet taken place in the world, a penultimate word of the world and about the world is always being prepared and always slowly changing, the world is more or less open and free within limits, everything comes from the past and is reworked in the present as we live into an open future. (419)

The parallel between this figuration of Goethe's sense of history and Bakhtin's sense of the novel as an ever-evolving genre marked by its close contact with contemporary reality is obvious. Indeed, Jennifer Wise suggests that Bakhtin's emphasis on the contemporaneity of the novel derives directly from Goethe and Schiller's 1797 essay (published in 1827) "On Epic and Dramatic Poetry." In this essay, Goethe and Schiller contrast the strong sense of current action in drama with the epic sense that all action is occurring in the past. In particular, they suggest that the drama is informed by "progressive" motifs (motifs leading to the furthering of action and plot development), while the epic relies principally on "regressive" motifs that retard action and slow the plot. Wise argues that Bakhtin's contrast between the novel and the epic is largely a reinscription of Goethe's contrast between drama and the epic.[20] Indeed, apparently incensed by Bakhtin's privileging of the novel over drama, Wise virtually accuses Bakhtin of plagiarizing this distinction from Goethe, referring to Bakhtin's essay "Epic and Novel" as a "generically purged version" of Goethe's essay which has "effaced all traces of the dramatic accents so definitive of Goethe's original discourse" (16).

Wise does not mention, however, that Bakhtin specifically cites Goethe and Schiller as a source of his characterization of the epic (*Dialogic Imagination* 13). And, while it is true that Bakhtin often seems unfairly to dismiss the dialogic potential of drama (and poetry, for that matter), it is also true that Bakhtin's apotheosis of the novel is part of a complex rhetorical strategy that is designed to counter a centuries-old critical tendency to consider the novel as an inferior or even subliterary genre. Indeed, Goethe himself has quite frequently been depicted as considering the novel inferior to drama or to lyric poetry. This depiction, however, is not entirely accurate, so Bakhtin's privileging of the novel in conjunction with his emphasis on Goethe's powerful chronotopic sense, can be read as an attempt to rehabilitate Goethe as a novelist.[21]

Bakhtin emphasizes that this chronotopic sense leads in Goethe's writing, especially the novels, to a sense of inevitable historical continuity from past, to present, to future. There are, in fact, numerous passages in the *Wilhelm Meister* volumes, especially *Wilhelm Meister's Apprenticeship*, that specifically indicate this intense sense of temporal connectedness. Early in the book, for example, the young Wilhelm exclaims to his lover Mariana his joy at being able to tell her about his past just as they share a present in which they can look excitedly toward the "blooming country" of their future together (11). But the most important use of temporality in the book is the overall bildungsroman form, which shows Wilhelm undergoing genuine change and development in response to the various experiences he encounters along the way. As Blackall puts it, "the novel is concerned with development, and how development takes place" (116). Granted, critics have disagreed over the precise nature of Wilhelm's development and whether he really achieves the maturity and education that are presumably his goal. Moreover, Wilhelm's development is perhaps atypi-

cal because his "apprenticeship" is overseen and to a certain extent
directed by the mysterious Society of the Tower (based on the Freemasons, of whom Goethe was one and Leopold Bloom is rumored in
Ulysses to be another). On the other hand, the point here may be that we
all develop within limitations set by external social conditions and that
none of us develop strictly on our own. In any case, that Wilhelm does
change during the course of the narrative is undeniable. The implication throughout the text is that time does work significant changes in
both individuals and societies.

There is, of course, a direct generic link between the *Wilhelm Meister* volumes (especially the first one) and Joyce's *Portrait*. *Portrait* is certainly a novel of the development of its protagonist, though Joyce
departs significantly from Goethe in his use of style as an indicator of
the growth of Stephen. The most striking stylistic feature of *Portrait* is
the way the development of Stephen's consciousness is figured
through the stylistic evolution of the narrative language of the text,
while Goethe's otherwise heterogeneous text is characterized by a consistency of style throughout.[22] As Kershner notes, "The text of *Portrait*,
with all its stylized incremental repetition and all its virtuoso verbal
effects, is nonetheless fundamentally bound to the narrative of
Stephen's consciousness" (*Joyce, Bakhtin* 161–62).

The thoroughly historicized model of subjectivity implied by the
stylistic movement of *Portrait* is highlighted through its contrast to the
desire of its central subject to escape from history. The suggestion by
Stephen in *Ulysses* that history is "a nightmare from which I am trying
to awake" is probably one of the two best-remembered proclamations
of his entire repertoire. Unfortunately, like that other best-remembered
quote—Stephen's earlier claim in *Portrait* that the artist, like God,
should remain invisible behind his work, "indifferent, paring his finger-
nails"—this remark is often quoted out of context and attributed to
Joyce directly as an expression of the author's own attitude. In both
cases, Joyce's texts then become an expression of the attitude of ahis-
torical aesthetic distance that is often associated with certain models of
literary modernism. The stakes in examining such statements are thus
particularly high, involving as they do issues that are fundamental to
an understanding not only of Joyce's entire project but of modern literary history as a whole. This is especially true as, in both cases, there is
no real justification for interpreting Stephen's remarks as providing a
statement of Joyce's own views. A yearning for an escape from the flow

of history is indeed a central characteristic of Stephen's entire psychic makeup. It is, however, a characteristic of which Joyce's texts are frequently critical, both by direct statement and by the dynamism of their textual mechanics. Reading Joyce alongside Goethe (especially Bakhtin's view of Goethe) highlights the intense engagement with history in Joyce's texts, an engagement that is far different from the idealist escape from temporality that Stephen seems to have in mind.

Stasis is central to Stephen's aesthetic vision; movement and change are the primary characteristics of the Joycean text. This difference highlights a tension between time and eternity that centrally informs not only the work of Joyce but much of western civilization from Plato onward, as figured perhaps most prominently in book 11 of Augustine's *Confessions*. Hugh Kenner notes the paradoxical character of the title of Joyce's first completed novel, since a *portrait* by nature pictures a static moment in time, while in *Portrait* Stephen constantly changes and develops through time: "The book is a becoming which the title tells us to apprehend as a being" ("Cubist *Portrait*" 171). Indeed, not only does Stephen develop, but the text itself changes and develops as well, with the narrative style evolving approximately in tandem with the growing sophistication of Stephen's consciousness. Kenner suggests that this development gives us a whole series of perspectives as opposed to the conventional single perspective of the portrait. He then suggests an artistic analogy for such use of multiple viewpoints in a single painting, arguing that "Joyce's *Portrait* may be the first piece of cubism in literary history" (173).

This analogy is certainly an interesting one, but Kenner's invocation of the simultaneous multiple perspectives of the cubist painting loses the temporal element that is so crucial to the presentation of Joyce's *Portrait*. We do see different perspectives on Stephen Dedalus, but we see them as an evolution through time rather than at a single moment. The book is fundamentally informed by a tension between being and becoming, as Kenner indicates, but this tension arises because of the conflict between the dynamics of the text as stylistic becoming and the attempts of Stephen himself to escape history into a world of static aesthetic being. One might say that the text of *Portrait*, with its constantly evolving style, is informed by a prosaic chronotope of the kind that Bakhtin associates with Goethe, while Stephen's own attitude toward time is more like that which Bakhtin associates with Dante. In this sense, then, *Portrait* is precisely the reverse of *Wilhelm*

Meister's Apprenticeship, in which the protagonist develops and changes but the style remains constant.

Goethe's consistent style, however, does not really conflict with the motif of development that informs his text. Instead, this style is simply neutral and unobtrusive, allowing Goethe to focus on Wilhelm's growth without distractions or contradictions. It is this focus that feeds the intense chronotopicity cited by Bakhtin in connection with Goethe's work. In Joyce's text, on the other hand, the style is anything but neutral, contributing a chronotopic voice of its own that challenges the chronotope represented by Stephen. In this sense, *Portrait* exemplifies Bakhtin's argument late in the chronotope essay that a given work may generally be informed by multiple chronotopes that interact dialogically: "Chronotopes are mutually inclusive, they co-exist, they may be interwoven with, replace or oppose one another, contradict one another or find themselves in ever more complex interrelationships" (*Dialogic Imagination* 252). The chronotopic structure of *Portrait* is thus less clear than that of *Wilhelm Meister's Apprenticeship*, but this loss of focus is compensated for by a contribution to dialogic encounters among different ideologies that greatly enrich Joyce's text.

Bakhtin's comments on characterization in the novel are also extremely useful in comparing Joyce's treatment of Stephen with Goethe's depiction of Wilhelm. For Bakhtin, one of the key advantages of the novel as a genre is its ability to reflect, through characterization, the way real people change through time. He argues that one of the most important differences between the epic and the novel as genres lies in the way epic characters are unified and whole, as opposed to the relatively fluid and provisional identities of the characters in novels. He suggests that "The epic wholeness of an individual disintegrates in a novel" and goes on to argue that in the novel "A crucial tension develops between the external and the internal man, and as a result the subjectivity of the individual becomes an object of experimentation and representation" (*Dialogic Imagination* 37). In particular, Bakhtin sees selfhood in the novel (and in the social world) not as a fixed identity but as an ongoing process: "As long as a person is alive he lives by the fact that he is not yet finalized, that he has not yet uttered his ultimate word" (*Problems* 59). In short, the self develops through an ongoing dialogue with others and with the external world, consistent with Bakhtin's vision of subjectivity as a boundary phenomenon between different consciousnesses, as something that arises not prior to inter-subjective exchange but as a product of that exchange.

Goethe at times points in *Wilhelm Meister's Apprenticeship* toward very much this same sense of the self as the dynamic product of ongoing social exchanges. Late in the book Wilhelm thus concludes that "True art . . . is like good company: it constrains us in the most delightful way to recognize the measure by which, and up to which, our inward nature has been shaped by culture" (484). But Joyce's Stephen rejects this phenomenon, believing that he, as an artist, can somehow create himself. During his musings on *Hamlet* Stephen argues that the artist is concerned not only with reproducing himself but also with creating himself in the first place. Indeed, from his first appearance in the opening of *Portrait* through his final departure late in *Ulysses*, Stephen's principal concern is the creation of a vision of himself with which he can feel comfortable and of which he can be proud. This process of envisionment is particularly central in *Portrait*, where the bildungsroman format, the title trope, and the underlying dialogue with Ovid's *Metamorphoses* all act to call specific attention to Stephen's attempts at forging (in both senses of the word) an identity for himself. But there is a critical flaw in all of Stephen's attempts at the development of a self-image, and that flaw is his inability to factor history into the equation. William Schutte notes, in regard to Stephen, that "*Portrait* is a record of his search for the one ideal to which he can dedicate himself forever" (96). Both *ideal* and *forever* are key terms here. Stephen seeks a single, ideal image of nobility that will be free from the tribulations and contingencies of history.

Stephen thus denies the constraints on individual development that are central to Bakhtin's notion of the prosaic, especially as exemplified in the writings of Goethe. For Stephen, the man of genius ideally can control his own fate without the intervention of the kinds of everyday influences that inhere in a fallen historical world. In attempting to create himself, Stephen seeks specific hero figures with whom he can identify, either from his own life or from among the great men of history. He also attempts a similar form of imaginary envisionment of himself through identification with idealized images from domains such as literature and religion. This envisionment often involves an attempt at identification with figures of authority, but Stephen also attempts a transgressive envisionment in which he seeks to establish his own sense of integrity and uniqueness through his rejection of authority. The two strategies are not, however, very different, at least in Stephen's case. As Vicki Mahaffey points out, by allowing his resistance to unitary authority to so determine his outlook, Stephen in fact remains inscribed within that authority (26–27). Or, as Joseph Buttigieg puts it, "If Stephen had truly dispelled God from his mind, he would have no need to take a stand against him" ("Struggle" 198).

Joyce's depiction of the construction of Stephen's identity begins with the very first words of *Portrait*, as he listens to the story told him by his father:

> Once upon a time and a very good time it was there was a moocow coming down along the road and this moocow that was coming down along the road met a nicens little boy named baby tuckoo. . . . (7, Joyce's ellipsis)

Stephen's reaction to this story involves the kind of bovarystic identification that will continue to characterize his reactions to literature throughout his appearances in Joyce's fiction: "He was baby tuckoo" (7). Meanwhile, on this same opening page we see the young Stephen surrounded by a somewhat bewildering (to him) array of adults with whom he seeks to identify and whom he seeks to impress, as when he dances to the clapping of Uncle Charles and Dante while his mother accompanies him on the piano. And, finally, still on the opening page, we find that Stephen is dimly aware of the existence of Michael Davitt and Charles Stewart Parnell, Irish political leaders who potentially serve as models for his own growing sense of self.

This early mention of Irish politics marks the importance that the political will play throughout *Portrait*. For Stephen, who seeks to evade politics, the significance of the political consists largely in his attempts at identification with Parnell. But this intrusion of the public discourse of politics into the private scene of the Dedalus home signals a major difficulty with this kind of envisionment. Stephen would like to imagine an identity for himself that sets him apart from those around him, that will make him a unique individual. But his efforts to do so are consistently couched in a language that is derived from the discourses of public institutions and traditions, indicating that there is no way to define the individual apart from the communal, the private apart from the public. As Trevor Williams notes, the first page and a half of *A Portrait* perform a constant dialectic between the public and the private spheres, the introduction of Eileen Vance being a clear sign that no private relationship can escape social contamination. (313)[23]

Stephen's attempts at identification, particularly with hero-figures or with images of authority, will continue to typify his efforts at imaginary envisionment throughout *Portrait*. In this vein, Simon Dedalus clearly occupies an important position as father figure, and Simon's failure to provide a model that Stephen considers adequate is central to Stephen's ongoing quest for a model that *is* adequate. Very early in *Portrait* we find Stephen mortified that his father lacks the social and professional status of the fathers of many of his classmates at Clongowes Wood College. So Stephen seeks to compensate for the lack of a positive father image by creating one, fantasizing about his father's accomplishments during a revery about his upcoming trip home for Christmas: "His father was a marshal now: higher than a magistrate" (20).

As Stephen grows older, Simon continually declines in effectiveness as a positive model, and the son will eventually reject the father entirely. Indeed, Stephen's relationship with his father deteriorates rapidly, ending in hostility and name calling that will eventually contribute to Stephen's decision to leave Ireland and to turn to the mythical Daedalus (who has the advantage of not being real) as a substitute father image. Failing to find an adequate model in his natural father, Stephen tries out a number of substitute figures. The search for a suitable father forms a major theme of *Ulysses*, though the theme is there deflated with a typical Joycean irony that undercuts Stephen's idealistic efforts as usual. As Watson puts it, "Joyce, connoisseur of anticlimax, shows Japhet in search of a father finding a place to pee" (55). But Stephen also seeks a number of substitute fathers in *Portrait*. Particularly important among such paternal models are the Jesuit priests by whom he is educated, and the fact that they are addressed as "Father" is not insignificant, especially given the powerful emphasis that Stephen places on words. Though somewhat threatening, the Jesuits serve as figures of mysterious and tantalizing occult power of the kind that Simon Dedalus lacks and that Stephen yearns to appropriate for himself. This motif becomes most clear when the director of studies at Belvedere College invites a newly pious, adolescent Stephen to consider turning to the priesthood as a vocation.

To receive that call, Stephen, said the priest, is the greatest honour that the Almighty God can bestow upon a man. No king or emperor on this earth has the power of the priest of God. No angel or archangel in heaven, no saint, not even the Blessed Virgin herself has the power of a priest of God. (*Portrait* 158)

Significantly, all the figures with whom the director compares the power of the priest are also figures that have served at various points as models for Stephen's efforts at envisionment. Stephen finds this invitation tempting; it offers him not only a clear role in which to formulate his self-image but a role that he has envisioned before: "How often had he seen himself as a priest wielding calmly and humbly the awful power of which angels and saints stood in reverence!" (158). Further, the priesthood offers Stephen a position from which he can be special, set aside from ordinary people. The director, in inviting him to consider the priesthood, is "offering him secret knowledge and power. . . . He would know obscure things, hidden from others" (159).

In a sense, the Jesuits play for Stephen much the same role that the mysterious Society of the Tower plays for Wilhelm—except that the Jesuits would move Stephen away from secular society, while the Society of the Tower seeks to help Wilhelm enter *into* German society. Of course, the Jesuits and the Freemasons are old enemies, so it is not surprising that they function in different directions. However, while the Society succeeds in engineering Wilhelm's apprenticeship, Stephen ultimately rejects the priesthood as a career and priests as models for his subjective development. Like Simon Dedalus, the priests Stephen encounters show themselves to be humanly flawed, so they cannot meet Stephen's requirements of perfection. It is significant, as Schutte points out, that Stephen never thinks of himself as a Catholic layman (96–97). He can consider being a Jesuit priest, or he can consider being a Satanic apostate, but his penchant for idealized visions leaves no room for the excluded middle in between. As a result, Stephen remains thoroughly inscribed within the authority of the Church, perhaps most so when he is at the height of his rebellion against it.

Indeed, one could argue that it is precisely his inability to escape the constraints of Catholic ideology that leads Stephen to reject the Church. He seeks poetic perfection and an escape from the prosaic realities of the everyday world, yet in Ireland the Church is thoroughly immersed in politics and in attempts to engineer the everyday lives of the Irish people. Importantly, though, Stephen's rejection of Catholicism is a purely personal matter that has little to do with the political realities of Ireland. Stephen lacks Joyce's intensely political vision almost entirely. And so, when the priests whom Stephen encounters in the course of his education ultimately fail as imaginary models, he simply raises his sights, seeking identification with the great men of Church history, much as he had sought identification with the heroes of ancient Greece and Rome. The scholastic philosophy of Aquinas forms a particularly important part of Stephen's own developing aesthetic theory, to the point where Stephen himself suggests that the philistine MacAlister might call that theory "applied Aquinas" (*Portrait* 209).[24] And those theories form an important part of Stephen's efforts to develop an ennobling self-vision. While exploring the philosophy of Aristotle and Aquinas, there are moments when Stephen's thoughts become clear, resulting in a concomitant moment of clarity in his self-image, so that "he felt that the spirit of beauty had folded him round like a mantle and that in revery at least he had been acquainted with nobility" (177).

St. Francis Xavier provides another model for Stephen, a particularly appropriate one. The inchoate "conversion" experience that puts Stephen in a position to consider the priesthood occurs at a retreat in honor of St. Francis, and in this light it is significant to note that Xavier, too, was a student of the philosophy of Aristotle. Perhaps more importantly, St. Francis's importance in Church history rests largely on his reputation as "apostle to the Indies." This reputation was obtained during an extended period of missionary service in the exotic East, a fact that no doubt would appeal to the romantic imagination of young Stephen in much the same way that it appealed to the young boy in "Araby."[25] In particular, St. Francis's career in many ways resembles that of Edmond Dantes, who similarly conducted a successful campaign in the exotic East—though unlike Xavier he was driven to the East by tormentors upon whom he wreaks vengeance after his return. Dantes is a classic example of the Byronic hero, and to Stephen "The figure of that dark avenger stood forth in his mind for whatever he had heard or divined in childhood of the strange and terrible" (*Portrait* 62).

Byron himself functions as one of Stephen's principal literary models of rebellion, while Stephen's conflict with his schoolmates over his loyalty to Byron also illustrates the alienation that informs all of his intersubjective relations. Adhering to a strict dichotomy of self and other, Stephen experiences his fellows as irreducibly alien, as objects rather than other subjects. Throughout *Portrait*, Stephen feels isolated and alone, different from his comrades. As a result, he gains very little in his efforts at envisionment through identification with his peers. Even very early in his career at Clongowes Wood College, we find that "All the boys seemed to him very strange" (13). And the cruelty of Wells in taunting him about the kissing of his mother or in pushing him into the ditch is incomprehensible to him. As a result of this lack of connection, Stephen generally associates his schoolmates with negative qualities from which he wishes to distance himself, using his sense of difference as a reinforcement of his hopes for uniqueness. Thus, he bolsters his own sense of nobility and sophistication through rejection of the "rude Firbolg mind" of Davin (180) and the "sharp Ulster voice" of MacAlister (193). On the other hand, Stephen again shows the beginnings of his "artistic" imagination by creating friends with whom he *can* identify. Stephen has heard and rejected the calls of his fellows in favor of the calls of his own imaginary creations: "He gave them ear only for a time but he was happy only when he was far from them, beyond their call, alone or in the company of phantasmal comrades" (84).

This turn to fictional friends is typical of the general movement by which Stephen uses art as a refuge for escape from historical reality. Again, this movement recalls the chronotope that Bakhtin associates with Dante and stands in stark contrast to the chronotope of *Wilhelm Meister's Apprenticeship*. Indeed, art is one of the central tools that Wilhelm Meister uses as he moves toward integration into society rather than escape from it. One could argue, then, that art functions for Wilhelm in a manner precisely opposite of that in which it functions for Stephen. In this sense it is not Wilhelm Meister but young Werther who is the true Goethean predecessor of Stephen. After all, the principal difference between *The Sorrows of Young Werther* and *Wilhelm Meister's Apprenticeship* is that Wilhelm Meister is able successfully to come to terms with the existing social order while Werther is an unusual, even pathological, individual who is unable to transcend his personal concerns and therefore is so radically at odds with the world around him that he is driven to suicide.

Werther in fact shares a number of characteristics with Stephen. Both characters are, for example, would-be poets. And, while one could argue that Stephen has talent whereas Werther does not, it is certainly true that neither really accomplishes much as a poet. In addition, Werther often anticipates Stephen in his longing to escape from the chronotopic reality of the temporal world. Unable to deal with the inevitable facts of human mortality, Werther rails against the transience of all things human.

> Can you say that anything *is*, when in fact it is all transient? and all passes by as fast as any storm, seldom enduring in the full force of existence, but ah! torn away by the torrent, submerged beneath the waves and dashed against the rocks? There is not one moment that does not wear you away, and those who are close to you. (Goethe, *Sorrows* 66)

Faced with the transience of the temporal, Werther longs "for the wings of a crane that passed overhead, to fly to the shores of the measureless sea," clearly paralleling the Icarus imagery that informs Joyce's depiction of Stephen. And, if Stephen's desire to escape from reality is most vividly figured in his attempts at the mortification of the flesh in part 4 of *Portrait*, Werther sometimes similarly turns toward thoughts of religious asceticism: "My soul is so beset that I long for the pampered ease of a hermit's cell, for a hair-shirt and a barbed scourge" (69).

Actually, the young Wilhelm Meister shares this view of art as an escape from reality; it is only after his years of apprenticeship that he learns to integrate the aesthetic with the prosaic. Indeed, one of the central oppositions that runs throughout *Wilhelm Meister's Apprenticeship* is that between the world of art and the world of business and commerce. One of Wilhelm's youthful poems, for example, depicts a struggle for his soul between the muses of "tragic art" and of "Commerce" (26). His youthful preference for the former, meanwhile, is made quite clear. He refers to the business career intended for him by his father as a "low profession," which he rejects in favor of the theater: "It was to the stage that I aimed at consecrating all my powers,—on the stage that I meant to seek all my happiness and satisfaction" (25).

One of the lessons Wilhelm must learn is that the stage, too, is a business, and much of the action of *Wilhelm Meister's Apprenticeship* involves Wilhelm's dealings with theatrical companies, whose problems and preoccupations frequently turn out to be more financial than artistic. Early in the book, he is appalled by this fact. He is, for example, unable to reconcile his idealized love for the actress Mariana with the behavior of the other actors in her company, who "seemed to think least of all on their employment and object: the poetic worth of a piece they were never heard to speak of or to judge of, right or wrong; their continual question was simply, How much will it *bring*? Is it a stock-piece? How long will it run?" (53–54, Goethe's emphasis). Wilhelm is initially repelled by the bourgeois materialism of the business world, especially by the rather vulgar materialism of his erstwhile friend Werner. Gradually, however, he comes more and more to appreciate the possible practical applications of drama as a means of influencing the general populace in positive ways. By the middle of the book, in fact, Wilhelm finds himself torn between the worlds of art and business, unable to decide finally in favor of either (264). He is thus willing to make certain practical compromises while he works in the theater company of Serlo in book 5 of the text. Eventually, Wilhelm rejects the theater almost entirely, viewing it as a locus of deception and pretense. However, late in the book (partially inspired by the aristocratic officer Jarno's suggestion that the world of the stage is not necessarily so different from the world at large) Wilhelm comes to recognize that his choice need not be entirely in favor of either business or art, but that a well-balanced life can include both (410).

This quick summary by no means does justice to the complex irony of Goethe's book, nor does it answer the concerns of some critics that Wilhelm's growing willingness to compromise with the everyday concerns of bourgeois society is a sign not of maturity but of degradation, of a loss of innocence and poetic vision. Reading Goethe through Joyce indicates the complexity of such questions, though by no means does it answer them. Numerous critics, for example, have seen the young Stephen, whose motto, significantly, is "all or nothing at all" as a figure of uncompromising single-mindedness. Compromise, on the other hand, is the great talent of Leopold Bloom, whose ability to reconcile opposing points of view is frequently cited by critics. Mahaffey, for example, sees Stephen and Molly as embodying diametrically opposed attitudes toward authority, while Bloom represents a compromise between these two extremes.[26]

Reading *Wilhelm Meister's Apprenticeship* through this interpretation of Bloom would suggest that Wilhelm does in fact learn something valuable by gaining an ability to compromise, thus moving from the position of Stephen (or even Werther) to that of Bloom in the course of his education. On the other hand, Bloom is hardly in control of his own compromises, and his inherent multiplicity may in fact merely be a reflection of the plurality of the bourgeois society by which he has been so thoroughly constituted and within the ideology of which he is so thoroughly trapped. In this sense, then, Wilhelm's growing willingness to compromise with the concerns of bourgeois society can be read as a capitulation and an admission of the difficulty of escaping the dominant ideology of the culture in which one lives.

It is this difficulty, especially as it functions within the paralytic constraints of Catholic Ireland, that informs the depiction of all of Joyce's characters, none of whom are truly able to break free of those constraints. Not wishing to present an overly sanguine picture of the possibilities for emancipation, Joyce shows his characters as thoroughly trapped within the various discourses that make them who they are. In addition, none of us, even in the most enlightened and democratic societies, can completely escape the constraints that society places on our subjective development. It is thus particularly crucial to recognize the folly of Stephen's attempts to do so, as opposed to Wilhelm's attempts to develop positively within the limits placed upon him by society. As Bakhtin emphasizes, it is social interaction that makes us truly human; individual liberty as freedom from social constraints is thus an impossible myth. If individuals are the products of discourses (rather than the other way around) true liberation begins not with changed individuals but with changed (and changeable) discourses. Thus, Joyce focuses in his career not on depicting characters who break free of the traditions of the past but in creating texts that challenge the conventions of literary discourse by engaging the literary tradition of forebears like Goethe in productive and critical dialogues. Joyce does not, however, seek literally to break free of the literary tradition, because texts take their meanings only within the context of that tradition. The dynamic and constantly changing nature of Joyce's own texts contributes to his dialogue with the past by assuring that Joyce's texts will themselves remain unfinalizable and therefore will avoid supplying new fixed conventions to replace the old ones.

Chapter Five

Shakespeare, Joyce's Contemporary: The Politics and Poetics of Literary Authority

Early in "The Dead" Gabriel Conroy debates with himself over whether to include a somewhat obscure quotation from Browning in his upcoming postprandial speech:

> He was undecided about the lines from Robert Browning for he feared they would be above the heads of his hearers. Some quotation that they could recognise from Shakespeare or from the Melodies would be better. The indelicate clacking of the men's heels and the scuffling of their soles reminded him that their grade of culture differed from his. He would only make himself ridiculous by quoting poetry to them which they could not understand. (179)

Gabriel, in short, recognizes that quotations from Shakespeare are apt to be more effective than quotations from Browning, if only because they are more likely to be recognized by his audience. It might even be said that Shakespeare is more contemporary than the Victorian Browning because the greater critical (and popular) attention paid to Shakespeare's work assures its continual revision in a contemporary context.

Similarly, in the "Sirens" chapter of *Ulysses*, Bloom thinks he recognizes a line from Shakespeare and muses on the richness of Shakespeare as a source of quotations for every occasion: "Music hath charms. Shakespeare said. Quotations every day in the year. Wisdom while you wait" (230). Both Conroy and Bloom thus indicate one of the principal reasons Joyce refers to Shakespeare more than to any other author—because Shakespeare is the one author allusions to whom are most likely to be recognized and understood by Joyce's readers. On the other hand, both of the above passages also call attention to the complexity of Joyce's use of Shakespeare. Conroy places Shakespeare's works in the same category as the *Melodies* of Thomas Moore, who for Joyce serves not only as an image of cultural banality but of Irish subjugation to the British. In *A Portrait of the Artist as a Young Man*, for example, Joyce sarcastically refers to Moore as the "national poet of Ireland" (180), a label that Gifford suggests has to do with the way Moore left Ireland for England and "advanced himself by currying favor in the drawing rooms of the influential in London" (*Joyce Annotated* 229).[1] Bloom, meanwhile, shows that lines from Shakespeare are sometimes "recognized" even when they do not come from Shakespeare at all—he seems to be remembering Congreve's "Music has charms to soothe a savage breast," though there is also a similar line in *Measure for Measure*.[2] In addition, Bloom indicates Shakespeare's status as a commodity in modern culture with his figuration of Shakespeare as a source of prepackaged wisdom.

Among other things, the easy (maybe *too* easy) recognizability of allusions to Shakespeare allows Joyce to use Shakespeare in extremely subtle ways, producing some of his most serendipitous intertextual effects.[3] Joyce's use of Shakespeare as *materia poetica* is also especially appropriate given that Shakespeare himself tended (following the standard authorial practice of his time) to build his work through appropriation and transformation of whatever materials happened to be at hand. As Stephen Dedalus says of Shakespeare in his disquisition on *Hamlet* in the "Scylla and Charybdis" chapter of *Ulysses*, "all events brought grist to his mill" (168). In fact, Shakespeare and Dante were probably the two authors from whom Joyce learned most in this regard. Of course, the importance of Shakespeare to Joyce is well known. Indeed, when John Eglinton in "Scylla and Charybdis" cites Dumas *fils* (or is it Dumas *père*?) to the effect that "after God Shakespeare created most," he might have been expressing Joyce's own attitude (175).

On the other hand, Joyce was certainly not above criticizing Shakespeare—for example, as a young man he sometimes expressed the opinion that Ibsen was superior to Shakespeare as a dramatist. Meanwhile, the attitude that Joyce displays toward Shakespeare in his fiction is certainly not reverential. It is, however, respectful, and the frequency of allusion to Shakespeare in Joyce's work can certainly be taken as an acknowledgment of Shakespeare's position at the center of the western cultural canon. In addition, Joyce's allusions to Shakespeare are often of crucial importance, contributing to an extensive dialogue between the two authors that is central to the texture of Joyce's writing, especially in *Ulysses* and *Finnegans Wake*. *Hamlet*, for example, is arguably at least as important as *The Odyssey* as a structural model for *Ulysses*. Similarly, noting the central importance of Shakespearean echoes in *Finnegans Wake*, Adaline Glasheen concludes that "Shakespeare (man, works) is the matrix of" Joyce's last novel (260).

Glasheen's emphasis on Shakespeare the man as a presence in the *Wake* appropriately indicates that Joyce's use of Shakespeare goes far beyond Shakespeare's texts themselves. Shakespeare is uniquely valuable to Joyce as an intertextual resource, both because his texts are so well known that Joyce can be reasonably confident that his allusions to Shakespeare will be understood and because Shakespeare himself occupies an important symbolic position in western culture. If Shakespeare's texts are almost universally acknowledged as great art, Shakespeare was himself firmly established by Joyce's time as the epitome of the great artist, making him a crucial figure for Joyce's engagement with the literary tradition.

There is, of course, much more at stake in this engagement than any mere "anxiety of influence." As Stephen Greenblatt puts it, Shakespeare's plays have become a "fetish of Western civilization" (161). In particular, Shakespeare functions as the leading representative of the culture of Elizabethan England, a culture that has frequently functioned for writers as the image of a Golden Age in comparison to which modern culture and society are fragmented, sterile, and degraded. The Elizabethan Age occurs before the "dissociation of sensibility" that T. S. Eliot diagnoses as a central factor in the decay of modern culture, and Elizabethan drama (especially Shakespeare's) functions for Virginia Woolf as the height of the kind of androgynous and nonegoistic art that she recommends as a counter to the social and cultural rifts that for her set the modern world against itself. Joyce uses Shakespeare in a variety of ways, drawing upon Shakespeare's works as intertextual material for use in constructing his own, engaging in dialogues with Shakespeare the man as a figure of cultural authority, and using him as a focal point for the initiation of historical dialogues between Elizabethan England and modern Ireland. In addition, especially when read through Bakhtin, the dialogue between Joyce and Shakespeare takes on special importance because it represents an encounter between two different genres and a resulting clash between the ideologies they represent. At the same time, it is crucial to recognize that "Shakespeare" is not by the time of Joyce an individual who lived in Elizabethan England—or even the body of work left by that individual. Shakespeare is an entire complex of cultural forces that includes the original plays, interpretations and performances of them, and their use as a major element of the ideological superstructure of the British Empire.

A great deal of critical energy and ink have been spent in the exploration of Joyce's specific allusions to Shakespeare. The most important critical exploration of the relationship between Joyce and Shakespeare is probably William Schutte's 1957 *Joyce and Shakespeare*, which not only added a great deal to the understanding of Joyce's use of Shakespeare but also served as a historically important milestone in literary criticism. As Mary Reynolds puts it, Schutte's book was "the first attempt to explain systematically the function of literary allusion in a major novel and the first large effort toward critical assessment of literariness in Joyce's work" ("Joyce's Shakespeare" 169).[4] More recently, Vincent Cheng has devoted an entire book to Joyce's use of Shakespeare in *Finnegans Wake*. In terms of sheer numbers, a convenient summary table at the end of Schutte's *Joyce and Shakespeare* counts 202 "quotations or adaptations of quotations" from 32 different works of Shakespeare in *Ulysses*, including 88 from *Hamlet* alone (191). Meanwhile, Weldon Thornton's *Allusions in "Ulysses"* identifies over 400 specific allusions to Shakespeare in *Ulysses*, including approximately 130 allusions to *Hamlet*. And Don Gifford lists in his *"Ulysses" Annotated* approximately 350 references to Shakespeare, including more than 100 to *Hamlet*.

Following Schutte's lead, critics have by now done a great deal not only to identify Joyce's allusions to Shakespeare but also to explore the significance of those allusions and their contribution to the generation of meaning in Joyce's texts. By far the single most frequently discussed instance concerns Stephen's Shakespeare theory in the "Scylla and Charybdis" chapter of *Ulysses*. Different critics have approached this episode in widely differing ways, indicating its richness. Schutte devotes an entire chapter of his book to this episode, focusing in an essentially New Critical style on Stephen's sources and on what this theory tells us about Stephen as a character. This episode also generates dialogues with a number of authors like Goethe. Meanwhile, both

Hugh Kenner (*Dublin's Joyce* 195) and David Hayman (*Joyce et Mallarmé* 2:7–9) point out that the links between Stephen and Hamlet in "Scylla and Charybdis" owe much to Mallarmé's *Hamlet et Fortinbras* and thus illuminate the relationship between Joyce and Mallarmé as well as that between Joyce and Shakespeare. Finally, in "Artist, Critic, and Performer," R. B. Kershner explores the way Stephen's Shakespeare theory enriches our understanding of Joyce's relationship to Oscar Wilde.

Critics have also noted that Stephen's disquisition on *Hamlet* not only represents Stephen's own theory of artistic creation but also opens dialogues with various other theories. In a study of Joyce's depiction of Stephen as a storyteller, Shari Benstock discusses the Shakespeare theory as an example of Stephen's narrative performance (726–34). And Colin MacCabe sees Stephen's presentation as an integral part of Joyce's dialogue with traditional modes of reading and writing, particularly informed by Stephen's inability to become an Irish Shakespeare because he must write not in the native language of Ireland but in the imperial language of England ("Voice of Esau").

MacCabe's reading points toward an awareness of the colonial roots of Irish English that runs throughout Joyce's work, informing in different ways both Gabriel Conroy's recognition in "The Dead" that "Irish is not my language" (*Dubliners* 189) and Stephen's famous complaint in *Portrait* that English "will always be for me an acquired speech. I have not made or accepted its words" (189). Granted, the lack of proprietorship of language shown by characters like Gabriel and Stephen goes beyond the effects of colonialism, characterizing to a certain extent the relationships of all speakers to all languages. But the importance of Joyce's status as a colonial and postcolonial writer in this respect should not be underestimated. Like Stephen, Joyce is using an English language acquired from Ireland's colonial masters. As a result, each time Joyce uses English his words bear traces not only of the cultural past of England but of the colonial past of Ireland. Joyce's heavy use of prior literary texts constitutes among other things an acknowledgment of the inherited nature of all language, and his allusions to Shakespeare (especially some of the more subtle of those allusions) illustrate this effect in an especially profound way, especially as Shakespeare stands not only as an icon of the past but as an icon of English culture in the present.

Language comes down to us already embedded in well-defined discourses that tend to limit the flexibility with which it can be used but also give to language a potential for political subversion through transgression of inherited linguistic norms. This effect can be illuminated through comparison of Joyce with Salman Rushdie, who has been treated more consistently by critics as a postcolonial writer than has Joyce, whose colonial/postcolonial status has been somewhat obscured by his position at the center of the modernist canon. Rushdie, like Joyce, is clearly a lover of the English language, noting in the London *Times* that "I don't think there's another language large or flexible enough to include so many different realities" ("Empire Writes Back"). But in this same article Rushdie also shows a profound appreciation for the historicity and political embeddedness of language, arguing that the vestiges of empire are still to be found in the "cadences" of the English language itself. On the other hand, Rushdie sees the political charge that inheres in language to be potentially energizing. Citing the great Irish writers Joyce, Beckett, and Flann O'Brien as predecessors, he argues that much "vitality and excitement" can be derived from attempts to "decolonize" the language, citing a number of contemporary writers such as Chinua Achebe and Ngugi wa Thiong'o who are resisting the history of imperialism that inheres within the language by "busily forging English into new shapes."

> But of course a good deal more than formal, stylistic alteration is going on in this new fiction. And perhaps above all, what is going on is politics. . . . There are very few major writers in the new English literatures who do not place politics at the very centre of their art. (8)

Rushdie's emphasis on the particular positioning of the former colonial within the English language recalls in a direct way Stephen's recognition of this effect in his encounter with the dean of studies in *Portrait*. Moreover, one could see the radical linguistic experimentation of *Finnegans Wake* as Joyce's attempt to engage in a dialogue with the echoes of colonization embedded in the English language through its relation to its association with British imperial history. Jacques Derrida thus reads the language of the *Wake* as a sort of allegory of resistance to linguistic imperialism very much in the manner of what Rushdie describes as decolonization. Derrida notes the Babelian multilingualism of the *Wake* and suggests that the interaction of English as the dom-

inant language in the text with the other secondary languages in the
same text is a mirror of the sort of imperialism that England imposed
on Ireland.

> English tries to erase the other language or languages, to colonize
> them, to domesticate them, to present them for reading from only
> one angle. But one must also read the resistance to this common-
> wealth, not only pronounce oneself but also write oneself against
> it. Against Him. And this is indeed what happens. Between islands
> of language, across each island. Ireland and England would be
> only emblems of this. What matters is the contamination of the
> master by the language he claims to subjugate, on which he has
> declared war. ("Two Words" 156)

In Joyce's writing, then, dialogues with the British colonial past of
Ireland can occur not only through specific allusions to great texts from
British culture but through very subtle linguistic effects due, above all,
to the fact that he is writing in the language of the British Empire. In
Joyce's work very subtle intertextual links can occur at what Bakhtin
calls the "sub-atomic level" of language, apart from any question of
direct allusion. At the same time, this "sub-atomic" effect is enhanced
by the presence of so many overt allusions, the various kinds of intertextuality that reside in Joyce's texts combining to create a fabric so
richly charged with intertextual energies that readers who approach
Joyce's texts through intertextual reading generally find that their
efforts will be well rewarded. Through the process of serendipitous
intertextuality that thus informs the experience of reading Joyce, readers who pursue intertextual associations (overt or not) in Joyce's texts
often find that this pursuit triggers a sort of chain reaction that results
in the activation of a number of other associations as well, contributing
in a powerful way to the already highly dialogic nature of Joyce's writing.

Intertextual connections can be created through resonances in language itself, through obvious allusion, and through more subtle kinds
of allusion. In general, as Michael Riffaterre points out,

> Intertextual connection takes place when the reader's attention is
> triggered by . . . obscure wordings, phrasings that the context alone

will not suffice to explain—in short, ungrammaticalities in the idi-
olectic norm . . . which are traces left by the absent intertext, signs
of an incompleteness to be completed elsewhere. (627)

In short, intertextual connection is triggered during moments of linguistic strangeness when oddities and peculiarities in tone or diction
indicate an absent intertext and thereby call attention to the dialogic
and intertextual nature of all language. Joyce deftly employs such
subtle intertextual triggers in his work, though of course this technique
cedes a great deal of the responsibility for generation of meaning to the
reader. Different readers might react differently to the same trigger,
some finding links to Shakespeare, others to Homer or Dante, others to
MTV videos, and so on. Indeed, many readers no doubt find echoes in
Joyce that Joyce did not anticipate or recognize. But Joyce's texts in a
sense authorize precisely this kind of multiplicity in readings, openly
inviting readers to contribute to the intertextual dialogue any voices
with which they might be familiar. And the serendipitous intertextuality that informs the dynamics of such readings can often be richly productive.

A look at Joyce's use of Shakespeare in a text like "The Dead"—
wherein Shakespeare is not an obviously central presence—can serve
to illustrate this phenomenon. For example, in "The Dead" the one sentence that has seemed most often to strike commentators as peculiar is
Gabriel's enigmatic note near the end: "The time had come for him to
set out on his journey westward" (223). Certainly the west is here associated with Ireland itself, and in this sense the "journey westward" can
be interpreted as a turn away from the antinationalist tendencies exhib-
ited by Gabriel in his earlier encounter with Molly Ivors. His journey
might then indicate his acceptance of the potential vitalizing effects of
the folk culture of his native land. In this light, it is important to note
that images of the East function throughout *Dubliners* as symbols of
exotic lands where one might escape the stifling atmosphere of Ireland.
Gabriel's westward turn, then, functions as an acceptance of current
reality as opposed to the dream of escape. There are also more symbolic
interpretations of this westward turn. Brewster Ghiselin finds a unify-
ing pattern in the religious connotations of the various eastward and
westward movements in *Dubliners* as whole, noting (among other
things) that Christians of the fourth century turned to the west to
renounce Satan and that Joyce must have "shared that profound

human feeling, older than Christianity, which has made the sunrise immemorially and all but universally an emblem of the return of life" (321). In contrast, the west is traditionally associated with sunset and with death—except that it is often a death associated with rebirth, since we all know that the sun will rise again tomorrow. Thus, Gabriel's turn to the west can be interpreted either as a rebirth and affirmative acceptance of his present life or as a surrender to death and despair.[5] Moreover, this duality in interpretation is inevitable; as that later Gabriel, Rushdie's Gibreel Farishta, tells us, "To be born again . . . first you have to die" (*Satanic Verses* 3).

The "westward journey" motif also potentially initiates a number of intertextual links, including Dante's use in the *Commedia* of the well-developed medieval topos of the *translatio imperii*, of movement from east to west—related to the westward movement of Aeneas from Troy to Rome—as a fundamental metaphor for history itself. "Modeled on the movement of the sun from east to west, this doctrine is conventionally based on the analogy between the duration of the day and the totality of history" (Mazzotta 99). Thus, "The sun is the foundation of history, its radical metaphor" (102). In this scheme, east is associated with the past and west with the future, so that Gabriel's turn to the west can be taken to represent his acceptance of the flow of history, as a rejection of the immersion in the past that characterizes the society around him, and as a turn toward the future.[6] This link to Dante potentially contributes to a reading of "The Dead" as a story of Gabriel's transcendence, but Joyce confounds any attempt to read Dantean transcendence as a model for Gabriel's "conversion" through references to numerous texts other than Dante's. In particular, "The Dead" includes a carnivalesque intermixture of echoes from "high" literature and "low." Just as surely as Gabriel's westward turn recalls the significance of westward movement in Dante's *Commedia*, so too does it recall the Wild West of those "chronicles of disorder" so beloved to the boys in "An Encounter." In fact, as Gerhard Friedrich has pointed out, it is quite possible that Gabriel's name is a reference to the western novel *Gabriel Conroy*, by Bret Harte. This connection also indicates a certain turn toward the future (the wagon master's cry of "westward ho!" manifesting a desire to get on with things) but in a prosaic way that does not imply transcendence of the physical world.

But the cry of "westward ho" predates the Wild West, having been used by westward-bound Thames boatmen at least as early as the sixteenth century. In literature it occurs in Shakespeare's *Twelfth Night* in a scene in which Olivia acknowledges that Cesario (Viola disguised as a boy) may be too young for her, that perhaps he/she needs some more seasoning before being ready for marriage.

> Olivia: Be not afraid, good youth, I will not have you;
> And yet, when wit and youth is come to harvest,
> Your wife is like to reap a proper man.
> There lies your way, due west.
>
> Viola: Then westward ho!
>
> (III.i.131–34)

Here, a westward journey is associated with a move toward greater maturity that will allow a man to become a better husband. In this light, Gabriel's plan to travel westward might be taken to indicate a resolve to be a better and more understanding husband to Gretta. In this case, then, the invocation of *Twelfth Night* as intertext appears to support affirmative interpretations of the ending of "The Dead" that would have Gabriel learning a valuable lesson and turning away from his former folly. Alternatively, one might interpret this passage as indicating that mature men make better husbands than do boys, so that Gabriel's invocation of the westward journey becomes a defensive attempt to elevate himself above Michael Furey. However, in the context of *Twelfth Night*, appearances can be (and almost invariably are) deceiving. Indeed, Feste's declaration that "Nothing that is so is so" (IV.i.8) can stand as a statement of the theme of the entire play. Despite Olivia's confidence, Viola will never become an adequate husband because she simply doesn't have what it takes to do so—and perhaps the implication is that Gabriel doesn't either.[7]

Of course, the relevance of *Twelfth Night* to "The Dead" is rather obvious. Since the identification by Julian Kaye some years ago, Joyce scholars have generally agreed that the Misses Morkan's annual dance occurs on Twelfth Night, though there has been some confusion and blurring of terminology (some of it by Kaye himself) between Twelfth Night and the Feast of the Epiphany.[8] This confluence of dates alone is enough to indicate that Shakespeare's play might be relevant to "The Dead," and indeed an examination of *Twelfth Night* shows a number of parallels between the two texts. For one thing, the central plots of the two works have a great deal in common. Kershner has pointed out the relevance of the tradition of courtly love in Gabriel's attitude toward Gretta (*Joyce, Bakhtin* 145), and surely one of the more vivid (and at the same time parodic) depictions of the courtly lover in all of literature is that of Duke Orsino in *Twelfth Night*. As the play opens, we find the good Duke pining away in fine fashion over his rejection by Olivia, his ideal true love. And his idealization of Olivia (like all idealism) results in a turning away from life—if only temporarily and comically.

> Duke: If music be the food of love, play on;
>   Give me excess of it, that, surfeiting,
>   The appetite may sicken, and so die.
>
>   (I.i.1–3)

In response, the Duke's aide Curio asks if he would like to go hunt the hart to take his mind off his troubles. Orsino, not too depressed to miss an opportunity to capitalize on an easy pun, responds:

> Duke: Why, so I do, the noblest that I have.
>   O, when mine eyes did see Olivia first,
>   Methought she purg'd the air of pestilence!
>   That instant was I turn'd into a hart,
>   And my desires, like fell and cruel hounds,
>   E'er since pursue me.
>
>   (I.i.17–22)

As M. E. Lamb points out in relation to this passage, "Orsino's comparison of himself with Actaeon is trite, and it shows him in the stereotype of the courtly lover" (65). Lamb further points out that by the sixteenth century it was common to interpret the various stories in Ovid's *Metamorphoses* as allegories of changing spiritual states, with Actaeon serving as a figure of failed metamorphosis who "has reached a point of inner stasis from which there is no apparent rescue" (66). In this sense, the Actaeon story is clearly relevant to the general spiritual paralysis that pervades all of *Dubliners*. Thus Gabriel, like Orsino, is being torn apart both by his own hyperbolic emotions and by a metaphorical pack of dogs.

But the relevance of the beginning lines of *Twelfth Night* to "The

Dead" does not depend upon this identification of Gabriel as a figure of Actaeon, though Actaeon is a traditional stock figure for the courtly lover. The Duke's reference to the traditional link between music and love puts in place a standard Renaissance topos that sounds throughout the play,[9] and his later reference to "That old and antique song we heard last night" (II.iv.3) provides a further link to the role played by songs such as "The Lass of Aughrim" in "The Dead." Also, it is important to note that the reason for Orsino's melancholy (other than the obvious fact that he enjoys his suffering so greatly) is that Olivia cannot give herself to him because she is mourning the recent death of her brother, no doubt a frail young lad who might have been mistaken for Cesario (or Michael Furey) on a dark night.

One of the more striking features of *Twelfth Night* as a play is the central importance of Viola's gender transformation into the boy Cesario and then back again at the end. This motif is a common one in Shakespeare, but, as Catherine Belsey points out, "Of all of Shakespeare's comedies it is perhaps *Twelfth Night* which takes the most remarkable risks with the identity of its central figure" (185). Indeed, the perfection of gender disguises in Shakespeare's Illyria points toward recent critical discussions of clothing as a metaphor for the socially determined nature of all gender roles. Even in the end of the play, when Viola's twin brother Sebastian has made his appearance and Viola's true identity is revealed, we find that she is *still* a boy for all practical purposes, at least as long as she remains clad in her boy's attire. To the Duke, she is still Cesario, despite all the revelations.

> Duke: Cesario, come—
>   For so you shall be, while you are a man;
>   But when in other habits you are seen,
>   Orsino's mistress and his fancy's queen.
>
>   (V.i.382–85)

Sandra Gilbert, among others, has emphasized that women modernist writers seem to regard gender identity as a matter of so much costuming and as something that can be put on and taken off like clothing. Moreover, "feminist modernist costume imagery is radically revisionary in a political as well as a literary sense, for it implies that no one, male or female, can or should be confined to a uni-form, a single form or self" (196). Gilbert appropriately invokes Woolf's *Orlando* as a central example of the effect she is describing, and it is significant that Woolf herself identifies Shakespeare as an important predecessor in the recognition of the fluidity of gender boundaries. Drawing on Coleridge's suggestion that the truly great mind is an androgynous one, Woolf notes that "one goes back to Shakespeare's mind as the type of the androgynous, of the man-womanly mind" (*Room* 102).

Reading "The Dead" through *Twelfth Night* helps to show that Joyce's writing also challenges traditional gender roles and that it was doing so even as early as *Dubliners*.[10] Kershner discusses the relevance of Harte's novel *Gabriel Conroy* and of the operas *Mignon*, *Dinorah*, and *Lucrezia Borgia* mentioned by Mary Jane Morkan and Mr. Browne during the dinner for a reading of Joyce's story, pointing out that "the major intertextual interventions in 'The Dead' point variously to male-female confusions, disguised and mistaken identities, and sexual ambivalences and frustrations" (*Joyce, Bakhtin* 148). Kershner does not mention *Twelfth Night*, though it would be difficult to produce a better description of Shakespeare's comedy than the one he provides. Further, Kershner convincingly demonstrates that these intertextual presences help to reveal Gabriel's constant movement toward the assumption of a feminine position in "The Dead."

A return to *Twelfth Night* helps to illustrate that destabilization of gender roles and of traditional metaphysical views of language as representation and direct reflection of the speaker's intention go hand in hand. Belsey notes that language involves "sets of terms and relations between terms in which a specific understanding of the world is inscribed" (166). She further notes (à la Derrida) that the metaphysical model of language depends upon well-defined systems of polar oppositions (of which the opposition male/female is paradigmatic) and that an insistence on this view of language involves an affirmation of the existing values of a society. Challenges to such a view of language, then, might be expected to arise during periods of crisis when these values are in question. Belsey recognizes that the tradition of female transvestism in literature goes back at least as far as Ovid's story of Iphis and Ianthe but suggests that the unusual frequency of such images in English Renaissance literature points to a fundamental contemporary crisis in the values of contemporary English society.[11]

Interestingly, Shakespeare himself centrally participates in one of many examples of the transgression of gender confusion that occur in *Ulysses*.

One of the many strange transformations that inform the "Circe" chapter occurs when Stephen and Bloom look into a mirror and see their images merge to form that of Shakespeare:

> *Stephen and Bloom gaze into the mirror. The face of William Shakespeare, beardless, appears there, rigid in facial paralysis, crowned by the reflection of the reindeer antlered hatrack in the hall.* (463, Joyce's italics)

This passage is extremely rich. Besides participating in the general blurring of the subjective boundary between Stephen and Bloom that informs the late chapters of *Ulysses*, it suggests that the great artist, exemplified by Shakespeare, must combine disparate characteristics. Indeed, we have been prepared for such a view of Shakespeare by Best's earlier allusion to Coleridge's characterization of Shakespeare as a "myriadminded man" (168). Here Shakespeare ostensibly becomes a sort of Everyman, a figure of the kind of wholeness associated by Eliot and Woolf with the English Renaissance. But the antlers of the hatrack, echoing Stephen's earlier depiction of Shakespeare as a cuckold, resonate with Bloom's similar condition and clearly undermine Shakespeare's position as a figure of cultural authority. This image of carnivalesque uncrowning challenges patriarchal mastery and suggests the incompatibility between artistic greatness and the monological attitudes represented by male dominance.

In this vein it is significant that the Shakespeare in the mirror in "Circe" is beardless, indicating an ambiguity in gender, especially in light of the common Renaissance belief (often reflected in Shakespeare's work) that young and beardless boys are still physiologically part female. Here Joyce powerfully anticipates Woolf, who would later argue that the great artist must be able to encompass simultaneously both male and female points of view. To Woolf, we all have both female and male components in our psyches, and it is the mark of the great artist that she can put these components into a productive dialogic relation in the phenomenon that Woolf refers to as androgyny.

> It is fatal to be a man or woman pure and simple; one must be woman-manly or man-womanly. . . . Some collaboration has to take place in the mind between the woman and the man before the act of creation can be accomplished. Some marriage of opposites has to be consummated. (*Room* 108)

Moreover, Woolf also recalls Joyce in her depiction of Shakespeare as a paragon of the androgynous attitude, her description of Shakespeare's "man-womanly mind" echoing Joyce's figuration of Bloom in "Circe" as the "new womanly man" (403).

In fact, Joyce's entire body of work from *Dubliners* onward is filled with instances of ambiguous sexuality and transgression of gender boundaries.[12] In *Ulysses* this motif is prominent in the treatment of *Hamlet* as intertext. While Stephen is clearly a figure of Hamlet throughout the text, Joyce's reinscription of Shakespeare's play involves a change of genders—it is Stephen's mother rather than his father who has died. Meanwhile, Hamlet himself is repeatedly associated with sexual ambiguity in *Ulysses*. Bloom, for example, muses on the implications of Hamlet's having been played in Dublin the night before by a woman, Mrs. Bandmann Palmer: "Male impersonator. Perhaps he was a woman." Then he adds a classic Bloomian touch: "Why Ophelia committed suicide" (62). And later John Eglinton tells us that "Vining held that the prince was a woman" (163).

The frequent play with gender boundaries in Joyce's work is accompanied by a consistent related challenge to patriarchal authority, which fundamentally relies upon the stability of gender boundaries. *Hamlet*, of course, is a play centrally concerned with the question of patriarchal authority. It is therefore not surprising that Stephen's disquisition on *Hamlet* in the "Scylla and Charybdis" chapter is in fact part of a larger meditation on paternity. As Stephen puts it, "Paternity may be a legal fiction. Who is the father of any son that any son should love him or he any son?" (*Ulysses* 170). This note of the difficulty of verification of paternity sounds throughout *Ulysses* in the repeated refrain that it is "a wise child that knows her father" (73).[13]

Stephen, disappointed and embarrassed by his own father, puts forth the theory that the artist, as the creator par excellence, has a unique ability to father himself, as it were. And he presents both God and Shakespeare (the two great creators in the history of western civilization) as the leading examples of such self-paternity. Citing the Sabellian heresy (which held that the Father, the Son, and the Holy Ghost were merely different names for the same being, so that God becomes both his own son and his own father), Stephen goes on to suggest that when Shakespeare wrote *Hamlet* "he was not the father of his own son merely but, being no more a son, he was and felt himself the father of all his race, the father of his own grandfather, the father of his unborn grandson." Or, as Buck Mulligan succinctly summarizes Stephen's point, Shakespeare was "himself his own father" (*Ulysses* 171).

Among other things, Joyce draws here upon the common Renaissance perception that the process of artistic creation (or any creation, for that matter) is inherently paradoxical. As Rosalie Colie points out, it was commonly held in the Renaissance that only God can create, ex nihilo, and that creation by human beings involves an imitation, however profound, of God's work. This perception, embodied in Dante's attempt to emulate God's method of writing in the *Commedia*, is also well expressed in Lear's claim that "Nothing can come of nothing." It is by now a cliché of Joyce criticism to note that Joyce draws this same parallel between the work of the artist and God, and when Colie notes especially that "Alchemical systems relied upon an elaborate analogy to the Creator's act" (61) she is describing a process of creation that bears a striking resemblance to the artistic technique of Shem the Penman, that "first till last alshemist" (*Finnegans Wake* 185.34–35). Indeed, Shem performs an alchemical operation to transmute his own waste matter into indelible ink for the writing of his own particular brand of literature (185.14–26). And the link to God in this operation is quite direct: Shem "creates his work as a Eucharist made from his own body in a mock liturgical passage" (Brivic, *Joyce the Creator* 15).

The metaphorical link between paternity and artistic creation continues throughout Stephen's argument in "Scylla and Charybdis," wherein Shakespeare is consistently associated with fatherhood. Stephen, for example, sees Shakespeare as playing the role of the ghost in productions of *Hamlet*—as in fact he may have done. The chapter also consistently blurs the boundary between sons and fathers, as in Stephen's reference to the Sabellian heresy and in Eglinton's confusion of Dumas *père* with Dumas *fils*. The characterization of Shakespeare cited by Eglinton does, in fact, belong to Dumas *père*, so that by attributing it to Dumas *fils* Eglinton inadvertently undermines paternal authority. Eglinton's comparison via Dumas of Shakespeare with God also participates in a continual association between Shakespeare and God throughout the chapter, an association that reaches back to Stephen's evocation in *Portrait* of the godlike dramatic artist and extends through Stephen's description here of God as "the playwright who wrote the folio of this world" (175). Importantly, however, Stephen continues this sentence with the suggestion that, in authoring the world, God "wrote it badly." Indeed, Stephen's thoughts in "Scylla and Charybdis" tend to undermine both Shakespeare and God as patriarchal creators. If in *Portrait* Stephen seems to endow the artist with godlike powers, in *Ulysses* God becomes an incompetent artist. Similarly, in the very passage in which Stephen views Shakespeare as the father of all his race (echoing Stephen's own desire at the end of *Portrait* to create the conscience of his race), he undermines Shakespeare's patriarchal role, suggesting that the actual authorship of Shakespeare's plays is uncertain. They were written, Stephen says, by "Rutlandbaconsouthamptonshakespeare or another poet of the same name" (171).

There are no strong, masterful father figures in Joyce's fiction. In *Dubliners* children tend to live with aunts and uncles rather than parents, and the characters who do specifically act as fathers in the book (such as Farrington and Little Chandler) do so in anything but exemplary ways. In *Portrait*, the inadequacy of Stephen's father triggers a series of attempts to find substitutes, all of whom also turn out to be inadequate. Leopold Bloom in *Ulysses* is perhaps the first father figure in Joyce's fiction to display anything like positive characteristics, but these are largely related to his ability to function as a father without mastery. And the humble, flawed, and fallen figure of HCE—much more like a Chaplin character in baggy pants than an authoritative, Godlike father—is Joyce's last and greatest depiction of paternal nonmastery. Margot Norris notes the subversion of paternal authority that runs throughout the *Wake*:

> In contrast to that certainty of identity which makes the Symbolic father the figure of the Law, the *Wake*'s father figure emerges as indeterminable, dependent, and variable by name. . . . The Wakean vision of a universe ever hurtling toward chaos is based on the theme of the fallen father. He is named rather than namer. He is uncertain of name and identity, unlocatable rather than a center that fixes, defines, and gives meaning to his cosmos. He is lawbreaker rather than lawgiver. As head of the family, he is incestuous rather than the source of order in the relations of his lineage. (61)

In a book-length study of Joyce's assault on the Law of the Father, Frances Restuccia notes that Joyce often employs the feminine as an instrument for subverting the authority of the Catholic Church: "It is as if Joyce thought that by aligning himself with the female position he could best free himself from the Church" (17). In this vein, note that the transgressions of gender roles in the *Wake* often have religious connotations. In the very first sentence of the book, the Church of Adam and Eve (as well as the biblical Adam and Eve) is referred to as "Eve and Adam's" (3.1).[14] Also particularly striking is ALP's reinscription of the Lord's Prayer in female terms: "In the name of Annah the Allmaziful, the Everliving, the Bringer of Plurabilities, haloed be her eve, her singtime sung, her rill be run, unhemmed as it is uneven!" (104.1–3).

Joyce's sustained attack on the Law of the Father participates in an incessant assault on patriarchal authority in general, as the figure of God the Father is the prototype of the kind of masterful father figure that Joyce seeks to debunk. That Joyce also implicates Shakespeare in many of the same motifs suggests a similar challenge to the authority of the literary tradition. But this challenge is highly dialogic. Far from simply rejecting Shakespeare as irrelevant to the modern world, Joyce acknowledges Shakespeare's role as a powerful predecessor for his own work and for modern literature in general. What he refuses to do, however, is to bow down before Shakespeare's greatness or accept that modern artists cannot reach similar levels of achievement. Joyce is also aware that Shakespeare the cultural icon epitomizes the kind of official art that has long been used to provide an implied justification for political abuses like imperialism. It is no accident, for example, that Baldyhead Dolan attempts to terrorize the students at Clongowes Wood by quoting *Macbeth* or that Garrett Deasy justifies his materialist ideology with a quote from *Othello* (*Portrait* 49, *Ulysses* 25).[15]

That Joyce uses Shakespeare so extensively as an intertextual source verifies the importance to Joyce of Shakespeare as a predecessor. However, Joyce approaches Shakespeare's texts not with awe and reverence but with scissors and paste in hand, ever alert for bits and pieces of discourse that he can coopt for use in constructing his own modern works. These intertextual raids on Shakespeare and other predecessors tell us a great deal about Joyce as an artist. They also say a great deal about modernism in general. After all, if Shakespeare functions in the modern imagination as the embodiment of the English Renaissance, Joyce has come more and more in recent decades to function as the embodiment of British modernism. As a result, Joyce's encounter with Shakespeare carries resonances that go far beyond the works of the two individual artists. In particular, the dialogue between Joyce and Shake-speare represents a confrontation between modernism and the Renais-sance, often seen as the two most important moments in western liter-ary history. But history (literary or otherwise) is not a series of important moments. It is a dynamic continuum, and by the modernist period the perception of the Renaissance had already been changed by centuries of scholarship. The Renaissance inherited by Joyce was pro-duced as much by Victorian writers like Pater as by Elizabethan writers like Shakespeare.

Joyce's use of Shakespeare provides important evidence of Joyce's attitude toward his literary predecessors and of his own participation in this continual rewriting of literary history. But this use is also extremely important to our understanding of the attitudes toward the past that inform modernist literature as a whole. Shakespeare is crucial to a number of modernist artists in this respect, especially in the way that he (and the Elizabethan culture he represents) often functions as an image of wholeness and integration as opposed to the visions of frag-mentation associated with modernity. For example, a central element of Eliot's indictment of the modern condition concerns his idea of the "dissociation of sensibility," a separation between thought and feeling that is central to the modern psyche and represents a fundamental sep-aration of humanity from experience in the world.

> It is something that happened to the mind of England between the time of Donne or Lord Herbert of Cherbury and the time of Ten-nyson and Browning; . . . Tennyson and Browning are poets, and they think; but they do not feel their thought as immediately as the odour of a rose. A thought to Donne was an experience; it modified his sensibility. When a poet's mind is perfectly equipped for its work, it is constantly amalgamating disparate experience; the ordi-nary man's experience is chaotic, irregular, fragmentary. The latter falls in love, or reads Spinoza, and these two experiences have nothing to do with each other, or with the noise of the typewriter or the smell of cooking; in the mind of the poet these experiences are always forming new wholes. . . . In the seventeenth century a dissociation of sensibility set in, from which we have never recov-ered; and this dissociation, as is natural, was aggravated by the influence of the two most powerful poets of the century, Milton and Dryden. ("Metaphysical Poets" 247)

Importantly, while Eliot specifically identifies the metaphysical poets as a counter to the psychic fragmentation that informs subsequent western culture, it is clear that Eliot means to suggest the metaphysical poets as the *last* representatives of an integration between thought and feeling that applies to the works of their Elizabethan predecessors as well. Moreover, the psychic fragmentation cited by Eliot is clearly related to a gradual process of cultural decline that he sees as informing western history from the seventeenth century onward. In poems like *The Waste Land* Eliot makes clear his belief that the great cultural monuments of the past (like the plays of Shakespeare) are no longer adequate to our situation in the modern world. But he also makes it clear that this inadequacy is a failing not of Shakespeare but of modern culture, which accordingly should attempt to strive to restore a condition in which the great works of the past can once again function.

Among other things, Eliot's notion of the dissociation of sensibility can be read as an assault on the status of science as the leading discourse of authority in the post-Enlightenment world. Frank Kermode, for example, sees Eliot's discussion of the dissociation of sensibility as an attempt to elevate the status of poetry as a discourse of epistemological authority. Eliot's argument, for Kermode, is merely

> the most successful version of a Symbolist attempt to explain why the modern world resists works of art that testify to the poet's special, anti-intellectual way of knowing truth . . . it is in search of some golden age when the prevalent mode of knowing was not positivist and anti-imaginative; when the Image, the intuited, creative reality, was habitually respected. (143)

Eliot's specific figuration of poetry as a potential means to heal the rift in the modern psyche—and especially his elevation of the poet over the "ordinary man"—would seem to support Kermode's analysis.

On the other hand, Eliot's historical model for the dissociation of sensibility is in many ways strikingly similar to Woolf's historical figuration of concepts like anonymity and androgyny, both of which also function as counters to the alienation and fragmentation that Woolf sees as central to modern society. Woolf's privileging of the anonymous artist involves a rejection both of masculine egotism and of individualism in general, which she sees (in an almost Marxist way) as a divisive and alienating force in modern society. As a counter to modern egotism, Woolf evinces the primal artist "Anon," a nameless, androgynous poet/singer whose oral art is produced without regard to personal recognition.

> The voice that broke the silence of the forest was the voice of Anon. Some one heard the song and remembered it for it was later written down, beautifully, on parchment. . . . Everybody shared in the emotion of Anons [sic] song, and supplied the story. Anon sang because spring has come; or winter is gone; because he loves; because he is hungry, or lustful; or merry; or because he adores some God. Anon is sometimes man; sometimes woman. ("Anon" 382)[16]

Woolf also links the concept of anonymity directly to the western literary tradition, especially Shakespeare. Indeed, Shakespeare functions for Woolf not only as a paragon of androgyny, but also as the "representative hero" of Woolf's theory of anonymity (DiBattista 15). For example, the title character of *Orlando* meditates on

> the value of obscurity, and the delight of having no name, but being like a wave which returns to the deep body of the sea; thinking how obscurity rids the mind of the irk of envy and spite; how it sets running in the veins the free waters of generosity and magnanimity; and allows giving and taking without thanks offered or praise given: which must have been the way of all great poets . . . Shakespeare must have written like that, and the church builders built like that, anonymously, needing no thanking or naming. (104–5)

As with Eliot's narrative of the dissociation of sensibility, Woolf's description of androgyny is a historical one. She sees the era of the Elizabethan playwrights (whose drama is by nature communal in form) as the last great heyday of anonymity, after which the rise of the printed book results in a cult of authorship and of the individual. Thus, Shakespeare becomes for Woolf the last great figure of Anon, and she ends her essay on the subject by noting that "The book after Shakespeare takes the place of the play. And Anon is dead for ever" ("Anon" 424).

Woolf's emphasis on artistic anonymity resembles, at least on the surface, the ideas of Eliot, who emphasizes that poetry should be impersonal, viewing (in a famous metaphor) the poet not as creator but as "catalyst":

> The point of view I am struggling to attack is perhaps related to the metaphysical theory of the substantial unity of the soul: for my meaning is, that the poet has, not a "personality" to express, but a particular medium, which is only a medium and not a personality, in which impressions and experiences combine in peculiar and unexpected ways. (Eliot, "Tradition" 56)

Woolf's particular use of Shakespeare as a symbol of this kind of impersonality also obviously parallels a number of conventional notions of Shakespeare as an impersonal artist, including Stephen Dedalus's description of the impersonality of the dramatic artist in *Portrait*. Of course, Stephen's later claim in *Ulysses* that Shakespeare was in fact the most autobiographical of artists reverses this position, but most conventional Shakespeare criticism sides with Stephen's earlier view, Shakespeare's greatness being largely attributed to his refusal to insert his personal opinions and prejudices into his texts.[17] Bakhtin himself participates in this tendency with his insistence on the absence of genuine polyphony in Shakespeare's plays, an absence that occurs both because drama as a genre is not well suited to polyphony and because Shakespeare does not place his own opinions in dialogue with those of his characters.

The depiction by both Eliot and Woolf of modern history as a gradual process of fragmentation recalls numerous similar diagnoses of the fragmentation of modern social and psychological life, ranging from Marx's analysis of the alienation resulting from the separation between workers and the products of their labor, to Nietzsche's vision of a separation between Apollonian and Dionysian energies, to Freud's evocation of a tripartite psyche torn by conflicting drives, to Jürgen Habermas's more recent discussions of the separation of cultural spheres in modern society. Woolf's suggestion that the printed book contributes directly to the alienation of modern humanity recalls similar arguments on the part of Marxist critics like Christopher Caudwell and Walter Benjamin. In his famous elegy on the demise of communal storytelling, Benjamin suggests that this demise begins with the invention of the printing press and occurs as part of the shift from oral to print culture (and from stories to novels) that has characterized western society for the past four centuries.

> The earliest symptom of a process whose end is the decline of storytelling is the rise of the novel at the beginning of modern times. What distinguishes the novel from the story (and from the epic in the narrower sense) is its essential dependence on the book. The dissemination of the novel became possible only with the invention of printing. (Benjamin 87)

Benjamin particularly emphasizes the contribution that the rise of the novel makes to the decline in the ability of individuals to relate to others.[18] In contrast to the communal activity of telling (and listening to) stories, both the reading and the writing of novels are solitary activities.

> The storyteller takes what he tells from experience—his own or that reported by others. And he in turn makes it the experience of those who are listening to his tale. The novelist has isolated himself. The birthplace of the novel is the solitary individual. (87)

For Benjamin the demise of storytelling functions as a part of a general movement toward cultural fragmentation that is imaged most vividly in his famous notion of the shattering of the quasi-religious "aura" that has traditionally surrounded works of art with an air of mystery and awe. Benjamin's vision here—especially in his central use of images of fragmentation—would seem to parallel Eliot's quite closely. One could indeed read a poem like *The Waste Land* through Benjamin as a kind of enactment of this shattering of the aura, with the broken images of Eliot's poem standing in stark contrast to the perceived wholeness of cultural artifacts like the plays of Shakespeare from which it draws so many of those images.[19] On the other hand, whereas Eliot seems to perceive (and depict) the shattered authority of the cultural/religious tradition as a sign of historical decay that he hopes to reverse, Benjamin by no means sees the loss of religious reverence for works of art in the modern world as an entirely negative development. Benjamin agrees with Eliot that developments in modern culture bespeak a general breakdown in authority, but (haunted by the specter of Nazi Germany) Benjamin hardly agrees that opposition to authority is necessarily bad. In particular, for Benjamin the fragmented works of modern mass-produced art (epitomized by film) can potentially contribute to the development of new, more actively engaged audiences. In turn, the members of these audiences may then learn a more critical mode of reception, which will presumably make them more resistant to political manipulation like that embodied in fascism, the aura of works of art being somewhat like the aura surrounding demagogues like Hitler. The shattering of the aura in modern art thus leads to "a tremendous shattering of tradition which is the obverse of the contemporary crisis and renewal of mankind" (223).

In short, while Benjamin does often seem nostalgic about the loss of traditional modes of cultural reception, he is able to find a positive potential in that loss that Eliot does not see. Similarly, Woolf's use of the cultural past, especially Shakespeare, is far more complex than Eliot's figuration of Shakespeare as an image of a lost past cultural wholeness. Woolf's writings on Shakespeare consistently express admiration for his work, though it should be pointed out that (like Joyce) Woolf actively appropriates Shakespeare and uses him for her own purposes rather than simply playing the role of apprentice to Shakespeare as master. Indeed, by making Shakespeare a paragon of androgyny and anonymity, Woolf is far from simply paying tribute to a great predecessor. Her praise for Shakespeare in this sense is in fact strongly transgressive (and to some extent intentionally perverse). After all, Shakespeare—as the "great man of British literature"—typically figures in the modern imagination precisely as the embodiment of the masculine individuality that Woolf is writing against, despite critical discussions of his impersonal artistry. Indeed, Woolf herself shows a clear awareness of the sinister side of Shakespeare's role as an official icon of English culture. If at times Woolf attempts to appropriate Shakespeare as an image of the kind of androgynous communal spirit she herself recommends, she does so in spite of (even *because* of) her full awareness that Shakespeare also functions as a leading symbol of the imperialistic, militaristic masculinism that she seeks to oppose. In *Mrs. Dalloway*, for example, it is largely the spirit of Shakespeare (and of Miss Poole, who taught him Shakespeare) that Septimus Smith seeks to defend in volunteering for service in World War I: "He went to France to save an England which consisted almost entirely of Shakespeare's plays and Miss Isabel Poole in a green dress walking in a square" (130).

Shakespeare's work thus serves as an emblem of English culture around which loyal Britishers can rally in a spirit of jingoistic nationalism. Given Woolf's horror of war, the negative implications of the potential use of Shakespeare's plays as a sort of recruiting poster for the war effort are quite clear. Meanwhile, as Seamus Deane notes, visions of Shakespeare as an embodiment of "English genius" lead directly to

> notions of national character, questions of the language appropriate to its proper expression and, by extension, to the stereotyping of groups, classes, races in relation to the kinds of writing (or music, architecture, whatever it may be) that they produce. (11)

In particular, Deane is interested in such questions in terms of the relationship between England and Ireland, and it is quite clear that Joyce, as an Irish writer, has his own special reasons to be suspicious of Shakespeare's role as the official embodiment of English cultural values. If for Woolf Shakespeare to a certain extent represents atrocities committed *by* her country, for Joyce Shakespeare is inevitably associated with the atrocities committed *against* Ireland by the British cultural forces that Shakespeare symbolizes.

Curiously enough, however, Shakespeare's status as a symbol of British imperial domination has received relatively little attention from critics of Joyce, who have tended to see in Shakespeare a great predecessor who functions for Joyce as an image of literary virtuosity. Indeed, when critics have acknowledged Shakespeare's status as an icon of Elizabethan culture, they have tended to imply by this acknowledgment a view of Shakespeare as a representative of the lost cultural greatness of the Renaissance while paying little attention to Shakespeare's specific Englishness or to the fact that the reign of Elizabeth I was a time of particularly harsh and violent imposition of English rule on Ireland.[20] Schutte, for example, concludes from Stephen Dedalus's obvious envy of Shakespeare that Shakespeare the man functions for Joyce as a "great artist and comprehensive soul" compared to whom the "lesser men" who populate the modern Dublin of *Ulysses* can hardly measure up. Thus, when Stephen and Bloom combine in the mirror of "Circe" to form a beardless, paralytic Shakespeare, the image functions for Schutte as a suggestion that, even with their respective abilities combined, Bloom and Stephen would still fall far short of

Shakespeare's greatness because cultural conditions in the modern world make artistic achievements on the order of Shakespeare's impossible.

Schutte largely describes the negative conditions that he associates with the modern world in terms of fragmentation metaphors reminiscent of Eliot. The "creative spirit," he suggests, "is inhibited by the fatal divisions of our world." Similarly, individual artists are incapacitated by the "division of man within himself" (145). In contrast, Shakespeare's Elizabethan England functions for Schutte as a standard of cultural achievement and social harmony.

> The plays written by Elizabethan Shakespeare reflect the integrated world which allowed him to be the great artist he was. It is a world in which values exist and in which relationships between man and woman are vital and lead through understanding to growth. It is informed with wit, vigor, and courage. Man is the measure of all things; he stands on his own feet, whether he is hero or villain, and asserts his right to be himself. (142–43)

Modern Dublin, on the other hand, is for Schutte a fallen city informed by cultural and moral collapse and by social fragmentation and alienation.

> The same cannot be said for the Dublin of 1904, where values are debased, where men cannot enter into any but the most casual relationships, where the characteristic forces in society act not to integrate but to divide, not to supply opportunity for vital, creative partnerships but to supply barriers for men to set up against one another. (143)

Importantly, Schutte suggests that his vision of both modern Ireland and Renaissance England is Joyce's as well. This vision, informed by an almost complete obliviousness to the fact that Joyce relates to the English literary tradition from the marginal position of colonial Ireland, is quite typical of critical approaches to Joyce at the time Schutte was writing, a phenomenon that is in itself highly interesting. Moreover, the figuration by Schutte (and most of his contemporaries) of Renaissance England as a time of social and cultural integration and wholeness has been seriously challenged by numerous recent studies. For example,

Jeffrey Knapp's wide-ranging examination of Elizabethan society demonstrates that the period was not at all the time of burgeoning English power and prestige that popular stereotypes would have it to be. In fact, looking at literary works from More to Shakespeare, and drawing upon a number of Elizabethan historical documents as well, Knapp concludes that the worldwide extent of England's political domination and influence was actually *decreasing* during most of Elizabeth's reign.

Knapp's new-historical style is clearly influenced by the work of Greenblatt, whose studies of Shakespeare and other Elizabethan writers have probably done the most to dispel visions of Elizabethan England as a utopian Golden Age. In *Shakespearean Negotiations*, for example, Greenblatt emphasizes again and again that Elizabethan cultural wholeness and grandeur have not only been exaggerated in the historical record but that they were already exaggerated during Elizabeth's reign. Elizabethan England was a place of famine, pestilence, and political violence, the true nature of which was obscured at the time (and for generations of historians) by a Renaissance version of the Big Lie, by an intentional strategy of pretending to cultural and political greatness. Assuming the throne in a time of chaotic social and political fragmentation, Elizabeth was able to hold that throne by patching together a makeshift political alliance of various noblemen and aristocrats. And she did so largely through sheer theater, through the production of spectacles that made her *seem* a grand and powerful ruler, even if she was not. Queen Elizabeth was

> a ruler without a standing army, without a highly developed bureaucracy, without an extensive police force, a ruler whose power is constituted in theatrical celebrations of royal glory and theatrical violence visited upon the enemies of that glory. (Greenblatt 64)

History attests to the success of Elizabeth's attempts to simulate power through official theater. At the same time, Greenblatt emphasizes that the spectacular surface of Elizabethan politics obscures what was in fact a time of intense social and political crisis, a time when powerful competing forces were already creating the rifts that would within a few decades explode in revolution and civil war. For Greenblatt, it is Shakespeare's singular ability to draw upon the energies generated by these conflicts that give his works their unique force. Shakespeare, in short, is special neither because his works reflect universal human truths nor because he writes in a time of unparalleled cultural greatness and integration. On the contrary, Shakespeare's works have a special energy precisely because they are so firmly embedded in their own historical context and because that context was a time of conflict, crisis, and fragmentation.

Greenblatt's Elizabethan England stands in stark contrast to the conventional myths upon which critics like Schutte draw in their attempts to describe the role that Shakespeare plays for Joyce. Moreover, it seems clear that Schutte's version of Joyce's attitude toward Shakespeare and Elizabethan England derives almost entirely from such myths and has very little to do with anything that can actually be found in Joyce's texts. Despite his rejection of Irish nationalism, Joyce makes quite clear throughout his work (especially in *Ulysses*) his awareness of the historical oppression of colonial Ireland at the hands of the British Empire. And one would be hard pressed to find in Joyce's work any indication that Joyce sees Elizabethan England as a time of lost, past wholeness to which the modern world should aspire. Indeed, about the only direct comparison that appears in the pages of *Ulysses* between the culture of 1904 Dublin and the culture of Elizabethan England is Buck Mulligan's irreverent suggestion that "life ran high in those days" in response to suggestions that Shakespeare might have been a pederast (168). Mulligan cites as his source the Trinity College professor Edward Dowden, an influential critic of Shakespeare who had noted in an 1877 introduction to Shakespeare's works written for schoolchildren that "in the closing years of the sixteenth century the life of England ran high" (cited in Kenner, *Ulysses* 113). Dowden's comments here and elsewhere on the "high" life of Elizabethan England were largely intended to defuse Victorian suspicions of Shakespeare's homosexuality. On the other hand (especially coming from Mulligan), this passage hardly depicts Elizabethan England as the cultural utopia that Schutte considers it to be. As Kenner points out, it was Oscar Wilde, with his 1889 suggestion that Shakespeare was "one of us," who spurred rumors of pederasty on the part of the bard, thus indicating that life ran rather high in Wilde's turn-of-the-century England and Ireland as well (Kenner, *Ulysses* 113). In short, Mulligan's characterization of life during the Renaissance calls attention to *similarities* between the cultures of 1904 Dublin and Elizabethan England rather than to differences between them.

Critics have often seen Joyce's use of Shakespeare, like his use of Homer, as an appeal to the authority of the cultural past the greatness and stability of which shores Joyce's texts against the fragmented cultural ruins that Joyce finds around him in the modern world. Indeed, Schutte at one point concludes that Joyce's use of Shakespeare is very similar to his use of Homer, seeing in both cases an attempt to contrast an integrated and heroic past with the degraded and fragmented present (143, 8n). Both readings, however, seem to derive more from widespread cultural and historical myths than from Joyce's texts themselves, which take a highly subversive stance toward the authority of the past in general and toward literary monuments like Homer and Shakespeare in particular. Further, these readings can be criticized not only for their lack of attention to what Joyce actually writes but for neglecting to challenge (or at least examine) the historical stereotypes upon which rest conventional visions of the greatness of classical Greece or Elizabethan England.

It should also be pointed out that the traditional equations "wholeness = good" and "fragmentation = bad" are themselves based on conventional cultural assumptions that have been challenged by a number of important modern thinkers, especially those of the postmodernist or poststructuralist variety. Ihab Hassan thus concludes that the tendency toward indeterminacy of meaning in postmodernist texts is part of a larger cultural tendency toward total pluralism that is "really compounded of sub-tendencies which the following words evoke: openness, heterodoxy, pluralism, eclecticism, randomness, revolt, deformation. The latter alone subsumes a dozen current terms of unmaking: decreation, disintegration, deconstruction, decenterment, displacement, difference, discontinuity" (27–28). This postmodernist privileging of plurality and fragmentation finds its most extreme expression in the works of radical postmodernist thinkers like Gilles Deleuze and Félix Guattari, but a tendency to embrace diversity and difference constitutes one of the most important currents in modern thought in general.

Critics who find in Joyce's work a nostalgic longing for the integration and wholeness provided by a mythical English Renaissance are ignoring not only the colonial past of Ireland but also the aesthetic principles upon which Joyce's mosaic texts are constructed. Especially when one reads Joyce through Bakhtin, it is clear that multiplicity and diversity of voices and attitudes are in Joyce's work positive virtues not signals of cultural degradation or disintegration. Indeed, Bakhtin him-self—with his emphasis on concepts like polyphony, dialogism, and heteroglossia—is clearly among the modern thinkers who question the desirability of unanimity. In this sense, it is interesting to note that Bakhtin's readings of Rabelais indicate that Bakhtin regards the Renais-sance not as a time of cultural wholeness and integration but an era of radical fragmentation resulting from the breakdown of the monologi-cal worldview of medieval Catholicism. Moreover, Bakhtin focuses on Rabelais largely because he can construct a credible description of Rabelais's times that applies suspiciously well to the modern context of Stalinism.

In his criticism of Bakhtin's dismissal of Shakespeare's polyphony in the 1929 edition of the Dostoevsky book, Lunacharsky suggests (in a mode that anticipates Greenblatt) that Shakespeare's polyphony arises from the cultural fragmentation of Elizabethan England.

> That colourful Renaissance, broken up into a myriad sparkling fragments, which had given birth to Shakespeare and his contem-poraries, was, of course, also the result of the stormy irruption of capitalism into the comparative calm of medieval England. Here, as in Dostoevsky's Russia, a gigantic break-up was getting under way. The same gigantic shifts were taking place and the same unexpected collisions between traditions of social life and systems of thought which had previously had no real contact with one another. (87)

Bakhtin, meanwhile, responds in the later version of the Dostoevsky book by essentially accepting Lunacharsky's description of the cultural fabric of Renaissance England and by acknowledging that as a result "early buddings of polyphony can indeed be detected in the dramas of Shakespeare" (*Problems* 33). Indeed, Bakhtin here figures Shakespeare (along with Rabelais, Cervantes, and Grimmelshausen) as one of the initiators of a long-term historical trend toward polyphony that reaches its culmination in Dostoevsky.

Bakhtin further acknowledges that it is quite possible to detect polyphony in Shakespeare's drama if one reads the plays together as a single work rather than individually. But Bakhtin remains adamant that drama as a genre is resistant to genuine polyphony because a given play "cannot contain *multiple worlds*; it permits only one, and not several, systems of measurement" (34). Of course, Bakhtin here is using polyphony in a highly specific technical sense that has to do with the relationship between the voice of the author of a text and the other, potentially oppositional, voices that arise in the same text. Lunacharsky certainly has a point about Shakespeare, but in his insistence on the polyphonic texture of Shakespeare's plays he may not sufficiently appreciate the technical specificity of Bakhtin's use of the term *polyphony*. Further, Lunacharsky does not pay sufficient attention to the fact that Bakhtin's discussions of particular genres should often be read symbolically rather than literally. Drama for Bakhtin can certainly be dialogic, if not polyphonic, as he acknowledges in his discussion elsewhere of the Italian commedia dell'arte, which is highly dialogic in its emphasis on slang and dialects and its numerous carnivalesque and folk-cultural elements. Bakhtin thus notes that "in the commedia dell'arte, Italian dialects were knit together with the specific types and masks of the comedy. In this respect one might even call the commedia dell'arte a comedy of dialects. It was an intentional dialectological hybrid" (*Dialogic Imagination* 82).

Among other things, the lack of polyphony that Bakhtin finds in drama seems related to traditional concepts like the Aristotelian unities that have been central to the genre for over two thousand years. Presumably, then, modern developments like the epic drama of Bertolt Brecht, which flaunts its violation of these unities and other dramatic conventions, might potentially overcome some of the limitations that Bakhtin sees in drama as a genre. Indeed, Bakhtin (in one of his rare mentions of modern literature) at one point suggests an interesting potential in Brecht's work when in the Rabelais book he cites Brecht as a modern practitioner of the "realist grotesque," which is "related to the tradition of realism and folk culture and reflects at times the direct influence of carnival forms" (*Rabelais* 46). Bakhtin does not follow up on this comment, but elsewhere in the book he categorizes Rabelais's work as grotesque realism in a way that can clearly be read as a veiled criticism of the Soviet privileging of socialist realism. And his subtle implication of Brecht in this motif is particularly apt given Brecht's own polemics with Georg Lukács and other proponents of socialist realism.[21]

For Bakhtin, genres are always associated with specific ideologies, the novel being unique in that it is by nature informed by multiple ideologies—and, in fact, by multiple generic influences. The ideology of a

genre poses limitations that individual authors can never fully overcome. Thus, Shakespeare may write in a time of radical cultural fragmentation, but his genre arises from a more monological past and
thereby limits the amount of polyphony that Shakespeare can inject
into his texts. Bakhtin's rejection of drama in favor of the novel is also
part of a larger attempt to overturn conventional cultural hierarchies,
the drama (especially Shakespeare) having traditionally been considered a "higher" form of literature than the novel. Bakhtin uses drama
and other "poetic" genres as a sort of metaphor for monological authority in general, whether that authority occurs in classical Greece, Renaissance England, or Stalinist Russia. Brecht's experimental drama constitutes a similar challenge to authority and to the ways high culture has
traditionally been used to justify and solidify bourgeois structures of
power.[22] Joyce, by confronting Shakespeare so extensively in his own
work, participates in a similar project. Joyce uses Shakespeare as a specific image of authority in much the same way as do Brecht and
Bakhtin, with the additional important element of dialogue with the
long history of British colonial domination of Ireland. Bakhtin's comments on Shakespeare and on drama, then, help to illuminate Joyce's
use of Shakespeare, just as Joyce's challenge to the authority of Shakespeare helps to explain Bakhtin's seemingly stubborn rejection of
Shakespeare. Meanwhile, both Joyce and Bakhtin present a powerful
challenge to those who, like Eliot, would employ Shakespeare's plays
as icons of an ideal past.

Chapter Six

Dostoevskian Problems of Joyce's Poetics: Narrative, History, and Subjectivity

Virginia Woolf once suggested that the works of Joyce are in danger of being ruined by an undue emphasis on "the damned egotistical self" (*Writer's Diary* 22). On the other hand, a little more than half a century later Hélène Cixous, whose project resonates with that of Woolf in a number of ways, was praising Joyce for his deconstruction of the traditional self, arguing that "Joyce's work has contributed to the discrediting of the subject" (15). Of course, Woolf's views on the subjectivism of Joyce's fiction are typical of early reactions to his work, while Cixous's comment is quite representative of more recent views, especially among poststructuralist critics.[1] Seemingly contradictory readings of Joyce like those by Woolf and Cixous are thus indicative both of the complexity of Joyce's work and of changes in critical styles. They are also indicative of a fundamental questioning of the nature of human subjectivity in the modern world. In the case of Joyce, much of this uncertainty is encompassed by two basic questions. First, is the subject a preexisting autonomous entity that goes forth into the world to encounter other subjects or is the subject in fact a product of those encounters? Second, if the subject is the product of such ongoing phenomena, how does one establish a stable sense of the continuity of identity over time? Both of these questions are very usefully illuminated by the work of Bakhtin, and especially by Bakhtin's discussion of the treatment of subjectivity in the fiction of Fyodor Dostoevsky. Subjectivity is, after all, one of Dostoevsky's great themes, and his exploration of the difficulty of establishing and maintaining a viable sense of individual identity in nineteenth-century Russia resembles Joyce's project in a number of important ways.

Granted, Dostoevsky is not a particularly obvious presence in

Joyce's work. Gifford, for example, does not mention Dostoevsky in either of his compilations of annotations to Joyce's work. Similarly, Thornton identifies no allusions to Dostoevsky in *Ulysses*, and Adaline Glasheen omits Dostoevsky from her "census" of figures alluded to in *Finnegans Wake*. Finally, Dostoevsky hardly appears in Ellmann's biography of Joyce, except for a passing mention of Joyce's suggestion that Shakespeare and Dostoevsky had little in common and for the relation of a minor anecdote in which Joyce dismissed his son Giorgio's claim that *Crime and Punishment* was the greatest novel ever written by quipping that "it was a queer title for a book which contained neither crime nor punishment" (*James Joyce* 430, 485). On the other hand, Joyce's comment (despite not being literally accurate) suggests a certain familiarity with Dostoevsky's book. Indeed, in *The Consciousness of Joyce* Ellmann lists both *Crime and Punishment* and *The Idiot* among the books left in Joyce's Trieste library (107).

The most extensive evidence of Joyce's engagement with Dostoevsky can be found in the volume *Conversations with James Joyce*, in which Arthur Power presents his recollections of his personal talks with Joyce during the 1920s and early 1930s. Many of these discussions focus on European literature, and one of the most important contributions of the book is that in it (in the words of Clive Hart's foreword to the volume) "Joyce's interest in, and knowledge of, the great tradition of Russian prose writing can be seen to be more profound than one might have suspected" (5). Moreover, Dostoevsky is singled out by Joyce in these conversations for special praise. For example, Power quotes Joyce as calling Dostoevsky

> the man more than any other who has created modern prose, and intensified it to its present-day pitch. It was his explosive power which shattered the Victorian novel with its simpering maidens and ordered commonplaces; books which were without imagination or violence. I know that some people think that he was fantastic, mad even, but the motives he employed in his work, violence and desire, are the very breath of literature. (58)

Joyce's identification of Dostoevsky as the creator of modern prose may seem surprising, but it is not especially unique—any number of critics have seen Dostoevsky as one of the principal initiators of literary modernism. Thus, Michael Holquist notes that "Dostoevsky has, of course, become an obligatory item in the catalogues Modernism invokes to define itself as a period" (*Dostoevsky* 33). One might also evince here the influence of Dostoevsky on Eliot, or Woolf's identification of nineteenth-century Russian literature as a powerful predecessor of British modernism in her famous essay "Modern Fiction." One can, in fact, find points of contact between the arch-Russian Dostoevsky and many modern (and even postmodern) western writers. In a recent general study of Dostoevsky's fiction, for example, John Jones suggests certain similarities between Dostoevsky and a number of such writers, including Samuel Beckett, Bertolt Brecht, and Franz Kafka, in addition to Joyce, Woolf, and Eliot.

Bakhtin's meditations on the human subject as a product of social interactions provide an initial point of contact between Joyce and Dostoevsky. Actually, "Bakhtin's" thoughts on subjectivity are presented most explicitly by V. N. Voloshinov in *Marxism and the Philosophy of Language* and in *Freudianism*.[2] In the latter, an extended Marxist polemic against Freudian psychoanalysis, Voloshinov describes the Freudian psyche as a sort of formalist self-contained entity and opposes to that notion a model in which subjectivity is generated through social experiences with language. Voloshinov dispenses with Freud's vision of psychological depth, replacing the notion of separate conscious and unconscious minds with that of a continuum of "official" and "unofficial" consciousnesses, both operating according to similar linguistic principles. Official consciousness is reflected in outward speech, while unofficial consciousness expresses itself through "inner speech," which is still a thoroughly social phenomenon.

> Every utterance is *the product of the interaction between speakers* and the product of the broader context of the whole complex *social situation* in which the utterance emerges. . . . Nothing changes at all if, instead of outward speech, we are dealing with inner speech. Inner speech, too, assumes a listener and is oriented in its constitution toward that listener. (*Freudianism* 79, Voloshinov's emphasis)

This dialogic model of selfhood thus posits a model in which speech is irreducibly social and subjectivity is meaningless apart from intersubjectivity: "Consciousness becomes consciousness only once it has been filled with ideological (semiotic) content, consequently, only in the process of social interaction" (Voloshinov, *Marxism* 11). The psyche is thus not a *thing* that exists internally in an individual so much as a series of *events* that occur in the process of intersubjective relations: "By its very existential nature, the subjective psyche is to be localized somewhere between the organism and the outside world, on the *borderline* separating these two spheres of reality" (26).

This vision of subjectivity is also reflected in Bakhtin's discussions of characterization in the novel, especially in *Problems of Dostoevsky's Poetics.* According to Bakhtin, Dostoevsky's characters have very little psychological depth in the conventional sense, despite Dostoevsky's reputation as a psychological novelist. Rather than attempt to probe the psychological depths of his characters, Dostoevsky stays on the surface, showing us the self-conscious images of his characters as they believe others perceive them. With a Dostoevsky character, "We see not who he is, but *how* he is conscious of himself; our act of artistic visualization occurs not before the reality of the hero, but before a pure function of his awareness of that reality" (*Problems* 49). What we see of any Dostoevsky character is determined at least partially by the Other. Dostoevsky does not create and describe fully-formed and finalized characters; instead, he lets those characters evolve in dialogue with their author and with the other characters. In short, Bakhtin suggests that Dostoevsky probes not the hidden depths of the individual subject but instead focuses on the surface interactions among different subjects. The implication, however, is that the subject is itself much more a surface phenomenon than is suggested by most "psychological" approaches to the self. Indeed, the human psyche for Bakhtin, as Caryl Emerson points out, is "a boundary phenomenon" that occurs in the interaction between subjects ("Outer Word" 249). Bakhtin's description of subjectivity in Dostoevsky should, then, have quite general applicability; in particular, it is clear that this description has great relevance to the work of Joyce, whose explorations of the nature of subjectivity very often echo Dostoevsky's.

Different critics have seen Joyce's treatment of subjectivity in widely differing ways. For example, critics like Leon Edel see Joyce's work as exemplary of a general modernist inward turn toward in-depth exploration of the minds of individual characters. Such critics focus especially on Joyce's use of stream of consciousness to depict interior speech in his characters.[3] Dorrit Cohn is typical of such views when she suggests that the "Penelope" chapter of *Ulysses* may be regarded as a paradigm of the autonomous interior monologue, as "the most famous and the most perfectly executed specimen of its species" (217). Indeed, though stream of consciousness and interior monologue per se are used extensively only in *Ulysses*, all of Joyce's work—through the use of free indirect style and other techniques—grants the reader access to the thoughts of characters in unprecedented ways. And when Joyce does depict interior thought processes different characters are sharply delineated, each thinking in his or her own distinctive, individual style.[4]

Other critics find the subjectivity of Joyce's work not in the minds of characters like Stephen Dedalus and the Blooms, but in the mind of Joyce himself. Joyce's work lends itself well to such interpretations, with the sheer magnitude of his achievement inviting apotheosis, despite the consistent self-parodic tone of his writing. Indeed, the figure of Joyce the "great author" looms above a great deal of the criticism of his work. Thus, Sheldon Brivic, believing Joyce to function as a godlike creator, argues that the informing "psychic structure" of both *Ulysses* and *Finnegans Wake* is the mind of Joyce (*Joyce the Creator* 22) and that "The central creation of Joyce's canon was his continuous development of his own mind" (44). Brivic reaches this conclusion within the framework of Lacanian psychoanalysis, and Brivic's own move from early Freudian-Jungian readings of Joyce (in *Joyce Between Freud and Jung*) to later Lacanian ones provides a sort of mininarrative of the ability of Joyce's work to maintain its relevance even as critical styles and emphases change.[5]

Critics like Edel, Cohn, and Brivic come to praise Joyce for his subjectivism, not to bury him, but this positive verdict is far from unanimous. For example, both feminist and Marxist critics have accused Joyce of an excessive emphasis on the individual subject, as shown by Woolf's comment, cited above, and by Georg Lukács's well-known concern that the modernist concentration on the internal mental processes of isolated individuals leads to an exclusion of the broader concerns of society as a whole. For Lukács, Joyce epitomizes the bourgeois reliance on the free autonomous individual as a paradigm of subjectivity. But Joyce's characters are hardly free; they are in fact constantly thwarted by the stifling limitations placed upon them by the stagnancy and rigidity of Dublin society. In this case, one might argue that Joyce's treatment of the individual acts to undermine rather than support the bourgeois myth of individual liberty. Jeremy Hawthorn thus responds to criticisms of *Ulysses* by Lukács and other early Marxist critics that the book embodied an artificial, formal order that rejected the real world of history and that it showed an inward turn toward subjectivity that denied the social dimension of life. Yet Hawthorn argues that, despite certain limitations, "one could counter-claim that few novels show their characters less as free, autonomous beings or more tied to their society and its history" (116). Granted, Joyce does in fact deal, in *Ulysses*, with the inner thoughts of his characters to an extent that is unprecedented in literature. But a close look at those thoughts shows them to be thoroughly constituted by prior discourses rather than originating in the mind of the thinking subject. It is rather obvious, for example, that the thoughts of Stephen Dedalus consist largely of allusions to literary and other sources. And Stephen is not alone in this regard—all of the characters in *Ulysses* seem to think primarily in quotations and allusions. Hawthorn suggests that the work of Lev Vygotsky points toward a way the subjective dimension of *Ulysses* can be related to the social:

> Vygotsky's account of the development of conceptual thought through the progressive internalisation of language advances hypotheses about the nature of the "language of thought" which offer a fascinating way in to the study of Joyce's presentation of inner cerebration in *Ulysses*. (117)

Anticipating Voloshinov, Vygotsky believes that language is first acquired as a thoroughly social phenomenon and that what he calls "inner speech" evolves from the progressive internalization of language. Inner speech evolves from the "egocentric" speech of children, which itself "grows out of its social foundations by means of transferring social, collaborative forms of behavior to the sphere of the individual's psychological functioning" (quoted in Wertsch 112).[6] Thus, Vygotsky's concept of inner speech would predict (correctly) that the interior monologues appearing in *Ulysses* are socially constituted rather than unique to the individual thinker.[7] For example, André Topia notes that Bloom's monologues include intertextual fragments of popular songs, folk ballads, operatic arias, religious hymns, poems, novels, plays, nursery rhymes, magazine and newspaper articles, proverbial phrases, advertisements, popular maxims, and (especially) Catholicism. Moreover, the intersection of different discourses in Bloom's

musings can result in some very Bakhtinian dialogue—a highly subversive example of intertextuality with Catholic discourse occurs when
Bloom associates *corpus* with *corpse* (Topia 66), implying that "the body
of Christ is no more than a cadaver" (115).

Fredric Jameson similarly emphasizes the political potential of
modernist "subjectivism." For Jameson modernist literature maintains
a viable notion of the self—epitomized by the strikingly identifiable
"personal styles" of modernist artists—that makes the modernist artist
capable of maintaining a critical perspective on developments in the
society around him. Jameson argues that the subjectivity of modernist
literature is what allows it a critical engagement with history, even as
Lukács and others argue that the subjectivity of modernism divorces it
from history. But Jameson also argues that the focus on individual
characters in Joyce and other modernists may in fact indicate a challenge to traditional notions of subjectivity.

> I want . . . to propose the alternative proposition that modernism's
> introspective probing of the deeper impulses of consciousness,
> and even of the unconscious itself, was always accompanied by a
> Utopian sense of the impending transformation or transfiguration
> of the "self" in question. (*Postmodernism* 312)

Jameson, in finding a positive role for the subjectivism of modernist literature, is reading modernism specifically against a postmodernism that he sees as informed by a radical loss of selfhood, a loss that
Jameson relates to the growing alienation of the subject in late consumer capitalism. For Jameson this growing alienation leads to a fragmented sense of self, and in particular to an inability to maintain a
sense of continuity in time that is reminiscent of the symptoms of the
schizophrenic patient:

> he or she does not have our experience of temporal continuity . . .
> but is condemned to live a perpetual present with which the vari-
> ous moments of his or her past have little connection and for which
> there is no conceivable future on the horizon. . . . The schizophrenic
> thus does not know personal identity in our sense, since our feel-
> ing of identity depends on our sense of the persistence of the "I"
> and the "me" over time. ("Postmodernism" 119)

Jameson suggests that literary texts participate in this loss of temporal continuity, since they are themselves products of the labor of writers who are alienated from their own texts. Therefore, in the age of late consumer capitalism, texts themselves become schizophrenic, depicting both time and the self as fragmented and discontinuous. Jameson particularly associates this movement toward schizophrenia with postmodernist texts, and indeed the "schizo-text" has become a standard category in the critical discourse surrounding postmodernism.

Jameson's discussion of the fragmentation of temporality (and thus of both texts and subjectivity) in postmodernism resonates in interesting ways with Bakhtin's treatment of Dostoevsky, which consistently parallels the narrative movement of Dostoevsky's texts with the subjective development of Dostoevsky's characters. For Bakhtin, if Dostoevsky's characters are fragmented, then so are his narratives, moving from one intense moment of crisis to another with little sense of temporal connection or impending narrative resolution. Such parallels between narrative and subjectivity also anticipate Paul Ricoeur's recent important study of the function of narrative in the human conception of time. In particular, Ricoeur suggests narrative as the critical link between subjectivity and history.[8] To Ricoeur, we confront history by formulating it in narrative form; in the process of constituting these narratives we also constitute ourselves. It is the connecting thread of such narratives that binds all the different moments of an individual life into a coherent whole.

> What justifies our taking the subject of an action, so designated by his, her, or its proper name, as the same throughout a life that stretches from birth to death? The answer has to be narrative. To answer the question "Who?" as Hannah Arendt has so forcefully put it, is to tell the story of a life. The story told tells about the action of the "who." And the identity of this "who" therefore itself must be a narrative identity. (246)

It is important to recognize that the "identity" cited by Ricoeur here does not imply a sameness over time but merely a narrative connectedness. Thus, narrative identity "can include change, mutability, within the cohesion of a lifetime" (246). The narrative subject, then, is constantly in the process of being constituted through the dynamic unfolding of the narrative in which she participates. The resultant flexibility suggests narrative sense as a potential antidote to the fragmentation of identity discussed by Jameson. Indeed, Richard Kearney, while largely agreeing with Jameson's depiction of postmodernism as a "postindividual" phase of history, concludes that Ricoeur's notion of narrative identity points toward a postmodernist notion of self that still allows for the conception of an ethical subjectivity. Kearney notes that ethics "presupposes the existence of a certain *narrative identity*: a self which remembers its commitments to the other" (395). This narrative self is not a permanent substance but constantly evolves.

> Such a model constitutes the self as the reader and the writer of his own life. But it also casts each one of us as a narrator who never ceases to revise, reinterpret and clarify his own story—by relating himself in turn to the cathartic effects of those larger narratives, both historical and fictional, transmitted by our cultural memory. The notion of personal identity is thus opened up by the narrative imagination to include that of a *communal* identity. The self and the collective mutually constitute each other's identity by receiving each other's stories into their respective histories. Self-identity, in whatever sense, is always a "tissue of narrated stories." (Kearney 395–96)

Woolf suggests that Joyce openly embraces (and contributes to the propagation of) traditional patriarchal notions of the strong autonomous individual, while Cixous argues that Joyce contributes to the deconstruction of such notions and embraces their passing. According to models like that proposed by Hoffman, Hornung, and Kunow, Woolf and Cixous might appear to be reading Joyce as a modernist and as a postmodernist, respectively. From Jameson's perspective, on the other hand, the difference between "modernist" and "postmodernist" writers in their approaches to subjectivity is not that the former accept conventional bourgeois notions of the self while the latter reject such notions. Indeed, both groups of writers show an awareness that the bourgeois vision of the strong, autonomous individual is a cultural myth that does not correspond to reality. The real problem for both groups of writers is the establishment of any authentic subjectivity whatsoever, and modernists differ from their postmodernist successors principally in the determination with which they seek a sense of self that can function in the modern world. In this sense (though Jameson does not mention him) Dostoevsky, whose characters strive mightily against their fragmented and unstable identities, becomes a paradigmatic modernist author.

Individual identity can be similarly problematic in Joyce. In *Dubliners* the movement from one story to the next involves a movement from one central character to another, which impedes the recuperation of the text as the continuous story of a single subject even while each of the characters shares much the same experience of Dublin life. *Portrait* focuses on a single character, Stephen Dedalus, but Stephen is very uncertain of his own identity, striving unsuccessfully throughout the book to find some suitable model after which he can pattern himself. Then, in *Ulysses*, Stephen "philosophically and existentially . . . seeks some reunion between his sense of himself as a series of so many flickering serial manifestations and his sense of himself as an enduring entity" (Maddox 34). Indeed, Stephen spends a great deal of time in *Ulysses* contemplating the enigma of the continuity of the self, signaled early on by his reflections on his schoolboy days at Clongowes Wood. The young boy we see in the early pages of *Portrait* both is and is not the one we see fifteen years later in the early pages of *Ulysses*. As Stephen himself puts it, "I am another now and yet the same" (*Ulysses* 10). Later, Stephen specifically links the question of the continuity of the self to that of individual responsibility. In the library scene of the "Scylla and Charybdis" chapter, he muses on the pound that he had borrowed five months earlier from the poet George Russell, attempting to produce an argument that he is not responsible for repaying the money, since it was an earlier, different self that received the loan: "Wait. Five months. Molecules all change. I am other I now. Other I got pound" (156). Late in *Ulysses* the boundaries between different characters become more and more diffuse, especially in the "Circe" chapter, where identities become extremely fluid and unstable. In the book's other later chapters characters begin to share thoughts and memories, and even names, with Stephen and Bloom at one point being supplanted by Blephen and Stoom (558). Joyce employs a similar strategy in *Finnegans Wake*, with (for example) Butt and Taff becoming Tuff and Batt (349.8–9). Indeed, the splitting, fading, and merging "characters" of the *Wake* mount one of the most powerful assaults on the notion of stable, unified identities in all of literature. They are not so much representations of individuals as textual forces, dissolved in the swirl and flow of Wakean language, and Joyce's entire textual practice in the *Wake* acts to undermine traditional notions of the self.[9]

Granted, Joyce does often focus on the inner minds of individual characters. Even in *Finnegans Wake* "characters" are identifiable by certain consistent characteristics, and the characters in *Ulysses* are in many ways among the most vivid and convincing in all of literature, despite reminders late in the book that they are fictional devices. Early judgments of Joyce's subjectivism arose largely because critics found his depiction of Stephen Dedalus in *Portrait* so entirely convincing, with most critics attributing the vividness of Stephen to a direct autobiographical link between Stephen and Joyce himself. But critics in recent decades have emphasized the irony in Joyce's relationship to Stephen, noting that a close reading of *Portrait* shows Stephen's self-importance to be continually deflated, even mocked. Indeed, "strong" individuals are invariably undermined in Joyce's fiction, with characters like the would-be Nietzschean Übermensch James Duffy, the pompously pretentious Garrett Deasy, the fiercely individualist Citizen of "Cyclops," and the prima donna poet Stephen Dedalus providing ample reminders of the fatuousness of individual pride and arrogance. And this duality in Joyce's attitude toward the subject also seems to inform his opinion toward himself as an artist. At times Joyce boasted of his greatness, suggesting that he could "do anything" with language and that he was perhaps exceeded only by Shakespeare as a writer of English-language literature; at other times Joyce proclaimed himself a mere "scissors and paste man," humbly assembling fragments of texts created by others.

One might wonder, of course, whether Joyce, like Laurence Olivier's Hamlet, was simply unable to make up his mind. But the complexity of Joyce's explorations of the nature of human subjectivity can also be taken as a reflection of a profound uncertainty about that nature in modern society as a whole. For one thing, Joyce was always intensely aware of the intricacies of language itself, and his dual depiction of the subject mirrors the way the word *subject* itself indicates both an independently active agent and a passive liege under strict authoritarian control.[10] And this linguistic "coincidence" represents far more than empty wordplay; the complex and contradictory nature of the meaning of the word *subject* and of Joyce's depiction of subjectivity both correspond to the real position of the subject in a bourgeois society that claims to value individual rights and freedoms above all else but then manipulates and controls its citizens to such an extent that no real individualism is possible.

Critics like Otto Kaus have suggested that the various contradictions inherent in Dostoevsky's work can be directly related to the contradictions in the budding capitalist society in which Dostoevsky lived and worked.[11] Similarly, the contradictions in Joyce's treatment of the subject resonate with the contradictory ideology of turn-of-the-century Irish nationalism, which was strongly informed by both a cult of individual heroism and a cult of individual self-sacrifice. Indeed, if Joyce's work supports both subjectivist and deconstructionist readings, it also undermines both, identifying the first with the cult of heroism and the second with the cult of selfless sacrifice. It is no surprise, then, that his work provokes multiple readings, though of course Joyce's work is not alone in this sense. For example, many critics follow Edel in considering Woolf in the company of psychological novelists, despite Woolf's own criticisms, in works like *A Room of One's Own*, of psychologism. When Anne Herrmann examines the work of Woolf and German writer Christa Wolf, she concludes that "Woolf deconstructs the centered, unified subject as such, while Wolf rewrites the traditionally male subject as female" (1). Thus, within Patricia Waugh's model of literary history, Herrmann would suggest that Woolf is a masculine postmodernist, while Edel would see Woolf as a masculine modernist. But Waugh lists Woolf as an exemplary woman writer for whom the masculine notion of the subject is largely irrelevant.

Waugh considers Joyce a masculine modernist, but he can also be seen as a "woman" writer by Waugh's definition, and indeed many French feminists (Cixous, Kristeva) have declared him an exemplar of feminine writing strategies, though the French feminist notion of the feminine comes closer to Waugh's characterization of postmodernism. But many critics have seen Joyce as conforming quite well to Waugh's notion of a communal alternative to masculine modernist and postmodernist attitudes.[12] Indeed, the possibility that Joyce's work supports alternative communal visions of subjectivity seems extremely promising, as it in a sense encompasses both the subjectivist and deconstructionist readings of Joyce. Cheryl Herr is typical of recent "cultural" critics who have argued that Joyce treats the subject not as an isolated monad but as a phenomenon defined by interaction with other subjects and with a complex of social conventions, codes, and discourses. For

Herr, Joyce's recognition of the social constitution of the subject has powerful political consequences, including the undermining of traditional notions of gender roles.

> From the notion that there's no "natural" or "nonalien" gender, *Ulysses* posits that there is no human nature in the ordinary sense of the term and no inner being that one struggles to understand, develop, or fulfill. Rather, *Ulysses* shows us cultural codes mingling in the minds of each character to the effect that the character—whether known through dialogue, thoughts, or action—is properly constructed as a narrative event. (Herr 154)

Franco Moretti parallels Herr, Topia, and Hawthorne in his recognition that Joyce's depictions of the "inner" thoughts of his characters in fact constitute a patchwork of quotations from public, social discourses. Indeed, for Moretti, Joyce's stream-of-consciousness technique is not an inward turn to the individual psyche but "the linguistic expression of the loss of individual identity" in the modern world (194). Joyce's streams of "consciousness" in fact indicate that individuals are unconsciously situated and manipulated by "arcane and uncontrollable" ideological forces (195). For Moretti this motif is most vividly represented in *Ulysses* through the continual reference to advertising and to the way advertising subtly maneuvers its audience into the role of consumer. One might also point to the way the fictions of popular women's magazines have constituted Gertie MacDowell as a consumer of romantic fantasy or to the way many of Molly's expectations concerning sexuality are derived from the reading of soft-core pornography. Such examples might suggest that Joyce conducts a sort of Adornian critique of the mind-numbing effects of popular culture. And indeed he does. But those who would see this critique as a typical modernist rejection of mass culture in favor of the elevated sphere of "high" art are looking at only half of the picture. It may be that popular culture is the most important constitutive force in the consciousnesses of characters like Gertie MacDowell and the Blooms, but it is worth keeping in mind that Stephen Dedalus is just as crippled by a bovarystic submission to writers like Shakespeare and Augustine as Gertie and the Blooms are by an immersion in writers like Paul de Kock.

De Kock is also a favorite of Dostoevsky's would-be intellectual Stepan Verkhovensky in *Devils*, and indeed the consistency with which

Joyce depicts his characters as being constituted by preexisting texts and discourses provides one of the strongest links between his work and Dostoevsky's. One of the clearest similarities between Joyce and Dostoevsky is that both authors construct their texts (and their characters) from bits and pieces taken from an almost astonishing range of genres and discourses. As early as 1925, Leonid Grossman described the generic multiplicity of Dostoevsky's texts in a manner that might apply almost equally well to Joyce's later works. Grossman notes that in Dostoevsky's novels

> the Book of Job, the Revelation of St. John, the Gospel texts, the discourses of St. Simeon the New Theologian, everything that feeds the pages of his novels and contributes tone to one or another of his chapters, is combined here in a most original way with the newspaper, the anecdote, the parody, the street scene, with the grotesque, even with the pamphlet. (cited in Bakhtin, *Problems* 15)

In fact, the similarities between Joyce and Dostoevsky are quite numerous, especially in their treatment of subjectivity. For example, as with *Ulysses*, a major focus of *The Brothers Karamazov* concerns the relation between fathers and sons, and particularly the ways in which individuals make the transition from being sons to being fathers, which can be seen as a fundamental trope for the development of individual identity.[13] Late in the book, the ace defense attorney Fetyukovich presents an ostensibly brilliant argument in favor of his client, Dmitri Karamazov, who is being tried for the murder of his father, the inveterate sensualist Fyodor Karamazov. Among other things, Fetyukovich argues that the evidence against Dmitri is so "unsubstantiated" and "fantastic" that there would be no question of a conviction were the crime involved not the particularly disturbing one of parricide (741–42). Such being the case, the lawyer then attempts to argue that, even *had* Dmitri murdered Fyodor, the crime would not really be a parricide, because old Karamazov had never been a real father to his son. In particular, Fetyukovich suggests that the connection between biological fathers and their sons is an extremely "mystical one, which I do not understand with my reason, but can only accept by faith" (745). He argues that, in a case like that of the Karamazovs, when (beyond the mystical act of conception) the father seems to have given little to his son except "an inclination to drink," there is no reason to consider the familial bond of father to son as anything more than a "mystical prejudice." In such cases, the so-called father is not a real father, "and the son is free and has the right henceforth to look upon his father as a stranger and even his enemy" (745–46).

Fetyukovich's argument is overly clever, of course, and his suggestion that old Karamazov probably got what was coming to him does not necessarily help his client. Indeed, when Dmitri is later convicted, there are hints that the jury of provincial peasants was at least partially reacting against the sophistication of Dmitri's fancy Petersburg lawyer. Like most things in *The Brothers Karamazov*, then, Dostoevsky's depiction of Fetyukovich's speech and its aftermath participates in a complex network of voices and countervoices, suggesting a parody of the lawyer's western rationalism, but at the same time providing anything but an unequivocal endorsement of the irrational prejudices of the Russian peasant.

For readers of Joyce, what is particularly striking about Fetyukovich's description of fatherhood is its anticipation of the very similar argument put forth by Stephen Dedalus in the "Scylla and Charybdis" chapter of *Ulysses*. Indeed, Stephen might almost be quoting Dostoevsky's Fetyukovich when he argues that

> Fatherhood, in the sense of conscious begetting, is unknown to man. It is a mystical estate, an apostolic succession, from only begetter to only begotten. On that mystery and not on the madonna which the cunning Italian intellect flung to the mob of Europe the church is founded and founded irremovably because founded, like the world, macro and microcosm, upon the void. Upon incertitude, upon unlikelihood. . . . Paternity may be a legal fiction. Who is the father of any son that any son should love him or he any son? (170)

Stephen goes beyond Fetyukovich in his attempt to draw conclusions about the authority of the Church from his argument about paternity, but there are strong religious resonances in Fetyukovich's speech as well. Among other things, Fetyukovich argues for a rational form of Christianity and calls for Christians to "foster only those convictions that are justified by reason and experience, that have passed through the crucible of analysis, in a word, to act sensibly and not senselessly as in dreams or delirium" (*Brothers Karamazov* 745). This argument is particularly suggestive in light of the East-West dialogue that so clearly informs Dostoevsky's depiction of Fetyukovich, becoming a western rational critique of the mysticism of Russian Orthodoxy. Indeed, especially when compared to Stephen's characterization in *Portrait* of Catholicism as "an absurdity which is logical and coherent" as opposed to the "illogical and incoherent" absurdity of Protestantism, Fetyukovich's rational version of Christianity carries unmistakable resonances of Catholicism (244). This interpretation is supported by Dostoevsky's consistent hostility toward Catholicism, which he saw as the epitome of all that was negative about western European culture.[14] And this connection is consistent with the general association in *Brothers* between Fetyukovich and western cultural influences in Russia.

Indeed, Dostoevsky's figuration of the Catholic Church as a sinister force that establishes and maintains its power through violence and intimidation suggests a number of possible parallels to the work of Joyce, despite the obvious differences in the cultural position of the Catholic Church in nineteenth-century Orthodox Russia and in turn-of-the-century Catholic Ireland. Even Dostoevsky's view of the Catholic Church as an image of foreign cultural contamination of his native Russia is not necessarily all that different from the attitude of Joyce, who also regarded Catholicism as a foreign force in Ireland (analogous to British imperialism), despite the centuries-long tradition of Irish Catholicism. The parallels between Stephen's and Fetyukovich's descriptions of paternity thus suggest the beginnings of a number of potentially rich dialogues between Joyce and Dostoevsky.

In *Eliot, Joyce, and Company*, which includes probably the most extensive comparative study of Joyce and Dostoevsky undertaken to date, Stanley Sultan builds upon Power's revelations of Joyce's interest in Dostoevsky to suggest ways Dostoevsky's work can be used to elucidate Joyce's, arguing especially that *Crime and Punishment* reveals aspects of Joyce's project in *Ulysses* that have otherwise received little attention from critics. Sultan notes certain similarities in content between the two books (like the fact that both present detailed evocations of daily life in specific modern cities) but pays special attention to structural similarities, arguing that both books depend unusually heavily on coincidence as a device of plot and structure. In particular, Sultan concludes that both books reach their eventual outcomes by "plot coincidences that signify the agency of a benevolent Providence—

by represented events that can be explained even in *Ulysses*, even with the most ingenious hermeneutic agility, in no other way" (*Eliot* 54).

Sultan, it should be pointed out, is engaged in a specific critical project—he wants to show that the vast majority of Joyce critics for the past seven decades have missed the point of *Ulysses*, which for Sultan is neither a social statement nor a reflexive literary and linguistic experiment so much as a good old-fashioned story about "real" people. Thus, Sultan sees Joyce's praise of Dostoevsky to Power as based on Dostoevsky's "commitment to portraying the events of psychological reality," which then for Sultan becomes Joyce's project as well. Sultan also wants to establish parallels between Joyce and the arch-Christian Eliot, and his attempt to divine from Joyce's texts a belief in God presumably contributes to both of these projects.

Unfortunately, Sultan's technique of declaring his conclusions indisputable does not eliminate the fact that his premises and his logic are extremely questionable. Outlining a number of instances of coincidence in both *Crime and Punishment* and *Ulysses*, Sultan concludes that both Dostoevsky and Joyce include networks of coincidences as a signal of the workings of God. He makes this conclusion on the basis of an unproven "thesis" that "an author who incorporates a system of coincidences in a fiction—some crucial to the plot, some more easily avoided than created—and who provides commentary on their significance, is saying 'straight out it's a miracle'" (61). Apparently, Sultan regards this conclusion as particularly obvious in the case of Dostoevsky, whom he then uses by comparison to suggest that the same must be true of Joyce as well.

There are, of course, a number of things wrong with this line of reasoning. For one thing, there are any number of reasons why an author might include elaborate systems of coincidences in a novel—to make parodic points about the use of coincidence as a plot device in other novels, to call attention to the artificiality of narrative in general and particularly to the difficulty of constructing viable narratives in the fragmented modern world, to comment upon theories of history, and so on. For another thing, it is far from unquestionable that Dostoevsky's fiction directly reflects the beliefs of its author—or that those beliefs are unequivocal. That the later Dostoevsky espoused conservative politics and Orthodox religion is well known, but for many readers one of the central sources of tension in Dostoevsky's later novels is the quest for faith in a modern world without God. Holquist, for example, concludes in *Dostoevsky and the Novel*, that the bulk of Dostoevsky's novels "put the existence of God into doubt" (127). Sultan seems to argue from the premise that Dostoevsky is a known quantity whose work can then be used as a reference point to illuminate Joyce's. But in point of fact Dostoevsky's work is as complex and enigmatic as Joyce's, and different critics have read Dostoevsky's work in radically different ways.[15]

One could, then, just as easily reverse Sultan's argument, assume that Joyce includes coincidences in *Ulysses* as a reflexive literary device to comment upon narrative, history, and subjectivity, and then conclude that Dostoevsky does likewise. Indeed, while it is true that Dostoevsky's work does not display the stylistic shenanigans of Joyce's, there is a great deal of literary artifice, even play, in Dostoevsky's fiction, including a number of the techniques of ostentatious artifice (allusion, parody, explosion of literary conventions) that have come to be associated with Joyce. The famous trial scene at the end of *The Brothers Karamazov* is the absolute climax of the book's story and is certainly charged with human interest. It also addresses the kinds of fundamental "psychological" and religious issues with which Sultan (correctly, to an extent) sees Dostoevsky as centrally concerned. Yet this scene is extremely literary in ways that radically subvert any interpretation of the book as a straightforward realistic narrative or statement of faith. The bulk of the trial scene consists of two orations, one by the prosecuting attorney Ippolit Kirillovich and the one by Fetyukovich. The prosecuting attorney presents a detailed narrative of the events leading up to, culminating in, and following the murder of old Karamazov, vividly depicting Dmitri as the killer. The prosecutor also constructs an elaborate portrait of Dmitri himself, painted in the blackest of colors. Yet all the while the seriousness of this narration is continually undermined by the prosecutor's penchant for literary allusion and by Dostoevsky's own sly parodic intrusions. At one point, for example, Ippolit Kirillovich describes Dmitri's "good" brother Alyosha (for purposes of contrast) but suggests that the pious Alyosha is in danger of falling into the typical Russian trap of "mistakenly ascribing all evil to European enlightenment" and of descending into "dark mysticism on the moral side, and witless chauvinism on the civic side" (697). These charges, of course, are precisely those that were commonly leveled against Dostoevsky himself, reinscribed here as a good-humored parody of his critics. Meanwhile, the climax of the prosecutor's speech is related in a chapter entitled "Psychology at Full Steam. The Galloping Troika. The Finale of the Prosecutor's Speech," clearly undermining Ippolit Kirillovich's conclusion via a comic tone that mocks his seriousness and via an allusion to Gogol that calls attention to the literariness of the entire speech.

When Fetyukovich gets his chance to respond, it is precisely the literary nature of his opponent's argument on which he focuses. In particular, he argues that the prosecutor's speech is pure fiction informed by "a certain, so to speak, artistic game, by the need for artistic production, so to speak, the creation of a novel" (726). Throughout his argument, Fetyukovich continually compares the prosecutor's narrative to a novel, suggesting that the "fantastic . . . novelistic suggestion" of the prosecutor is far too unreliable to be used as the basis for a murder conviction (731). Moreover, Fetyukovich argues that Ippolit Kirillovich has made Dmitri into a fictional character who bears little resemblance to the "real" Dmitri: "you have created a different person!" (732). Of course, Fetyukovich then proceeds to produce his own narrative and create his own Dmitri, a sensitive soul whose tender heart is immersed in Schiller and in a love for "the beautiful and the lofty" (743).

Fetyukovich's speech threatens radically to destabilize the entire narrative of *The Brothers Karamazov*. For one thing, Dostoevsky again includes an element of self-referential textual play in the speech. Fetyukovich's characterization of the murder charges against his client as "fantastic" recalls charges like that of the contemporary critic G. Z. Yeliseyev that Dostoevsky's exploration of murder in *Crime and Punishment* was fantastic (cited in McDuff 10). Similarly, Fetyukovich's evocation of "the beautiful and the lofty" in relation to Dmitri clearly echoes one of the leitmotivs of the Underground Man. Meanwhile, pointing to the prosecutor's seeming ability to delve into Dmitri's mind and to read his deepest motivations, Fetyukovich "praises" his adversary's argument for employing "the wealth of psychological gifts with which God has endowed our abilities." Indeed, he concludes that Ippolit Kirillovich is "a profound and subtle psychologist, who has long deserved special renown for this quality" (726–27). But this praise is immediately undermined when Fetyukovich proceeds to produce a counternarrative, also based on psychology, "in order to demonstrate that one can draw whatever conclusions one likes from it. It all depends on whose hands it is in. Psychology prompts novels even from the most serious people, and quite unintentionally" (728).

The obvious referent of the parody here is legal investigative psychology itself, which Dostoevsky clearly saw as a dehumanizing attempt to reduce human identity to an object of scientific inquiry and description. As Bakhtin puts it, Dostoevsky was consistently critical of such psychology as an approach that at best "permits mutually exclusive solutions to be accepted with an equal probability of being true" and at worst was "simply a lie degrading the individual" (*Problems* 61). Or, as the ace investigative psychologist Porfiry Petrovich continually points out in *Crime and Punishment*, the results of psychological inquiry are "a matter of conjecture." The entire courtroom sequence in *The Brothers Karamazov* can be read as an extended parody of legal proceedings in general, and the legal officials of the provincial town of Skotoprigonyevsk are satirized in a manner reminiscent of Gogol's *The Government Inspector*. But the echo here of contemporary critical responses to Dostoevsky's work in Fetyukovich's description of Ippolit Kirillovich as a psychologist is obvious, and the suggested parody of those responses gains energy from Dostoevsky's own disavowal of them: "They call me a *psychologist; this is not true.* I am merely a realist *in the higher sense*" (cited in Bakhtin, *Problems* 60, his emphasis).

Beyond such instances of self-parody and textual play, Fetyukovich's response to the prosecutor is undermined by its own literariness, especially when combined with the constant characterization of the prosecutor's version of events as a "novel." Indeed, Ippolit Kirillovich answers by suggesting that Fetyukovich himself has offered nothing but "novel upon novel," possibly inspired by the poetry of Byron (748). It would seem, then, that both attorneys regard the appellation *novel* as synonymous with *unreliable* or *untrue*, a suggestion that is particularly significant coming as it does within a novel. Moreover, this evocation of the liar paradox of Epimenides (which would seem to anticipate the self-referentiality of recent postmodernist fiction) is reinforced by the entire structure of the novel. Coming into these courtroom speeches, readers have just traversed a detailed narrative of the events surrounding the death of old Karamazov, events that seem to make it clear that the murder was actually committed by Dmitri's half-brother Smerdyakov. Thus, we have an apparent advantage over the jury in the trial in that we "know" what happened. But the continual reminders by both Ippolit Kirillovich and Fetyukovich that the information presented in novels cannot be believed tends to call our knowledge into question, especially given that the narrator of *The Brothers*

Karamazov seems highly unreliable at times and may in fact have invented his narration in much the same way as the two lawyers do. The entire book is narrated in a mode of rumor and innuendo that never offers an authoritative account of events with which to compare the fictional narratives of the lawyers. Almost all readers of the book come away feeling that Smerdyakov did, in fact, commit the murder with the subtle collaboration of Ivan Karamazov. But this information is available to us only through the account of Smerdyakov's confession to Ivan in the chapter "The Third Meeting with Smerdyakov," the contents of which could only have been revealed to the narrator by Ivan (who is by this point apparently mad)— unless, of course, the narrator simply made them up.

Dostoevsky's refusal to provide an authoritative perspective on the events related in *The Brothers Karamazov* seems a far cry from Sultan's suggestion that Dostoevsky's project is to reveal the hand of God in the playing out of human events. Robert Belknap's description of *The Brothers Karamazov* as a "willfully 'ill-made' novel" seems extremely apt, but it hardly seems consistent with the attempt to suggest the guiding hand of God in constructing the plot (83). In the same way, Dostoevsky's depiction of the "events of psychological reality" is far from simple. As the reconstructions of Dmitri Karamazov by both attorneys show, human identity in Dostoevsky is far from a stable, monolithic structure. Identity for Dostoevsky is, in fact, consistently a narrative construct, something that happens in the course of events rather than something that preexists and then participates in those events.

Dostoevsky's novels are filled with illustrations of the notion that subjectivity is at base a narrative phenomenon. In *Devils*, for example, the superfluous man Stavrogin is largely superfluous because he is unable to find an effective narrative in which to participate. Indeed, as Holquist has emphasized, the characters in this novel are as a group so incapable of establishing an effective sense of temporal sequence that the very notion of individual identity is put into question. And, if individual identity is the stuff of which novels are made, then *Devils* puts the whole genre of the novel—that ultimate genre of the bourgeois individual—radically into question. The book thus "has as its theme as well as its structure the impossibility of its putative genre. Novel-ness, the search for a unique coherence, collapses into anti-novelness, the recognition that coherence can never be unique" (Holquist, *Dostoevsky* 147). Indeed, *Devils* is even more "ill-made" than *The Brothers Karamazov*. As much as it is a critique of nineteenth-century utopian socialists (and a sometimes striking anticipation of twentieth-century communism), *Devils* narrates the failure of narrative, its incompetent *skaz*-like Shandean narrator serving to illustrate the difficulty of establishing a stable sense of narrative identity in Dostoevsky's contemporary world.[16] Dostoevsky's treatment of personal psychology in *Devils* thus results not in an affirmation of traditional theologically-based notions of identity but in an exploration of the inefficacy of those notions that simultaneously challenges related literary conventions.

Such challenges are, of course, quite familiar to readers of Joyce. Indeed, the problematic relationship between narrative and personal identity is crucial to Joyce's fiction. One could, for example, summarize the spiritual paralysis of the characters of *Dubliners* as an inability to participate in narratives other than the strictly stereotypical ones provided by the cultural rigidity of the society in which they live. Much of the plot of *A Portrait of the Artist as a Young Man* can be summarized in Stephen's attempts to establish a notion of temporal sequence in his life that will lead to a sense of self with which he can be comfortable. The bildungsroman form of the book clearly contributes to this motif, but the disjunctive ending—which contrasts radically with the social reconciliation typical of the genre—suggests the difficulty of attaining such reconciliation in Dublin while still preserving a working artistic imagination.

Holquist relates the instability of narrative identity in Dostoevsky to a generally fragile historical sense in nineteenth-century Russia as a whole, a fragility that also relates to the place of literary tradition in Russian culture. For example, Holquist notes that "doubts about the existence of a national literature, not pious affirmations of Russian culture, carried the day in the early nineteenth century" (*Dostoevsky* 13). Holquist discusses the work of nineteenth-century thinker Pyotr Chaadaev, noting that Chaadaev's work

> cut to the heart of all doubts about the history of particular Russian institutions, political as well as cultural, by declaring, in effect, the Russians had no history at all: "Historical experience does not exist for us. Generations and ages have passed without benefit to us. With regard to us it is as if the general law of mankind had been suspended. . . ." He goes on to speak of the Russians as "being somehow out of time." (14)

Holquist also notes that, because of this sense of being outside the mainstream of history, nineteenth-century Russians typically relied especially on literature as a source of national identity. As a result, "history was more often than not in Russia equated with literary history" (28). Of course, the same might be said of Ireland, given the centrality of literature to the definition of an Irish national identity in the Irish Renaissance. Interestingly, though, Holquist specifically contrasts the Russian difficulty in finding a way to enter history with Stephen Dedalus's expressed desire in *Ulysses* to escape from history: "History during this period was less, as Joyce would say, a nightmare to awaken from than it was a dream to realize" (15).

The problematic nature of narrative identity in Dostoevsky is a particularly prominent motif in *Notes from Underground*, whose protagonist desperately strives to find a narrative form in which he can make sense of his experience but finds his life hopelessly fragmented, his inability to connect one moment to the next clearly illustrating the problematic sense of temporal continuity that Holquist associates with nineteenth-century Russian culture. On the other hand, the temporal fragmentation of the Underground Man also anticipates Jameson's discussions of schizophrenia in modern and (especially) postmodern western culture, suggesting an interesting point of comparison between Dostoevsky and Joyce. Indeed, the issues raised by Dostoevsky's depiction of the Underground Man are often remarkably similar to the issues raised by Joyce's fiction, especially in the depiction of Stephen Dedalus.

Stephen and the Underground Man are alike in many ways. Both are extremely self-conscious, both feel a strong sense of isolation and difference from others, both display consciousnesses that are overtly constituted by literary discourses. Both also employ narrative as a central strategy in their attempts to formulate a coherent and continuous sense of selfhood from these discourses, but both have a great deal of difficulty in doing so.[17] Indeed, though Holquist's mention of Stephen's notorious desire in *Ulysses* to awaken from the nightmare of history would seem to suggest an overly rigid sense of narrative identity that stands in strong contrast to the fragile and fragmented identities of Dostoevsky characters like the Underground Man, in point of fact Stephen's sense of being trapped in history and the Underground Man's sense of being exlcuded from it are merely opposite sides of the same coin.

Holquist notes that the Underground Man constantly constructs narratives in his attempt to lend continuity to his fragmented experience of reality: "He seeks to make a coherent story out of his life by imposing on it a literary pattern" (62). This project fails miserably, however. The Underground Man is in fact quite good at constructing plots, but his excessive self-consciousness makes him all too aware of the blatant fictionality of the patterns he thereby imposes on reality. In addition, he is well aware that his highly literary plots are extremely derivative. To a certain extent, he—as much as Stephen Dedalus—is tormented not by a lack of connection with the past but by an inability to break free of it and a desire "to curse the past and cover it with dust" (*Notes* 80). The Underground Man feels thoroughly entrapped by past literature. He is a great reader, and he shows a continual awareness that most of his attitudes and insights are derived from his reading, that his most "personal" dreams and fantasies are "entirely ready-made, largely stolen from poets and novelists and adapted to serve every need and demand" (67). Indeed, this sense that the narratives he constructs are little more than collections of literary clichés is often quite specific. At one point, the Underground Man envisions a lengthy fantasy of humiliating the officer Zverkov in a duel that is so affecting he is moved to tears, a reaction immediately followed by intense shame at his realization that the entire fantasy was lifted "from Silvio and from Lermontov's *Masquerade*" (99).[18]

The Underground Man's sense of literary belatedness, his sense that all plots have been used before, frequently figures in Dostoevsky's work. For example, the Underground Man's highly derivative duel narrative will be largely repeated in the story of Father Zosima in *The Brothers Karamazov*, where the motif thus becomes doubly belated. And Rodion Raskolnikov characterizes his murder of the old pawnbroker in *Crime and Punishment* as (among other things) an attempt to assert his originality, to break free of what he sees as the central terror of the common Russian populace—the fear "of doing something new, saying a new word of their own that hasn't been said before" (*Crime* 34). Yet Raskolnikov's own thoughts are far from original. As his friend Razumikhin tells him, "you steal from other authors. There's not a spark of independent life in you!" (213). And Raskolnikov's difficulty in asserting his own orginal and independent selfhood is one that haunts Dostoevsky's characters all the way from Devushkin in *Poor Folk* (who is convinced that Gogol's "The Overcoat" is the story of his own life) to the Karamazov brothers (who often feel that their lives are predetermined by their family heritage).

The hyperconscious Underground Man differs from most other major Dostoevsky characters only in his heightened awareness of his own mind as a patchwork of quotations. As a result, he is also particularly bitter about his lack of uniqueness and originality. The narratives from Pushkin and Lermontov that inspire the Underground Man's fantasies of vengeance against Zverkov are themselves (like *The Count of Monte Cristo*, which is so important for Stephen Dedalus) centrally concerned with the theme of revenge, and this desire for revenge is a central motivating factor in the Underground Man's life. Michael André Bernstein describes *Notes from Underground* as "a pastiche of countless prior texts, in part because that is all the Underground Man himself really consists of, except for his additional burden of finding this existence-as-pastiche intolerable" (109). In an extensive study of the dark side of the Bakhtinian carnival, Bernstein suggests *Notes from Underground* (which is clearly both dialogic and carnivalesque in Bakhtin's sense) as a key example. Bernstein compares the Underground Man's bitterness to Nietzsche's notion of ressentiment, which is informed both by a resentment at being constituted by others and a generalized desire for revenge against this situation. In particular, Bernstein notes that the Underground Man's Nietzschean ressentiment involves a "nagging rage at the human experience of temporality. . . . As a creature of ressentiment, haunted by memory and fashioned by citations, he can have no present except for his impotent misery at the process of time itself" (108–9).

Bernstein notes that the Underground Man's sense of "time-as-oppression" echoes one of the most important "imaginative crises of nineteenth-century thought" in both Russia and the West. For our purposes, it is clear that this sense closely resembles Stephen Dedalus's characterization of history as an oppressive nightmare. Stephen and the Underground Man are also quite similar in the way both respond to a sense of being constituted by others with an attempt to establish their difference from and independence of others, an attempt that leads to a radical sense of isolation and alienation in both characters. Bakhtin notes the tendency of the Underground Man to view the world in terms of his difference from it.

The world for him falls into two camps: in one, "I," in the other, "they," that is, all "others" without exception, no matter who they are. Every person exists for him, first and foremost, as "the other person." And this definition of the person directly conditions all the Underground Man's attitudes toward him. He reduces all people to a single common denominator—"the other." (*Problems* 253)

This mode of intersubjective relation is strikingly reminiscent of that of Stephen, especially in *Portrait*, where it leads Stephen to a sense of isolation that is accurately summarized by Cranly: "Alone, quite alone. You have no fear of that. And you know what that word means? Not only to be separate from all others but to have not even one friend" (247). Despite this isolation Stephen, like the Underground Man, is literally constituted by the discourse of others, a discourse that is often highly literary. When he seemingly rejects conventional Catholic rules of behavior and goes out to encounter the Otherness of Dublin's prostitutes, he does so largely within a narrative fantasy derived from *The Count of Monte Cristo*, just as the Underground Man appeals to literary models in his dealings with the prostitute Liza.

Indeed, the Underground Man's speeches to Liza are so obviously composed of literary clichés that even the ill-educated Liza recognizes the nature of his discourse, responding to his initial story of love and marital bliss by noting that "it's like out of a book" (115). The Underground Man bitterly responds with a narrative about the dark future that awaits Liza in her life as a prostitute, a narrative specifically designed to bring her pain. This narrative is itself a cliché, as the Underground Man well knows: "I knew that I was speaking stiffly, artificially, even bookishly; indeed, I was incapable of speaking otherwise than 'like out of a book'" (121). Still, the narrative allows the Underground Man to demonstrate that his command of literary cliché is far superior to Liza's, and his images of her future are so vividly abject that she is driven to tears.

The Underground Man's use of literary cliché to establish his domination over Liza (the only mode in which he can envision interaction with others) is particularly significant given that this relationship is itself a cliché. Liza, of course, is the stereotypical whore with a heart of gold, a motif that functions frequently in Dostoevsky's fiction, perhaps most prominently in the depiction of the meek Sonya in *Crime and Punishment*. It seems clear in *Notes from Underground* that Dostoevsky is to

some extent parodying the lack of moral imagination in both sentimental fictions of the 1840s and socialist fictions of the 1860s in his use of
this motif. What is particularly telling, however, is that from all appearances Dostoevsky himself falls into the same trap, employing Liza's
willingness to offer love and acceptance to the Underground Man
(despite his nastiness) as an image of the kind of Christian self-sacrifice
that Dostoevsky himself seems to recommend as an antidote to the
moral bankruptcy of his contemporary world. But, if the Underground
Man enacts one cliché after another in his gestures toward Liza, the fact
is that Liza responds with a cascade of clichés of her own. Bernstein
thus suggests that the net result of this motif in *Notes from Underground*
is to undermine Dostoevsky's own Christian ideology, making it
appear to be just another cliché. Bernstein further notes that such readings of Dostoevsky's fiction as being inimical to his own thought are
fairly common; indeed, the inability (or refusal) of Dostoevsky to dominate his fiction with his personal ideology lies at the heart of what
Bakhtin sees as the polyphony of his texts. At the same time, Bernstein
notes that readers have typically been oddly "committed to siding with
Dostoevsky *against* his fiction as soon as the pressures of the split
become too acute" (111, Bernstein's emphasis).

The phenomenon Bernstein cites is exemplified by Sultan's view of
Crime and Punishment as a "doctrinaire, didactic novel" that supports
Dostoevsky's Christian views, despite its complexities (*Eliot* 73). Such
readings of *Crime and Punishment* are no doubt enhanced by the book's
ending, in which Raskolnikov apparently undergoes a religious conversion, which caps the preceding narrative with a suitably Christian
conclusion. Thus, Raskolnikov in a sense completes the Underground
Man's suspended quest for a viable narrative of personal identity. This
may well have been what Dostoevsky intended to convey. However,
the many parallels between Dostoevsky and Joyce suggest ways of
reading Dostoevsky through Joyce that emphasize the ability of Dostoevsky's texts to generate meaning that goes far beyond any question of
authorial intention.

When read through Joyce, even the ending of *Crime and Punishment*—often criticized as being an overly reductive expression of Dostoevsky's Christian message—becomes potentially subversive of that
message. Joyce's work powerfully challenges the whole notion of religious conversion, as demonstrated in Stephen's comic failed conversion in *Portrait*. It is significant, for example, that *Portrait* so closely par-

allels the *Confessions* of St. Augustine up until the time of Augustine's conversion, which presumably succeeds where Stephen's fails. Given Augustine's insistence that his conversion led to a complete transformation that literally made him a different person, Joyce's challenge to the ideology of conversion has clear implications in terms of his explorations of the continuity of identity and history. Seen through Joyce, then, Dostoevsky's apparent suggestion of religious conversion as a solution to Raskolnikov's fragile sense of self seems highly peculiar. If Raskolnikov's fundamental difficulty is an inability to establish a continuous sense of self over time, the kind of radical temporal break implied by the Augustinian conversion experience seems anything but an effective cure. Moreover, following in the footsteps of predecessors like Augustine hardly seems to answer Raskolnikov's desire for originality.

Read in this way, the "conversion" of Raskolnikov at the end of *Crime and Punishment* seems highly suspect. Like the Underground Man, Raskolnikov has lived his life by trying to find an appropriate narrative in which to participate, though (as Holquist notes) Raskolnikov's candidate narratives tend to involve history rather than fiction. In particular, Raskolnikov commits murder in order to explore the possibility of making a radical change in his life through a single mighty deed that will place him in the category of Napoleon or other great figures of history. In short, he has been seeking "conversion" all along, and in the end he has not changed his fundamental goal or strategy but has simply switched from a historical narrative to a religious one. Now he will attempt to make a grand gesture that will place him in the company of Augustine, just as he earlier sought to emulate Napoleon. Indeed, Dostoevsky's epilogue directly supports this reading. Raskolnikov ends with a sense that he will have to perform a "great heroic deed" in order to complete his conversion—which places him in precisely the same situation he was in at the beginning of the text. And the text closes with an acknowledgment that "at this point a new story begins," though the current story has been completed. In short, Raskolnikov is still attempting to establish and stabilize his identity through narrative—it is just that, his previous narrative having failed, he has decided to try a different one.

Raskolnikov's move from historical to religious narratives closely parallels that of Stephen Dedalus in *Portrait*. As Stephen marches to the office of the rector at Clongowes Wood to demand rectification for his unfair pandying, he is determined to perform a heroic act like one that might have "been done before by somebody in history, by some great person whose head was in the books of history. And the rector would declare that he had been wrongly punished because the senate and the Roman people always declared that the men who did that had been wrongly punished" (53). Indeed, Napoleon himself is one of Stephen's favorite role models among historical figures. Later, Stephen switches from history to religion in his attempted conversion, an attempt that Joyce undermines through the comic depiction of Stephen's attempts to mortify his senses and thereby become more devout. This motif, along with Joyce's general parodic assault on the Christian apotheosis of suffering, powerfully challenges Dostoevsky's apparent presentation of suffering as the key to Christian salvation. Read through Joyce, Raskolnikov's "conversion" becomes merely an ironic repetition of his earlier decision to kill the old pawnbroker, while Sonya becomes not a Christian ideal but (like Liza of *Notes from Underground*) a parodic victim of that ideal, rendered pathetic and ridiculous through her overly literal acceptance of the Christian narrative of suffering.

Of course, the numerous affinities between Joyce and Dostoevsky also suggest ways of reading Joyce through Dostoevsky. In particular, comparisons between Joyce and Dostoevsky demonstrate that many of Joyce's most modern motifs (problematic subjectivity, awareness of belatedness in the literary tradition, exploration of nontraditional narrative forms, mosaic construction of multigeneric texts) have important precedents that go far back into the nineteenth century. Moreover, read through Dostoevsky, Joyce's treatment of subjectivity becomes neither an endorsement of individualism nor an attempt to undermine it but an exploration of the difficulty of true individuality in the modern world. In addition, the parallels between Dostoevsky and Joyce suggest the relevance to Joyce's work of the description by Bakhtin and his circle of human subjectivity as an ongoing social phenomenon. Further, Bakhtin's continual insistence on a metaphorical relationship between selves and texts suggests clear parallels between Joyce's exploration of alternative models of subjectivity and his exploration of alternative narrative forms through his experimental writing practice.

Conclusion: Modernism, Postmodernism, Joyce

This study has emphasized Joyce's relationship to the western literary tradition by initiating dialogues between Joyce and predecessors from Homer to Dostoevsky. To suggest that the works of such predecessors can provide important insights into the work of Joyce is, of course, not a very surprising move. On the other hand, the particular dialogues enacted in this study suggest readings of Joyce that often conflict markedly with long-popular perceptions of modernist art as elitist, aestheticist, subjectivist, and sealed off from social and political concerns. My readings of Joyce's relation to literary predecessors like Homer, Dante, Rabelais, Shakespeare, Goethe, and Dostoevsky certainly reinforce the common perception that both considerable literary knowledge and extensive interpretive dexterity are of great use in reading Joyce's work. However, my Bakhtinian readings as a whole counter the notion that Joyce's work is divorced from reality because of its literariness or that it seeks an elite audience through its difficulty. On the contrary, Joyce's often highly subversive dialogue with the "great" texts of the literary condition acts to undermine conventional high-low cultural hierarchies and to situate Joyce's work in close contact with historical reality.

Any reading of Joyce that seeks to argue the powerful political potential and historical embeddedness of his work must at some point come to grips with the fact that these characteristics run strongly contrary to many received notions about modernist literature, despite Joyce's perceived centrality to modernism. Such is the prominence of Joyce's work (especially *Ulysses*) in the modernist canon that when Maurice Beebe set out in 1974, in "*Ulysses* and the Age of Modernism," to catalog the "cardinal points" of modernism, he did so not by examining a broad range of modernist works but simply by analyzing *Ulysses*. Beebe cites Leslie Fiedler as one of his authorities for consider-

ing *Ulysses* as the most representative modernist work, but it is important to note that Fiedler comes to praise Joyce in this way in order to
bury him, declaring in 1970 that "The literary movement which we
have agreed to call 'Modernism,' and at the center of which Joyce
stands, is a literary movement which is now dead" (21). Beebe himself
declares modernism dead in another 1974 essay, "What Modernism
Was," delivering a eulogy that again identifies Joyce's corpus as the
principal corpse.

But, like that resilient Irish hod carrier, Tim Finnegan, Joyce has
shown a stubborn refusal to stay dead. The death certificate that Fiedler
hands to modernism is meant to announce the coming of the new age
of postmodernism, and in the two decades since Fiedler's announcement Joyce has gradually worked his way into a position of eminence
in the postmodernist canon (oxymoron though such may be) that rivals
the one he once held in modernism. According to this revised assessment, modernism is still dead, but Joyce is alive and well because he
turns out secretly to have been a postmodernist all along.

Clearly Joyce is a crucial figure for any exploration of the interface
between modernism and postmodernism, and a close examination of
his ex post facto metempsychosis from modernist to postmodernist
promises to yield a great deal of information about the dynamics of
modern literary history in general. For one thing, a number of other
prominent modernists have experienced similar postmodernist rein-
carnations, and erstwhile modernist figures like Proust, Woolf, Stevens,
Williams, Pound, Eliot, Beckett, and even Yeats have recently been
"postmodernized" by various observers. In fact, so many modernists
have been discovered to have "actually" been postmodernists that one
begins to wonder whether there *were* any modernists in the first place.
Perhaps the implication is simply that modernism is at least as much a
product of the ways texts are read as of any inherent properties in the
texts themselves.[1] More generally, the recent "postmodernization" of
so many modernist writers may simply serve to illustrate the way that
literary history always consists of a process of rewriting and updating
previous literary works. If recent criticism has transformed our understanding of modernist writers, it has changed the way we see Victorian,
romantic, Enlightenment, Renaissance, medieval, and classical writers
as well.

In any case, there has been much critical debate over the nature of
modernism in recent years. In particular, it has recently become more

common to read Joyce and other modernists as political writers. For example, Russell Berman notes the efforts of critics like Matei Calinescu and Peter Bürger to distinguish between modernism and the avant-garde but suggests that this distinction tends to deemphasize the significance of the modernist break with nineteenth-century bourgeois culture. Berman himself uses the terms *modernism* and *avant-garde* interchangeably and sees a genuine political engagement on the part of modernist/avant-garde artists like Joyce and Thomas Mann, who both actively seek to transfer their aesthetic ideals from an autonomous world of art "into social practice: social revolution via aesthetic innovation" (72).[2] Even Marxist critics, who earlier tended to follow Lukács in rejecting Joyce as a bourgeois writer, have frequently embraced Joyce's work in recent years.[3] Fredric Jameson's arguments in favor of Joyce and other modernists are well known, and even critics like Franco Moretti, who concludes that Joyce himself "considers the aesthetic sphere incapable of being either an example to, or a compensation for, the state of the world," still see much positive political potential in *Ulysses* as a critique of bourgeois society (208).

Terry Eagleton's comments on the autonomy of the modernist text—and on Joyce's texts in particular—are indicative of the complexity of this issue. In a relatively conventional way, Eagleton sees the modernist text in general as having turned its back on the world of history. For him,

the modernist work brackets off the referent or real historical world, thickens its textures and deranges its forms to forestall instant consumability, and draws its own language protectively around it to become a mysteriously autotelic object, free of all contaminating truck with the real. ("Capitalism" 67)

However, Eagleton grants that this distaste for the real has its positive side, and in this resistance to "instant consumability" he acknowledges a movement by which the autotelic modernist text battles the tendency of capitalist society to reduce the work of art to a mere object, exchangeable like any other commodity. But for Eagleton the modernist text avoids one form of commodification only to fall prey to another: "The autonomous, self-regarding, impenetrable modernist artefact, in all its isolated splendour, is the commodity as fetish resisting the commodity as exchange, its solution to reification part of that very problem" (67).

Eagleton's point is well taken, and his observation of the double movement inherent in the autonomous, self-reflecting text seems sound. On the other hand, Eagleton does little to demonstrate that modernist texts in fact *are* autonomous and self-reflecting, and his comments on the radical divorce between text and reality in modernism certainly seem to have little to do with *Ulysses*. *Ulysses* constantly calls attention to its language and to its methods of composition, constantly reminds us that we are not reading the story of "real" people on a "real" day in Dublin. But surely this does not mean that the text thereby avoids all "contaminating truck" with the realities of 1904 (or 1922) Dublin. Indeed, the complex multilayered processes of signification at work in Joyce's writing constantly slip and slide among a variety of levels of meaning, including strictly reflexive commentaries on language and writing, but also including very specific commentaries on real-life Dublin, and more general commentaries on modern society in general. In comments elsewhere on *Ulysses*, Eagleton himself notes that the book gains much of its power by maintaining elements of the naturalistic novel, thus allowing its readers to develop traditional expectations, which are then undermined (*Criticism* 156). Eagleton here even grants that Joyce's famed reflexivity effects a certain engagement with reality, arguing that Joyce seems to have regarded the world itself as a sort of aesthetic artifact.[4] For Eagleton, Joyce does not turn away from the realities of modern urban life as do Yeats, Eliot, and Lawrence. Instead "Joyce remains a progressive, prototypically urban producer, exploiting difference, disconnection, splitting, permutation and simultaneity as the very forms of his art" (157). And in still another discussion Eagleton calls *Ulysses* "scandalous and subversive" and suggests that the polyphonic, punning discourse of Joyce's later texts "pulverizes" the "bourgeois myth of immanent meaning" (*Ideology* 375).

Eagleton is very much aware that there is a contradiction between his view of the modernist text as eschewing all contact with reality as it succumbs to fetishization and his depiction of Joyce's writing—which in many ways seems to epitomize his comments on the modernist text—as potentially radical. But he suggests that the contradictory movement in Joyce's writing parallels a similar contradiction in capitalism itself. Capitalist society is caught up in a western metaphysical tradition in which signification operates by a process of naming that depends upon a clear distinction between what is a thing and what is not that thing. In short, meaning is based on difference, especially on a series of clearly defined polar oppositions like high and low, sacred and profane, male and female, and so on. But in the sphere of production capitalism acts inexorably to level all differences, commodification reducing anything and everything to a faceless interchangeability. Joyce's commodification of signification itself (what I have called sliding signification) thus turns the economic underpinnings of capitalism against its philosophical foundations, effecting a conflict that reveals the profound contradictions that lie at the heart of capitalist society. Further, this translation of commodification from the realm of economics to the realm of literature undermines the traditional separation between culture and bourgeois civil society, thus making it impossible for the former to continue to be used "to mystify and legitimate the raw appetite" of the latter (Eagleton, *Ideology* 376).

Such indications of the complex relationship between modernist art and capitalist society suggest that conventional notions of modernism as disengaged from social concerns need to be reconsidered. Indeed, modernism for Jameson is distinguished from postmodernism by modernism's greater extensive critical engagement with history. If anything it may well be that what we typically call modernist art is characterized by an unusually high degree of social concern and by a strong belief in the power of art to effect genuine social and political change.[5] Yet many critics still see modernism as politically disengaged—or even reactionary. Such critics continue to round up the usual suspects, charging that modernist works are elitist and aestheticist, that they are concerned with individual psychology rather than social reality, and that they represent an attempt to escape from temporality and historicity. The readings of Joyce in the present study can be summarized in terms of the same charges, all of which appear from these readings particularly ill-founded.

Modernist Difficulty, Cultural Elitism

The novelist-narrator of Flann O'Brien's *At Swim-Two-Birds* offers the following advice to other would-be authors of modern literary works:

> The entire corpus of existing literature should be regarded as a limbo from which discerning authors could draw their characters as required, creating only when they failed to find a suitable existing puppet. The modern novel should be largely a work of refer-

ence. Most authors spend their time saying what has been said before—usually said much better. A wealth of references to existing works would acquaint the reader instantaneously with the nature of each character, would obviate tiresome explanations and would effectively preclude mountebanks, upstarts, thimbleriggers and persons of inferior education from an understanding of contemporary literature. (33)

While it is true that the narrator's friend Brinsley (playing Lynch to the narrator's Stephen) immediately ironizes this statement with his response of "That is all my bum," it is also true that this passage stands as a striking commentary on the kind of allusiveness that has frequently been seen as a central tendency of modernist literature. Most obvious among these is O'Brien's text itself, but this method of composition by appropriation brings to mind the works of a number of other authors as well, among whom Joyce looms as the most prominent. Further, O'Brien's passage takes a parodic swipe at such authors (including himself) by suggesting a specific motivation for the dense allusiveness of their texts—to identify an educated elite that is somehow worthy of access to the products of high culture.

O'Brien's passage thus directly addresses the common critical view that literary modernism reduces art to a self-contained system that attempts to avoid engagement with the real world and that such art shows an elitist contempt for the masses and mass culture. For example, Andreas Huyssen has argued that modernism is distinguished from postmodernism precisely in the way modernism preserves the "great divide" between "high" and "low" culture, while postmodernism challenges this hierarchy. Huyssen uncritically accepts the conventional categorization of Joyce as a modernist, though he does not present any evidence from Joyce's work to back up this categorization, apparently regarding it as self-evident.[6] And it is certainly true that Joyce's works, with their dense networks of allusions and their unconventional uses of language, can be extremely difficult and recondite, raising the question of whether they do not in fact deny access to the uninitiated rabblement.

Joyce's bricolage texts are indeed constructed from other texts and from other preexisting discourses, but this method of construction hardly represents an unequivocal elitism. For one thing, Joyce's attitude toward his sources in high culture is frequently critical, and his dialogues with his literary predecessors tend to undermine the authority of high culture. In addition, his sources are not exclusively, or even principally, of a literary nature. Joyce's allusions to Shakespeare, Dante, Homer, and others are often particularly striking because of their aptness and wit (and because those are the sorts of connections professional scholars are trained to find), but Joyce's primary *materia poetica* is always derived from the real historical setting of his own Dublin. *Ulysses* garners much more from *Thom's Dublin Directory* than from *Hamlet* or the *Odyssey*, and Joyce's texts in general are packed with references to real people, places, and events to a greater extent than almost any others before or since. And, even when Joyce's sources are "literary," they are often derived from decidedly nonelitist forms such as newspapers, magazines, pornography, and the popular stage.[7]

Furthermore, Joyce does not divest these materials of their historical embeddedness when he imports them into his texts. Rather than aestheticizing (or canonizing, as Bakhtin would call it) the various languages that make up the fabric of his own discourse, Joyce shows a profound recognition of the sources of those languages and of the social and political ramifications of those sources. The many social voices that sound in Joyce's work are allowed positions from which to speak, even when the spirit of his work seems radically antithetical to those positions. The resultant clash of discourses mirrors in a dramatic way the clash of discourses that constitutes the society in which Joyce's texts arise.

But, if Joyce's work is not limited to literary concerns, then neither is the work of most other leading modernists. Certainly it helps to be familiar with Dante, Shakespeare, and Wagner when reading *The Waste Land*, but it is quite possible to read that poem (especially the notes) as a parody of the kind of intellectual pretentiousness with which it is itself sometimes charged.[8] Moreover, the poem also makes extensive use of materials like popular songs, and it is as helpful for reading the poem to know the milieu of London taverns as to know the plot of *The Tempest*. Such observations hold for other important "modernists" as well. Recent readings (especially feminist ones) have uncovered an intense social and political orientation in the work of Virginia Woolf, and Woolf's work is also replete with information and material from nonliterary sources, as studies like those by Hussey and Zwerdling have shown.

Bertolt Brecht presents perhaps the best example of a writer frequently labeled as modernist whose work is highly allusive and extremely literary yet at the same time engaged with contemporary political and social issues in an obvious way. Brecht's Marxist political commitment is well known, yet his intertextual method of constructing his texts is a classic modernist strategy. Beginning with the early *Baal* (a parodic response to Hanns Johst's *Der Einsame*) and extending through works like *Edward II, The Threepenny Opera, Roundheads and Peakheads, Coriolan,* and *Antigone,* Brecht's plays are quite often adaptations of specific works from the western dramatic tradition. Even plays that are not direct adaptations draw quite heavily on this tradition, making extensive use of materials from predecessors like Shakespeare, Goethe, Schiller, and Büchner, in addition to materials from nondramatic artists ranging from Dante, to Grimmelshausen, to Hašek, to Upton Sinclair. Brecht also draws heavily upon the work of his contemporaries and associates, authoring many of his plays in conjunction with collaborators like Lion Feuchtwanger while deriving significant inspiration from the work of modern writers and directors like Klabund, Wedekind, Piscator, and Meyerhold. Finally, Brecht utilizes a great deal of material from sources in popular culture, ranging from the German *Volksstück,* to cabaret, to detective thrillers, to the films of Charlie Chaplin. Indeed, Brecht's intermixture of materials (and styles) from both "high" and "low" culture is one of the ways his work resembles Joyce's most closely. While rejecting Joyce as an elitist modernist, Andreas Huyssen thus acknowledges Brecht's "immersion in the vernacular of popular culture" as an attempt to "destabilize the high/low opposition" that informs traditional western culture (16). But Frederic Ewen's description of Brecht's heteroglossic manipulation of language might just as easily describe much of the writing of Joyce:

> Brecht revolutionized poetic language. He domesticated its brutality, tamed its cloacal aspect. Such speech as was found in *Baal* had not been found on the German stage before. Here was the popular idiom of the marketplaces and the fairs, caught directly "from the mouth" of the speakers, but fused with the language of Luther's Bible, and fitted into the broken patterns learned from Büchner— but all unmistakably Brecht. (96)

Keith Dickson notes that "Brecht's magpie method of composition borders at times on plagiarism" (192). Of course, this "plagiarism" is largely the point of Brecht's technique, which is designed both to mock the typical bourgeois emphasis on ownership and to challenge the hegemony of a western literary tradition that has long served to provide cultural underpinnings for the economic and political machinations of capitalism. And Joyce's scissors-and-paste technique is not all that different from Brecht's "magpie method."[9] Brecht's epic theater presents itself specifically as an alternative to a western dramatic tradition still rooted in the Aristotelian principles of ancient Greek drama. Combined with Brecht's frequent subversive use of Shakespeare, this rejection of the techniques of Greek drama acts to undermine the two most important "Golden Ages" of the western cultural past, just as Joyce's work also challenges the authority of both classical Greece and Renaissance England.[10]

One of Brecht's favorite alienation effects is the use of intrusive and inappropriate styles, a strategy quite familiar to readers of Joyce. In Brecht this technique quite often takes the form of the use of elevated poetic style to depict the most sordid workings of capitalism, as in the use of blank verse to describe the manipulations of Mauler and his associates in *St. Joan of the Stockyards* or in the use of high Elizabethan style in the scene in *Roundheads and Peakheads*, in which de Guzman asks his sister Isabella to submit to the sexual extortion of the political thug Zazarante. This technique thus serves both to highlight the contradictions of capitalism itself and to indicate the complicity of high culture in those contradictions. Brecht's dialogue with the western literary tradition consistently suggests that this tradition has long been used to disguise the ugly reality of capitalism through the beauty of high style and to reinforce the workings of bourgeois sentimentality through its exploitative appeal to the emotions.

When Brecht has Arturo Ui (his Chicago-gangster version of Adolph Hitler) rehearse lines from Shakespeare in order to perfect his rhetorical techniques of crowd manipulation, he makes an important statement about his view of the traditional function of high culture in bourgeois society.[11] Of course, Elizabethan drama is an ideal choice as a focal point for Brecht's assault on the authority of bourgeois high culture, both because of the centrality of Elizabethan drama in bourgeois culture and because of the obvious parallels between the theatricality of the techniques of official power in Elizabethan England and the aestheticization of politics in Nazi Germany. As in Joyce, Shakespeare is a particularly crucial figure in Brecht's subversive appropriation of the classics of western culture. As Matthew Wikander points out, Brecht's epic theater draws heavily upon the techniques of the Elizabethan stage, even as Brecht himself powerfully rejected what he saw as the protobourgeois attitude of Shakespeare: "Brecht's imperialistic co-optation of Shakespeare's techniques—possibly *vandalism* is a better word—is always accompanied by rejection of Shakespeare's ideology" (234).[12]

Joyce similarly questions the implications of high poetic style, both in his own dialogic mixtures of widely differing styles and in terms of specific thematic content. As with Brecht, this project often involves a subversive dialogue with Shakespeare. Meanwhile, the conflation of lyricism and urination in the punning title of *Chamber Music* perfectly summarizes Joyce's attitude toward conventional categories of "high" art. A similar attitude can be seen at the end of part 1 of *Portrait*, when Stephen muses on the sounds of the cricket bats at Clongowes Wood: "In the soft grey silence he could hear the bump of the balls: and from here and from there through the quiet air the sound of the cricket bats: pick, pack, pock, puck: like drops of water in a fountain falling softly in the brimming bowl" (59). The "brimming bowl" passage that describes the sound of the cricket bats at Clongowes repeats an earlier passage (p. 41) and also recalls the sound of Father Dolan's infamous pandybat, which makes its appearance in the intervening pages. Indeed, the pandying episode contributes greatly to the reaccentuation of the sound of the cricket bats from one occurrence to the next, adding an ominous dimension. This dimension is further reinforced by the specific cultural coding of cricket as a locus for the perpetuation of the values of Ireland's British colonizers. The poetic intonation of the "brimming bowl" passage thus suggests a complicity between British imperial power and the traditions of British high culture. In addition, the lofty status of this literary language is further challenged at the beginning of part 2 as Stephen's Uncle Charles smokes his pipe in the jakes: "While he smoked the *brim* of his tall hat and the *bowl* of his pipe were just visible beyond the jambs of the outhouse door" (60, my emphasis). Clearly, the language of the previous page is still lingering in the air around this passage, and the resultant dialogue between the earlier poetic language and the later prosaic outhouse context undermines the pretensions of the former in a highly carnivalesque way.

Brecht and Joyce may be special cases, but in point of fact it is relatively easy to see the engagement of many "modernist" texts with the

real world, despite their overt literariness. However, the charge of difficulty is harder to counter. Even so ostensibly simple a text as *Dubliners* turns out to be simple only on the surface, with a vast array of subtleties and nuances dancing just beneath. And the immense difficulty of
Finnegans Wake is undeniable. There is no question that writers like
Eliot, Woolf, and (especially) Joyce *are* difficult. Even Brecht was often
criticized by fellow Marxists for producing plays that were too intellectually subtle for a mass audience. After all, the subversive assaults of
writers like Brecht and Joyce on the bourgeois cultural tradition are
largely lost on those who are unfamiliar with this tradition. And the
polyphony of voices that sound in the texts of Brecht and Joyce—democratic though such multiplicity may be in principle—contributes significantly to the complexity of those texts, as readers are forced to try to
weave their way through dense thickets of competing discourses in
order to recuperate any meaning from them at all. Moreover, this difficulty goes beyond the sheer density of information in the texts, extending to Joyce's innovations with language and form.

Richard Poirier summarizes a traditional view of the motivation
behind the extreme difficulty of so many modernist works, suggesting
that, with no widely shared common culture in modern society, this
difficulty creates a subgroup of dedicated and qualified readers willing
to work toward understanding the author and thus sharing his culture
(126). In a similar vein Wayne Booth argues that "Virginia Woolf . . .
was haunted by the sense that older writers could depend upon an
audience with public norms, while she must construct her private values as she went, then impose them, without seeming to do so, on the
reader" (392). But this view of modernist difficulty as a strategy for the
creation of a private cultural system to counter the growing fragmentation of public life clearly has little or no relevance to the work of Joyce
or Brecht. The works of both of these authors are resoundingly public
in nature, and furthermore their range of cultural reference is so broad
and all-inclusive that there can be no question of developing a private
"in group" of initiated readers who share Joyce's or Brecht's own cultural perspective. There is no secret handshake that gives one access to
Brecht or Joyce, and their references to popular culture can be expected
to be as baffling to many literary scholars as allusions to Dante, Goethe,
and Aristotle might be to *Mother Courage* or to the old Irish milk-
woman in "Telemachus."

Eliot's *The Waste Land*, for many *the* modernist poem, arises from

an ideological perspective radically different from that of Brecht or
Joyce, but it still provides an excellent example of the difficulty of modernist literature.[13] The special demands that the poem places on its
readers—the knowledge required to understand its intertextual references and the cleverness required to decipher its portent—are well
known and suggest especially clear parallels to the work of Joyce.
Indeed, the poem even includes a direct challenge for reader involvement: "You! *Hypocrite lecteur!—mon sembable,—mon frère!*" (*Collected
Poems* 55). Eliot is a particularly interesting case for the exploration of
aspects of modernism, since he was a leading modern theorist as well
as a poet.[14] He argues that much of the difficulty of contemporary literature arises because the author simply feels that he is unable to express
himself in any other way (*Use of Poetry* 143). Elsewhere, amid a sort of
capsule manifesto of the modernist style, Eliot states the necessity of
difficulty in more direct terms as a symptom of life in the modern
world:

> it appears likely that poets in our civilization, as it exists at present,
> must be *difficult*. Our civilization comprehends great variety and
> complexity, and this variety and complexity, playing upon a
> refined sensibility, must produce various and complex results. The
> poet must become more and more comprehensive, more allusive,
> more indirect, in order to force, to dislocate if necessary, language
> into his meaning. ("Metaphysical Poets" 248, Eliot's emphasis)

Eliot's attitude here seems curiously similar to that of Marxist critics of modern culture like Jameson and Adorno, and indeed Eliot's key
concept of the "dissociation of sensibility" partakes of many of the
same perceptions of the fragmented condition of modern psychic life as
does Jameson's notion of schizophrenia. Yet this idea that modernist
difficulty is mimetic of modern reality runs directly counter to the fact
that much of the difficulty of modernist literature seems to arise from
the impact on modernism of the symbolist aesthetic with its disdain for
representation of the real world. Eliot, himself strongly influenced by
French symbolists like Laforgue, echoes this disdain in suggesting that
meaning in poetry is chiefly useful "to satisfy one habit of the reader, to
keep his mind diverted and quiet, while the poem does its work upon
him: much as the imaginary burglar is always provided with a bit of

nice meat for the house-dog" (*Use of Poetry* 144). This passage suggests that much of the difficulty of modernist texts is not inherent in the texts themselves, but simply arises from improper reader expectations. In this vein, Eliot lists the other two sources of modernist difficulty as "novelty" and "consternation" on the part of a reader intimidated by the anticipation of difficulty (143–44).

Joyce, like Brecht, often seems intentionally to provoke such consternation, but in both cases this provocation can be interpreted as attempts to stimulate critical analysis on the part of their audiences rather than attempts to exclude the masses from access to their work. The alienation effect on which Brecht's epic theater relies is ultimately designed to bring the audience more actively *into* his work. Similarly, if Joyce's texts make unprecedented demands on the reader, they also allow the reader to participate in the generation of meaning to an unprecedented extent.[15] The extraordinary degree of reader involvement allowed (and required) by Joyce's texts creates a situation in which those texts have an enhanced ability to encourage the reader to challenge received ideas. In fact, Gabriel Josipovici sees a similar function for the difficulty and artificiality of modernist texts in general, arguing that the modernist artist who writes in a symbolist vein

> holds that the work of art is meaningful precisely because it reveals to us the "otherness" of the world—it shocks us out of our natural sloth and the force of habit, and makes us see for the first time what we had looked at a hundred times and never seen. ("Modernism and Romanticism" 192)[16]

Thus, even symbolism has a potential political power, and the echo here of Brecht's alienation effect is clear. In the case of Joyce, this is particularly true because the identifiably symbolist strain in his work never exists in pure form but is combined with other, ostensibly more realistic modes of writing. It is thus a commonplace of Joyce criticism to note the simultaneous presence of symbolism and realism in his work, and in fact the multilayered generation of meaning in Joyce's work is even more complex than this binary model indicates. Moreover, the self-conscious and autocritical nature of Joyce's work is such that symbolist aesthetics itself becomes an object of inquiry in the text, much as does poetry in the plays of Brecht. These interrogations help to highlight the fact that the desire for an escape from history embodied in symbolism—and in bourgeois art in general—was itself a symptom of a specific sociohistorical moment.

Modern Authorship and Modernist Subjectivism

Apparently Joyce's work does not conform to traditional notions of the elitism and formalist solipsism of modernist works, but then again neither does Eliot's or Woolf's. In his essay "The Lessons of Modernism" Josipovici takes a common position when he argues that modernism arises from a crisis of authority that infected all of western society sometime around the end of the nineteenth century. In particular (as far as art was concerned), this crisis involved a questioning of "the authority of the author or creator" (109). According to this model, artists became increasingly less confident in their privileged status as interpreters of reality, leading to a reticence of which Eliot's Prufrock is perhaps paradigmatic.

Eliot himself, in "Tradition and the Individual Talent," provides perhaps the most important theoretical statement of this new view of the relationship between art and artist with his model of the artist as catalyst.

This removal of the artist from the work (a foreshadowing of the New Criticism)[17] led Hugh Kenner to entitle his book on Eliot *The Invisible Poet*, and that phrase brings to mind the emphasis on authorial anonymity in Woolf as well as the famous statement on artistic invisibility made by Stephen Dedalus in Joyce's *Portrait*. Sultan, in fact, suggests that "concealing the authorial voice" is a "general modernist practice" ("*Ulysses*," "*Waste Land*" 62) and cites authorial invisibility as one of the basic similarities between *The Waste Land* and *Ulysses* (72).[18]

It would appear to be a short step from the modernist emphasis on invisible authors to the more ostensibly postmodern questioning of authorship embodied in the work of thinkers like Barthes and Foucault. Indeed, Huyssen argues that poststructuralism is not postmodernist, but modernist, and that the poststructuralist "death of the subject" is

> nothing more than a further elaboration of the modernist critique of traditional idealist and romantic notions of authorship and authenticity, originality and intentionality, self-centered subjectivity and personal identity. (213)

A conventional counter to this claim would be to suggest that, while both modernists and poststructuralists acknowledge the decentering of authorship and subjectivity, the poststructuralists welcome this decentering while the modernists are nostalgic for the more centered past and show that nostalgia by attempting to create a substitute center in the work of art itself. Indeed, common narratives of the differences between modernism and postmodernism very often directly parallel narratives of the distinction between structuralism and poststructuralism.[19] Joyce clearly participates in the modern trend toward decentered authorship, but at the same time he curiously subverts both of these positions. He undercuts the modernist autonomy of the work of art by the constant insertion of material from outside the work, and he denies the postmodernist death of the author by making his authorial presence felt in a way that is anything but invisible. Even Stephen Dedalus, apparently a much more conventional modernist than Joyce, seems to change his position from *Portrait* to *Ulysses*, arguing in the latter that all great art is to some extent autobiographical—though contributing additional confusion by claiming (à la Dostoevsky's Underground Man) not to believe his own arguments.[20]

The modernist emphasis on works of art as well-crafted artifacts clearly implies the presence of a talented artisan who produces the work. And, if modernist views of authorship are thus paradoxical, the general modernist attitude toward human subjectivity (of which authorship is a subcategory) is no less complex. Time and again modernist works are concerned with questions of identity, of self and Other, to the point that a focus on the interior workings of the human subject is often considered *the* representative gesture of modernist works. Some critics have distinguished between modernism and postmodernism precisely on the basis of the thesis that postmodernism deconstructs the subject while modernism accepts and explores the autonomy of the self. Hoffman, Hornung, and Kunow are typical of such critics when they argue that modernism deals with subjectivity and postmodernism with the lack thereof.

> The perceivable signs of a tendency toward the disappearance of a subjectivity in modern literature become a fact in postmodern works. Thus a radical gap between modern and postmodern literature is reflected in the opposition of two *epistemés*: subjectivity versus loss of subjectivity. (20)

This scheme makes for an extremely neat distinction between modernism and postmodernism, and it is one with a fairly widespread currency. Unfortunately, the issue of subjectivity in modernism and postmodernism is probably quite a bit more complicated than these scholars seem to indicate. For one thing, modern writers show a range of attitudes toward human subjectivity, and it seems unlikely that all of these attitudes can be encompassed by a neat separation into two *"epistemés."* After all, one need not abandon the category of the subject altogether in order to challenge the bourgeois notion of the unified autonomous individual; both Marxist and feminist thinkers have challenged that notion by proposing alternative conceptions of subjectivity that emphasize intersubjective relation rather than subjective autonomy.[21] Patricia Waugh thus agrees that modernism relies on a relatively traditional notion of the self and that postmodernism deconstructs traditional notions of the self. But for Waugh both modernism and postmodernism are primarily masculine movements that are largely irrelevant to the concerns of women writers who neither accept nor oppose traditional male-oriented models of subjectivity. Instead, women writers propose new models of the self, especially those based on intersubjective relation as prior to individual subjectivity. Waugh suggests that

> for those marginalized by the dominant culture, a sense of identity as constructed through impersonal and social relations of power (rather than a sense of identity as the reflection of an inner "essence") has been a major aspect of their self-concept long before post-structuralists and postmodernists began to assemble their cultural manifestos. (3)[22]

Yet the treatment of subjectivity in modernism, influenced as it was by the then-new theories of Freud, was anything but strictly traditional at the time, as critics like Jameson have pointed out (*Postmodernism* 312).

Robert Langbaum has discussed at some length the new concepts of identity and modes of characterization evidenced in *The Waste Land*, seeing these developments as one of the principal organizing features of the poem.

> The point is that Eliot introduces a new method of characterization deriving from the reaction against the nineteenth-century belief in the individual as the one reality you could be sure of. Eliot's name-

less, faceless voices derive from the twentieth-century sense that the self, if it exists at all, is changing and discontinuous, and that its unity is as problematical as its freedom from external conditions. ("New Modes" 110)

Of course, this same "twentieth-century sense" of the self as "changing and discontinuous" dates back at least to Dostoevsky, as Bakhtin has shown. One might also compare here the famous conclusion to *The Renaissance*, in which Walter Pater speaks of the human subject as a fragile entity, infinitely variable over time in the flow of sense impressions that constitutes life: "It is with this movement, with the passage and dissolution of impressions, images, sensations, that analysis leaves off—that continual vanishing away, that strange, perpetual weaving and unweaving of ourselves" (236).

What seems in this modern sense of the self to be a source of great anxiety for Eliot has for writers like Joyce and Brecht served as a source of hope for potential liberation from the oppressive structures of the past. Eliot, for example, seems highly nostalgic when he discusses the modern fragmentation of the self in his idea of the "dissociation of sensibility," a separation between thought and feeling that represents a fundamental change in methods of thought, a fundamental separation of man from experience in the world. Still, Eliot's privileging in this same discussion of the poet's ability to merge different perspectives is highly reminiscent of Woolf's suggestion that androgyny is necessary in the great artist, and it is not entirely clear that either of these attitudes differs greatly from the kind of Bakhtinian dialogism that so obviously informs the work of Joyce. On the other hand, one could argue that both Eliot and Woolf display a rather un-Joycean nostalgic hope that somehow art might heal the scissions in modern society. Both, for example, sometimes figure Elizabethan England as a lost past time of cultural greatness and subjective wholeness, a figuration that Joyce's subversive use of Shakespeare radically challenges.

Brecht again provides perhaps the most obvious example of a modernist artist who openly embraces the subversive political potential of new conceptions of subjectivity, though his seemingly easy acceptance of a postindividualist notion of the self might also be identified as a postmodernist gesture. Janelle Reinelt, for example, argues that in his explorations of decentered models of subjectivity Brecht "anticipated and developed practical demonstrations of several of the key operations of deconstruction and postmodernism" and cites *A Man's A Man* as exemplary: "Galy Gay may be seen as post-Derridean man" (349).[23] Clearly, Brecht's concern in plays like *A Man's a Man* with the malleability of human identity participates in his career-long assault on individualism, an assault that functions as a sort of Marxist counterpart to Woolf's feminist attack on the "damned egotistical I." But this motif is highly complex. If identity is changeable, that fact might make it possible for individual subjects to elude the official forces that seek to interpellate them into rigidly predefined subjective positions—or it might simply present an opportunity for further inter-pellation. For Brecht, the establishment of a better society requires that human behavior be modified, and the possibility of such change remains at the heart of his work from *A Man's a Man* (written in 1924–25) onward. In this play the meek Irish porter Galy Gay under-goes a transformation of identity that makes him into the British soldier Jeraiah Jip, a human fighting machine.

In his own later comments on the play Brecht suggested that Gay's transformation was to be taken as an optimistic indication of the possi-bility of human change. However, the fact that Gay passively under-goes his transformation at the hands of others gives his change of iden-tity a dark undertone. From a Joycean point of view, for example, it is obviously significant that Gay is an Irishman who is conscripted into the service of the British, who then remake him in their image. And modern history in general suggests that the availability of effective techniques for modification of human behavior can have disastrous consequences in the wrong hands. Thus, Martin Esslin argues that the play shows that Brecht had "grasped the essence of later brainwashing techniques" (284). Similarly, Frederic Ewen reads the play in a highly dystopian vein, finding that "Brecht has foreshadowed the alienation of the machine-made man, and social conformism. The will to be meta-morphosed into nonentity arouses in him, at this time, a mixture of admiration and contempt" (138).

Brecht might attribute the modern crisis in subjectivity to the inevitable alienation of the individual in capitalist society. Woolf might cite the suppression of human potential inherent in the stereotypical expectations of patriarchal society. Joyce might adduce the extremely narrow range of subjective roles available to individuals in a society ruled by rigidly conventional structures of power. And Eliot might point more toward the breakdown in such structures, arguing that the lack of authority in the modern world gives individuals no stable and dependable source of subjective models. But, whatever the different perspectives of specific individual artists, the modernist perception of a crisis in subjectivity appears so widespread that it clearly responds to something very real in the historical moment of modernity. Different writers respond to this crisis in very different ways, but on the basis of strict textual evidence in their literary works it is difficult if not impossible to differentiate among the attitudes toward subjectivity taken by authors as ostensibly different as Eliot, Woolf, Joyce, and even Brecht.

Now-popular arguments that Eliot is nostalgic for past theocentric wholeness, that Woolf is engaged in the adumbration of exciting new feminist modes of subjectivity, that Joyce produces a politically powerful social conception of the self, and that Brecht depicts a social subject that is particularly amenable to participation in historical change are largely dependent upon information that we bring to these texts from the outside. For example, we know from other evidence that Eliot was a conservative Christian, that Woolf recognized the artificiality of gender, that Joyce sympathized with various left-wing political ideas, and that Brecht was committed to Marxist principles despite his nonmembership in the Communist Party.

This kind of extratextual information is not irrelevant, no matter how wary of the intentional fallacy one might be. As Jameson has argued, a total separation between a writer's artistic production and her own ideological stance "is not possible for any world-view—whether conservative or radical and revolutionary—that takes politics seriously" (*Political Unconscious* 289). Bakhtin's work, in particular, emphasizes the importance of considering the position from which the author writes. At the same time, in a writer like Joyce one has to deal with the paradoxical fact that often his authorial intention is apparently that one should not grant interpretative authority to authorial intention, just as Bakhtin's work also emphasizes the importance of the position from which the reader reads. From this point of view it seems clear that the political ramifications of a given work of art arise at least as much from the ideological leanings of the reader as from those of the writer. And the reader's ideology involves not only personal attitudes but a whole range of contextual and ideological positionings from which the work is read, just as the writer's ideology is itself encompassed by the historical conditions in which the work is produced. But these contexts change with time, and some aspects of the work of Joyce (or anyone else) that are visible now simply could not have been seen, say, fifty years ago. In a sense they were not *there* fifty years ago. It is here that literary history becomes particularly critical. If there is an almost irresistible temptation to read works within the framework of periods or movements, it is also clear that the conceptions we have of such schemes of categorization largely determine which elements of a given text will be revealed and which ones will remain hidden in such procedures. History thus becomes doubly important in any attempt to interpret literary texts within such frameworks because the general relationship to history that we find within a text is so heavily dependent upon the model of literary history that we impose from without.

Modernism and the "Nightmare" of History

Of course, history itself has been a central topic of study for critics of modernism, which has often been read as centrally informed by a desire to escape from the messiness of history into an ideal aesthetic world of order and stasis. In the opening lines of *Burnt Norton*, Eliot summarizes what is for many the representative modernist attitude toward time and history:

> Time present and time past
> Are both perhaps present in time future,
> And time future contained in time past.
> If all time is eternally present
> All time is unredeemable.

This attitude is, presumably, an attempt to deny that time and history even exist, a claim that all times are one—or, at least, a claim that there is a perspective greater and more important than the one we can gain from within time. In the case of Eliot this perspective is God's, and the echo of Augustine in these lines may be no accident. But one need not be a practicing Christian to desire an escape from temporality, and this Augustinian notion of the presentness of both past and future is also echoed in the apostate Stephen Dedalus's vow to "Hold to the now, the here, through which all future plunges to the past" (*Ulysses* 153).

This kind of denial of history has understandably brought modernists under considerable attack from critics (especially Marxist critics) who see it as politically irresponsible. In an influential article Robinson and Vogel charge that modernism seeks to intensify isolation. It forces the work of art, the artist, the critic, and the audience outside of history. Modernism denies us the possibility of understanding ourselves as *agents* in the material world, for all has been removed to an abstract world of ideas. (198)

Robinson and Vogel also add a feminist orientation to this argument, and in general they appear to regard modernism itself as a sort of massive, worldwide, white-male-capitalist conspiracy designed to shore up the powers that be and to prevent women and other marginal groups from gaining a slice of the political pie.

Such complaints have a certain validity, though the exact identity of the "modernism" against which they are being leveled is unclear. It is hard to see how the characterization of modernism as antihistorical could apply to Brecht or how the charge of antifeminism could apply to Woolf. Joyce is perhaps a less clear case, and he has indeed sometimes been implicated in such charges. For example, William Spanos identifies Stephen Dedalus as a paragon of the kind of spatialization of time he sees as characteristic of the desire for an escape from history in the New Criticism, noting that Stephen's stated aesthetic position "constitutes a remarkably accurate *résumé* of New Critical poetic theory" ("Modern Criticism" 97). This analysis of Stephen seems sound, and it is also true that the New Critical emphasis on the text itself tended to divorce the text being read from its historical context, even if it is not true that the New Critics specifically sought to escape history. But in a later essay ("Postmodern Literature and Its Occasion") Spanos transfers most of his earlier assault on the New Critics directly to modernism itself, and here the picture becomes more complicated. Against what he sees as an ethically irresponsible "modernist" denial of history Spanos proposes as paradigm the historical engagement he finds embodied in the existentialism of Heidegger. Heidegger writes: "As authentically futural, *Dasein* is authentically as 'having been' (*gewesen*). Anticipation of one's uttermost and ownmost possibility (death) is coming back understandingly to one's ownmost 'been'" (373).[24] Yet Heidegger's existentialist description of the connectedness of past and future in *Dasein* sounds strangely similar to Eliot's statement of yearning for a timeless eternity. How can we, as Prufrock might say, presume to tell the difference?

The answer is that we must consider the context from which the equally enigmatic statements of Eliot and Heidegger are taken. In the long run this may come close to saying that we can tell Eliot from Heidegger because we know Eliot is a conservative Christian and Heidegger is an antimetaphysical existentialist. In other words, we can distinguish between these two passages because we have already decided in advance what they mean based on other information. With Heidegger this kind of interpretation might be based on other evidence in his philosophical texts, though such evidence might still not provide an unambiguous solution—one might keep in mind the remark by Georg Lukács that Heidegger's supposed historicity looked an awful lot like ahistoricity. And the lines from Eliot can be interpreted unequivocally as a rejection of temporality only through access to information external to his poetry itself. After all, the first three lines suggest temporal connectedness as easily as atemporality, and the next two lines are preceded by an "if" that renders their meaning irreducibly ambiguous.[25] Again, there is nothing wrong with introducing such external information, but it should be done carefully, with close attention to ideological implications. There is little to be served by imposing a prefabricated model of modernism on Eliot's poem, and thus declaring that it shows a contempt for temporality, because we already know that's what modernist poems are about.

Joyce's work is an excellent example of the potential for impoverishment in such models, since any interpretation of his writing as a statement of typical modernist yearning to awake from the nightmare of history clearly misses much that is valuable in his work. Granted, Joyce sees a great need to escape the tyranny of the past, as evidenced by the powerful subversive challenge to the authority of the great classics of the western cultural tradition implied in his dialogue with predecessors like Homer and Shakespeare. But this challenge is not so much a rejection of history as a recognition that a nostalgic privileging of past moments of cultural glory like classical Greece or Renaissance England is fundamentally inimical to progressive historical change. It is in this sense—and not in the sense of a desire to escape from social and political reality—that history is a nightmare for Joyce, just as Marx hopes in *The Eighteenth Brumaire* to encourage people actively to make their own history when he declares that "the tradition of all the dead generations weighs like a nightmare on the brain of the living" (595). A comparison with Brecht's similar challenge to the authority of the monuments of the western cultural past helps to highlight the potential political power of Joyce's demythifying treatment of the literary tradition. Similarly, my comparisons in this study of Joyce with writers like

Dante and Goethe suggest that Joyce's attitude toward history is far closer to the prosaic engagement that Bakhtin attributes to Goethe than to the idealist escapism that Bakhtin associates with Dante.

History itself is a central concern of Joyce's writing. For example, according to the "handlist" compiled by Steppe and Gabler, the word *history* (in various grammatical forms) occurs forty-six times in the Gabler edition of *Ulysses*, while Hart's *Concordance to "Finnegans Wake"* lists approximately forty-seven such occurrences. This frequency already indicates that history is a major subject of inquiry in Joyce's last two major works. Moreover, one of the most striking features of both of these works is the sheer mass and diversity of real-world historical information that Joyce has imported into them. The topic of history takes center stage very early in *Ulysses*, where we once again encounter Stephen Dedalus, that arch-enemy of all things temporal, now employed as a teacher of (among other things) history. And we are presented within the first two chapters with no fewer than four different models of history that we can mull over. In the "Nestor" chapter, Stephen reflects on Blake's poetic alternative to history and on Aristotle's notion of history as the passing of possibility into realization, potential into entelechy. But later Stephen shows a growing maturity as he rejects the vision of aesthetic escape from temporality offered by Blake. Unlike many of his contemporaries among Irish poets, Stephen refuses to "creepycrawl after Blake's buttocks into eternity" (153). Aristotle, on the other hand, functions as a sort of opposite pole to Blake, representing a view of history as concrete fact that will also be shown to be lacking in the course of the book.[26]

Two other characters in the early pages of *Ulysses* also offer theories of history. As Stephen prepares in the Martello Tower to go off for his day of teaching, he remarks on the imperialistic domination of Ireland by both the Catholic Church and the English government. So the Englishman Haines offers a halfhearted (and condescending) "apology" for the treatment Ireland has received at the hands of his countrymen over the centuries: "We feel in England that we have treated you rather unfairly. It seems history is to blame" (17). In short, Haines denies any English responsibility for the treatment of Ireland, placing the blame instead at the doorstep of some impersonal force called "history," which apparently pursues its inexorable course independent of human intervention.

A similar theory of history will be espoused in "Nestor" by Mr.

Deasy, who announces the teleological view that "All human history moves towards one great goal, the manifestation of God" (28). Deasy here, after his fashion, echoes a long-standing Christian tradition that includes Augustine's notion of God's eternal plan. But the most direct referent here would seem to be Hegel's scientific/rational version of providential history.

> That world history is governed by an absolute design, that it is a rational process—whose rationality is not that of a particular subject, but a divine and absolute reason—this is a proposition whose truth we must assume. (28)

This view of the divine plan behind history leads Hegel to the ethnocentric conclusion that his contemporary European culture is the culmination of that plan and to the nationalistic belief that Germany is supreme among the nations of the earth. The echoes here both of British imperialism and of the Irish nationalism that Joyce so opposes are clear, and it is obvious why Joyce, always sensitive to concrete political implications of abstract philosophical ideas, would make Hegel's model a target for criticism.

For Joyce, as for Marx, history is very much a matter of human agency and intervention. Spanos himself does not seem to know quite what to do with Joyce in his critique of modernism as antihistorical, though he does properly note the irony in the fact that the New Critics should seem to cite Stephen's theories of aesthetic stasis as "scriptural authority" even as most readers were already interpreting *Portrait* as a satire of that theory ("Modern Criticism" 97). My readings suggest that Stephen's viewpoint in this matter is not Joyce's, and that Joyce's texts are themselves intensely temporal as well as profoundly embedded in history. But the very historical embeddedness of Joyce's work implies that it partakes of much of the same cultural milieu as did the contemporary New Criticism. And, if Joyce's ironic treatment of Stephen Dedalus shows that Joyce's works potentially take a stance far different from that of the New Critics, it is also true that Joyce's extremely dialogic discourse still allows "New Critical" voices to sound within his texts. A reader who comes to Joyce's work, then, with the expectation that it will conform to New Critical aesthetic principles will doubtless find much to confirm those expectations. The same might be said for any number of other modernist writers as well, so that one begins to suspect that much of the difficulty in characterizing modernism arises simply from a confusion between modernism and the New Criticism.

Spanos seems to partake of this confusion when he identifies a recognition of the importance of the interpretive position of the reader as a postmodern stance.

> The objective interpretive methodology of modernism, in other words, is grounded in an ideology sealed off from dialogic encounter. A postmodern hermeneutics, on the other hand, recognizes, with Heidegger, that there can be no presuppositionless understanding of literary texts. ("Postmodern Literature" 224)

But, if Spanos here seems in danger of confusing modernism with the New Criticism, or at least of confusing works of art with certain historically contextualized interpretations of those works, he is certainly not alone. As Eliot suggests (and exemplifies), in any period "there is a significant relation between the best poetry and the best criticism of the same period" (*Use of Poetry* 20). However, the relationship between modernism and the New Criticism is probably stronger than similar relationships in any preceding periods. Partly because the difficulty of modernist works made explication necessary, and partly because of educational and social changes that made criticism viable as a profession, modernist works of art exist in a partnership with the criticism of that art to an unprecedented extent.[27]

Views that modernism is based on a formalist aesthetic that represents a turning away from engagement with the real world may, then, partially result from an identification between modernism and the New Criticism. But, if this view is unfair to modernism, it is somewhat inaccurate in relation to the New Criticism as well. It may be that New Critical reading strategies were built around close readings of texts rather than on dialogues with discourses from outside those texts, but the New Criticism itself arose in a specific historical context and in direct opposition to certain trends in the modern world. The ideology of the New Criticism may have been conservative, even reactionary, but it was a conscious ideology, nevertheless, and one with which its practitioners actively sought to intervene in history. The New Critics sought not to divorce art from history but to mobilize art as a force with which to oppose the rising cultural hegemony of science and the resultant dehumanizing technologization of the modern world. For them this mobilization required a clear delineation of the boundaries between art and the rest of society in order to establish a critical perspective for art, a notion that is not so far from the neo-Marxist ideas of Theodor Adorno. Indeed, there is a clear way in which the rightist New Critics were the direct forerunners of a variety of leftist cries against the tyranny of reason that have become prominent in the past few decades.

Both Adorno and the New Critics had much in common with modernist artists in that they both genuinely believed in the potential of art to exert an important influence in society, though they had very different notions of the direction in which that influence should move. Both Adorno and the New Critics also believed that the critical potential of art could best be realized if art maintained a distinctive identity apart from the rest of society, a suggestion that observers like Bakhtin would strongly question. Indeed, a Bakhtinian approach to Joyce's work suggests a clear movement toward integration of art into the swirl of competing discourses that constitutes modern society. This attitude recalls the goal influentially attributed by Bürger to the avant-garde, and the avant-garde is certainly one of the contexts within which Joyce's work can fruitfully be read.

A principal characteristic of Joyce's texts is that they constantly point beyond themselves and therefore cannot be adequately understood without recourse to extratextual information. Of course, modernist allusiveness is in itself no threat to New Critical principles, and allusion can in fact help to solidify culture as a social force of the kind embodied in Eliot's "Tradition." But the information imported into Joyce's texts (or Eliot's, for that matter) from outside is far from exclusively literary, and a central feature of Joyce's work is that it calls attention to what Jameson has called (in reference to allusive works in general) "the roots such texts send down into the contingent circumstances of their own historical time" (*Political Unconscious* 34). By my reading, Joyce's texts are much more amenable to interpretation through the hermeneutic mode that Spanos identifies with postmodernism, but virtually any other "modernist" can be read in this way as well. It is no accident that virtually all major modernist writers have gradually become postmodernists after two decades of postmodern criticism. In the case of Joyce, we have a writer whose work apparently was once apolitical but now is political, but what has happened is that his work was once read in apolitical ways and now is increasingly being read in political ones.

I am not, however, suggesting that this apparent transformation in the ideology of Joyce's work is a simple figment of the critical imagination. On the contrary, Joyce's texts *have* changed over the past fifty years because the critical framework within which we read them has changed and because that framework itself is in a very real sense constitutive of the texts. The bottom line is that it makes little sense to categorize individual works of literature as modernist or postmodernist, even if we can figure out what we think those terms mean. It is simply not possible to separate the characteristics of a work from the characteristics of the method of interpretation being used to read that work. Any given text is open to a variety of reading strategies, though the texts of Joyce may be unique in the extent to which they can offer themselves to readings according to so many different strategies. The extreme formal complexity and reflexivity of Joyce's work, combined with his own intense political commitment, seem to cry out for modernist readings. Yet there is in Joyce a skepticism toward the possibility of genuine and radical change (especially in Ireland) and an insistent tone of parody (especially self-parody) that suggest clear points of entry for postmodernist readers. Finally, Joyce's parody can often be so violent (especially when he cracks apart the bones of language, as in *Finnegans Wake*) that avant-garde readings seem appropriate.

Meaning in the Joycean text operates very much like the principle of complementarity in modern physics. If one designs an experiment to demonstrate that subatomic particles are in fact particles, then lo and behold one will find particles—but one will be unable to see waves at all. And, if one designs an experiment to demonstrate that these so-called particles are in fact waves, then one will find waves, but at the expense of no longer being able to find particles. But Joyce's texts are even more complex. Their complementarity extends not just to two alternative readings but to many, each with a particular ideological charge.

Joyce's work has thus been particularly ill-served by the tendency to regard him automatically as one of the highest of all high modernists and thereby to assume that he shares certain characteristics usually attributed to high modernism, even though Joyce's work in many ways differs radically from that of most writers—like Pound and Eliot—who are also typically included in this category. As a result, viewing Joyce as a high modernist often makes unavailable much of the range of possible readings of his work. It might seem that this problem could be rectified either by recategorizing Joyce as something else (perhaps a post-modernist) or by redefining what we mean by modernism. However, the multiplicity of Joyce's work makes it inherently resistant to catego-rization—no matter how one describes a category like modernism, there will inevitably be aspects of Joyce's writing that are not consistent with that description. My conclusion is that such categories should probably not be used to describe literary texts and authors at all. Instead, they should be used to categorize reading strategies. A mod-ernist reading of Joyce would then emphasize certain characteristics of Joyce's writing, a postmodernist reading would emphasize others, and so on.

Of course, this shift in categorization from texts to readers does not imply that different reading strategies will not prove more or less fruit-ful for different texts. Some texts might yield richer results for mod-ernist readings, others for postmodernist readings, or the same text might respond better to modernist readings in some of its aspects and to postmodernist readings in others. This categorical shift also tells us very little in itself about what modernist and postmodernist reading strategies might entail. Indeed, these terms are already so thoroughly contaminated by their use as labels for texts and authors that there would be clear advantages to abandoning them altogether. However, the fact that these terms are so thoroughly charged with the resonances of former use might also prove advantageous by opening up important dialogues and by posing certain important questions. If, for example, one asks why Joyce is so widely regarded as a modernist when his work has so little in common with conventional descriptions of mod-ernism, the answer inevitably highlights the way readers have so often read texts according to certain critical assumptions without paying suf-ficient attention to the potential for alternative readings. Similarly, a recognition that modernism is more properly a kind of reading than a kind of writing can potentially clear up a number of perplexing prob-lems that have plagued historians of modern literature and culture. If nothing else, this recognition focuses critical attention on the strategies used in reading texts in a way that can only be beneficial. For complex texts like those of Joyce, the worst mistake any reader can make is to assume that she is reading the texts in "pure" form, without the filter-ing effect of her own critical assumptions and prejudices. The remedy for such mistakes, however, is not to eliminate the filter (since that would be impossible) but to maintain an awareness of the filter and seek an understanding of the filtering effect. As Joyce's reference in *Finnegans Wake* to criticism as a "warping process" shows, he was also well aware that this process is unavoidable and that criticism plays a crucial role in the realization of a literary text.

Literary texts are complex cultural products, and they continue to be produced as long as they are read. Joyce's work is particularly relevant to this process because of the central importance of his own "warping," or rereading of his literary predecessors. But it should be clear that the constitutive power of criticism goes well beyond the work of Joyce or even the issue of modernism vs. postmodernism. All periodizations and categorizations are products of reading, and all readings are inescapably shot through with ideology. Our task as readers is not somehow to escape this ideology but to recognize it. We should not attempt to prevent our own cultural and ideological perspectives from coloring our readings of literary works; we should instead attempt to maintain an awareness that our readings are ideological and thereby seek to avoid mistaking specific ideological readings for the "truth" of the text at hand. Of course, certain conservative critics would point to such a view of literature as a prime symptom of its death and of the contemporary decay of cultural authority and values. I would argue that such self-consciously constitutive readings are our best means of ensuring that culture and literature remain alive. If the dead are to speak to us, we must also be prepared to reply.

Notes

Introduction

1. Citations from *Finnegans Wake* are given with page numbers followed by line numbers throughout this study.

2. The obvious relevance of Bakhtin's theories to the work of Joyce has led many to wonder why Bakhtin himself hardly mentions Joyce. Clark and Holquist provide an answer, noting that Joyce was a persona non grata within the context of Stalinist culture. "As of at least the First Writers' Congress in 1934, *Ulysses* could no longer be praised in print. . . . Thus, Bakhtin effectively had two choices as regards Joyce, to attack him or not to mention him" (317). Indeed, in Stalinist Russia it was politically dangerous to deal with most contemporary texts, though it is also true that Bakhtin (who was trained as a classicist) seemed to prefer older texts as a matter of taste.

3. Joyce himself seems to have regarded Shakespeare and Dostoevsky as opposites. Remarking on the incongruity of a Bach oratorio based on the Gospel of Matthew, Joyce once remarked that such a combination was "like lumping together Shakespeare and Dostoevski" (Ellmann, *James Joyce* 430).

Chapter One

1. That there are in fact twelve of these muses, not nine, is typical of the ontological confusion (and mathematical inaccuracy) of the "Circe" chapter of *Ulysses*.

2. See Levin and Shattuck for an argument that even as early as *Dubliners* Joyce was drawing significantly on *The Odyssey* as a structural model in his work.

3. Many of these arcane materials were identified by Joyce himself, but critics like William Schutte have concluded that much of the material supplied by Joyce to Gilbert was little more than a series of practical jokes at the expense of the overly gullible Gilbert (*Joyce and Shakespeare* 3). See McCarthy ("Stuart Gilbert's Guide") for a survey of Gilbert's book and its reception by later critics.

4. For a recent example of such elaborations, see Hardy, who stresses the differences between Joyce and Homer but concludes that in this case "to contrast is to compare" (189).

5. On the masculine orientation of ancient Greek culture, see Michel Fou-

cault's *The Use of Pleasure*. For a feminist commentary on Joyce's reinscription of Homer, see Doherty.

6. Morson and Emerson note that western appropriators of Bakhtin have focused on aspects of his work that make him seem to resemble Bakunin as well. However, they conclude that on balance Bakhtin is a less radically libertarian thinker than is his Russian predecessor (42–43).

7. The multiplicity of voices in Joyce's fiction becomes more and more obvious as his career proceeds, but this kind of polyphonic voicing is already used to good effect as early as *Dubliners*. See Thompson.

8. Joyce claimed not to have read Marx, except for the first sentence of *Das Kapital*, which he reportedly found so absurd that he stopped reading (Ellmann, *James Joyce* 142n). Of course, Joyce's own comments are not entirely reliable in such matters.

9. Note Stephen Heath's suggestion that the exact relationship between Joyce's writing and the texts he parodies is complex and often ultimately undecidable: "What is in question in Joyce's writing is not the proclamation of irony or ridicule *against* the model imitated, but a copying that fixes no point of irony between model and imitation, that rests, in this respect, in a hesitation of meaning" ("Ambiviolences" 41–42, Heath's emphasis).

10. One might compare here M. H. Abrams's characterization of the romantic project as a "secularization of the sublime," or as an attempt to reinscribe the energies of traditional religion within the framework of secular discourse.

11. Stephen here has a great deal in common with Eliot. In fact, Bakunin's description might apply more to Eliot than to the English romantics, despite Eliot's own distaste for romanticism.

12. *Ulysses* is, in fact, seeded with a number of parodies of bourgeois sentimentality, ranging from the story of Athos, the faithful dog left behind on the suicide of Bloom's father, to that of Jumbo and Alice, the lovestruck elephants separated by the philistine machinations of P. T. Barnum.

13. On Joyce's (along with Thomas Pynchon's and Samuel Beckett's) subversive use of rats as images to undermine Christian pretensions of idealistic purity, see my essay "The Rats of God."

14. Bakunin criticizes Lamartine for his "vain and ridiculously envious desire to rise to the poetic height of the great Byron" (82).

15. Hamlet, Shelley, and Napoleon all appear as figures of identification for Stephen in *Portrait* as well, though it may be that he, too, is Byron chiefly.

16. Tennyson is, of course, the ultimate "establishment" poet of Victorian England. Note, for example, the habitual quoting of Tennyson by the patriarchal Mr. Ramsay in Woolf's *To the Lighthouse*.

17. Significantly, Joyce parodies this particular phrase several times in *Finnegans Wake*.

18. Pecora discusses Joyce's skepticism toward the tradition of the self-sacrificial hero in his treatment of Conroy, noting that "Gabriel might be one of the bloodiest impostors of all, caught within the whole structure of a heroism . . . derived from the life of Christ" (237).

19. The link between this cult of self-sacrifice and Christ as a figure of sacrifice is quite direct. For example, note Jim Connolly's pronouncement in the *Irish Worker* of February 5, 1916: "Without the slightest trace of irreverence but in all due humility and awe, we recognise that of us, as of mankind before Calvary, it may truly be said 'without the shedding of blood there is no redemption'" (quoted in MacCabe, *James Joyce and the Revolution of the Word* 169).

20. See *Vargas Llosa Among the Postmodernists*.

Chapter Two

1. John Kidd suggests in a later article that the Rabelaisian echo Rea finds in *Portrait* may in fact be a direct echo of Plutarch, Rabelais's source in the passage in question.

2. This prayer translates as "Bright as lilies. A throng gathers about. Jubilant you of virgins. Chorus rescues." That St. George's is a Protestant church does not, of course, prevent Stephen from reading in the bells a Catholic message.

3. For additional affinities between Joyce (especially in *Finnegans Wake*) and Rabelais in terms of their attitudes toward language, see Jacquet. On the other hand, Sidney Monas has argued that the most important link between Joyce and Rabelais (especially as read through Bakhtin) is "folklore—a deep involvement in the most ancient, most basic and universal folkloric traditions" (cited in Clark and Holquist 388n.41). But see Kinser for an argument that this view of Rabelais is a distortion arising from reading his work from a twentieth-century perspective rather than from Rabelais's own sixteenth-century perspective (257).

4. Morson and Emerson make this point convincingly several times in their excellent book. Indeed, they see *Rabelais and His World* as a kind of aberration in Bakhtin's career, especially in the way that carnival figures there as a kind of utopian escape from the normal flow of history. As a result, the western critical emphasis on Bakhtin's work on carnivalization has led to "a number of very peculiar appropriations of Bakhtin, from Marxist to deconstructionist, and, in our view, it has tended to obscure the larger and more consistent shape of his thought" (67).

5. Anatoly Lunacharsky, whose own work with the medieval carnival probably influenced Bakhtin, concluded that the carnival, as a realm of officially *authorized* transgression, merely acted as a sort of safety valve that would allow for the harmless release of social tensions that might otherwise lead to genuine subversion (see Clark and Holquist 313). Many later critics of Bakhtin have made the same point as Lunacharsky. Terry Eagleton, for example, argues that "Carnival, after all, is a *licensed* affair in every sense, a permissible rupture of hegemony, a contained popular blow-off as disturbing and relatively ineffectual as a revolutionary work of art" (*Walter Benjamin* 148, Eagleton's emphasis).

6. For an extended treatment of the abject side of the carnival, see Michael André Bernstein.

7. That Bakhtin would employ the Catholic Church as a symbol of oppression is obviously highly reminiscent of Joyce's criticisms of the Church in Ireland. For a discussion of some of the parallels between Stalinist oppression in the Soviet Union and Joyce's figuration of Catholic oppression in Ireland, see Juraga and Booker.

8. On anti-Stalinist resonances in Bakhtin's career as a whole, see Booker and Juraga, *Bakhtin, Stalin, and Modern Russian Fiction.*

9. These totalizing tendencies derive directly from orthodox Marxist insistence on the centrality and solidarity of the working class. For a critique of such tendencies from the perspective of a postmodernist acceptance of fragmentation (and for an outline of pluralistic "post-Marxism" forms of radical politics that might escape such tendencies) see Laclau and Mouffe.

10. Franco Moretti similarly argues that the setting of Joyce's books is not the real historical Dublin but a sort of exemplary city of advanced capitalism (189–90). But for Moretti this allegorical use of Dublin allows Joyce to make profound criticisms of modern capitalist society in his work. Moreover, Moretti argues that the very structure of *Ulysses* mirrors the structure of capitalist society itself (190). Thus, the self-conscious concern of *Ulysses* with its own structure and composition does not prevent the book from commenting on bourgeois society at the same time.

11. See, for example, Spears.

12. Thus, in an implicit dialogue with Bataille (among others), Foucault's later work calls into question the view that writing or talking about sexuality is inherently subversive, arguing instead that such an emphasis may work directly with rather than against existing structures of power. I consider the complexities of transgression in bourgeois society at more length in my book *Techniques of Subversion in Modern Literature.*

13. Similarly, in his discussion of the abject side of the Bakhtinian carnival, Bernstein specifically excludes Joyce, noting that Joyce's writing "remained not only untouched by, but programmatically opposed to" the abjection and Nietzschean ressentiment that informs the texts of writers like Céline (132).

14. Margot Norris also suggests that the *Wake* is the product of a single dreamer (9) and notes that virtually every one of the "typical dreams" described by Freud in *The Interpretation of Dreams* constitutes a major theme in the *Wake* (6). Her analysis is, however, somewhat more sophisticated than that of Campbell and Robinson and includes a detailed analysis of the "dream language" of the *Wake.*

15. Freud predictably interprets Schreber's fantasies of gender transformation as evidence that "The exciting cause of his illness . . . was an outburst of homosexual libido" (426). A more detailed reading of Schreber's case in terms of the relationship between psychosis and sexual identity is performed by Jacques Lacan in his important essay "On a Question Preliminary to Any Possible Treatment of Psychosis," in *Écrits* 179–225.

16. Jung diagnosed Joyce's daughter Lucia as schizophrenic and offered to

analyze Joyce, citing certain similarities between the use of language by Joyce and his daughter. Joyce refused. See Ellmann, *James Joyce* (679–80). Lacan had a long and intense involvement with Joyce's texts, teaching a number of seminars on Joyce in the period 1971–76. Aubert's recent collection *Joyce avec Lacan* contains much of Lacan's commentary on Joyce as well as related essays by other commentators.

17. In the *Phaedrus*, Plato notes that "there were two kinds of madness, the one caused by sicknesses of a human sort, the other coming about from a divinely caused reversal of our customary ways of behaving. . . . And of the divine kind we distinguished four parts, belonging to four gods, taking the madness of the seer as Apollo's inspiration, that of the mystic rites as Dionysus', poetic madness, for its part, as the Muses', and the fourth as that belonging to Aphrodite and Love" (101).

18. There are, of course, numerous affinities between Joyce and Flaubert as writers, as the quotation from Kain at the beginning of this chapter suggests. The most extensive examination of these parallels is Cross's *Flaubert and Joyce*.

19. Feasts in general are favorite scenes in carnivalesque literature (compare the "Dinner with Trimalchio" segment of Petronius's *Satyricon* [51–91]). Indeed, the *Satyricon* resonates with the work of Joyce in a number of ways. Note, for example, that Trimalchio's chef is called "Daedalus" because of his cleverness.

20. Interestingly, the LeClerq translation of *Gargantua and Pantagruel* renders the title of this chapter as "The Palaver of the Potulents." Joyce, of course, would have seen the earlier Urquhart version, which translates this chapter title more literally. The Cohen translation, which I cite throughout, renders it as "The Drunkards' Conversation."

21. See Cheyfitz for a useful discussion of the source of the word (and the concept) *cannibalism* in the early encounters of Spanish explorers with the native inhabitants of the Caribbean (41–43).

22. I discuss this motif in my essay "The Rats of God."

23. One might compare here the dialogue between cannibalism and communion that informs the story of Ugolino in Canto XXXIII of Dante's *Inferno*. For Dante, of course, cannibalism and communion are different indeed, and conflating the two (as does Joyce) represents a serious perversion and misreading of the spiritual significance of the Eucharist. On this canto, see Freccero (152–66).

24. Indeed, the reader of *Dubliners* is clearly invited to see certain parallels between Father Flynn and the old josser. And the old josser's near-ecstatic reveries on the whipping of young boys anticipate the sadistic Father Dolan of *Portrait*.

25. Such images of transgressive sexuality are particularly prevalent in *Finnegans Wake*. Thus, Clive Hart suggests that in the *Wake* "It seems to have been a part of Joyce's design to include allusions to every possible form of sexual deviation, and to use the most common perversions as primary material" (*Structure and Motif* 205).

26. See Don Gifford's gloss on the passage in question in *"Ulysses" Annotated* 556.

27. Foucault himself identifies the Catholic sacrament of Confession as a central example of the conversion of sex into discourse that he sees as a central movement of modern western society.

28. Indeed, for Joyce the Catholic God Himself is a sadist, as in *Ulysses*, where Stephen describes "the lord of things as they are whom the most Roman of catholics call *dio boia*, hangman god," a characterization that links up with the motif of the hanging of the croppy boy to make an obvious comment on Catholicism as an enemy of Ireland (175).

29. Such passages suggest that Stephen may have been at least partly named by Joyce in reference to St. Stephen, a Greek who served as the prototype for all Christian martyrs.

30. Joyce had a lively interest in this issue and treated it extensively in his work. For a discussion of this interest within the context of Joyce's broader interest in the modern redefinition of sexuality, see Brown 63–78. For a discussion of this interest within the context of the general Irish concern with population levels, see Lowe-Evans 58–99.

31. I discuss elsewhere certain parallels between the Bloom/Cohen encounter and Dante's initial meeting with Beatrice in his *Purgatorio* ("From the Sublime to the Ridiculous"). In terms of Foucault's argument, note that Beatrice immediately demands of Dante a confession of his sins: "tell, tell if this is true; for your confession / must be entwined with such self-accusation" (XXXI, l. 5–6). Beatrice's accusations include some of a clearly sexual nature, including a mention of Dante's involvement with a "pargoletta," or young girl. Most Dante scholars identify this girl as at least partially being an allegorical embodiment of philosophy, but many agree that she may well have had her roots in a real indiscretion on the part of the poet.

32. Similar images of bodily fragmentation do, however, occur in Rabelais. See Bakhtin for a discussion of such images as a carnivalesque parody of the proliferation of saints' relics in medieval Catholic Europe (*Rabelais* 349–50).

Chapter Three

1. It would appear that Reynolds's identification of this particular triumvirate of illustrious predecessors is informed especially by *Ulysses*. In *Finnegans Wake*, on the other hand, Samuel Beckett (who was as much as anyone in a position to know) suggests that Joyce's three most important influences were Dante, Vico, and Bruno. Joyce himself in *Finnegans Wake* clearly identifies Dante, Goethe, and Shakespeare as the three most canonical poets of western literature (539.5–8). It is interesting to note that Dante is the only figure who appears on all three lists.

2. This process differs from what Jacques Lacan calls floating signification in that it allows a greater role for authorial agency rather than being an inherent property of language.

3. I trace some of these precedents in my essay "Western Culture in the *Wake* of Joyce."

4. As Freccero notes elsewhere, the motif of turning to stone is a conventional Pauline sign of interpretive blindness (158).

5. See Freccero (152–66) for a discussion of the Ugolino episode as an allegory of the damaging effects of overly literal interpretation. For example, note that, when Ugolino and his sons are locked in the tower, the Count says "sì dentro impetrai" [I turned to stone] (l. 49).

6. Dante explains his use of this mode of allegory in his famous letter to Can Grande. And, although the authenticity of this letter is somewhat in dispute, reading the *Commedia* as a fourfold allegory is extremely productive. For a thorough discussion of this and other issues relating to Dante's allegorical method, see Robert Hollander, *Allegory*.

7. See, for example, Craig Werner's suggestion that Joyce's work gains its force from the fact that Joyce refused to lean too far toward either the realist or the symbolist pole (3). This does not mean, of course, that individual critics never choose one side or the other in this debate. Thus, Stanley Sultan argues that there have always been two fundamentally opposed traditions in Joyce criticism, one focusing on his works as self-referential texts (identifiable with Werner's "symbolism"), and one focusing on realistic representation (*Eliot* 262–68). Sultan himself is firmly in the realist camp.

8. For Sollers these four levels in Joyce include a literal and obscene level, a historical level, a mythical level, and a level of "pleasure, of joyance, of coming."

9. The list continues for another half page in the same vein.

10. The classic discussion of Joyce's "mosaic" procedure in assembling materials for *Ulysses* is that provided by A. Walton Litz in *The Art of James Joyce*. Litz also extends his discussion to *Finnegans Wake*, demonstrating numerous affinities between Joyce's methods of composition in the two texts and concluding that the *Wake* "developed gradually and inevitably out of the method of *Ulysses*" (76).

11. Collagelike techniques have always played a large part in the construction of the multigeneric texts in the tradition of Menippean satire. In addition, such techniques were quite central to the composition of medieval texts in general, as the well-known examples of writers like Dante and Chaucer clearly demonstrate.

12. All English translations from the *Commedia* are those of Mandelbaum.

13. Freccero quotes the suggestion by Bernardus Silvestrus that Daedalus represents the journey of the intellect and a complete attention to the study of philosophy (17). He further notes that Augustine preceded Dante by viewing Ulysses as a figure of the "presumptuous philosopher who would reach the truth unaided" (20). The link between Ulysses and Daedalus in medieval thought is a strong one, prefiguring the links forged by Joyce between Leopold Bloom and Stephen Dedalus in *Ulysses*.

14. Callow also sees in these lines an allusion to Boccaccio's *Decameron*, further indicating the richness of Joyce's allusive technique.

15. It may also be significant that the Italian word for "wings" used by Dante here is *penne*. Through the kind of multilingual pun that he employs more and more as his career proceeds, Joyce exploits the etymological relationship

between pens and feathers to make the inadequate wings of Icarus a metaphor for the faltering pen of the poet Stephen.

16. These quotations derive originally from Samuel Butler and from John Howard Payne, respectively, but by Joyce's day they were already clichés of common speech.

17. It is indicative of Dante's approach to poetry that he did not feel that he could create a fictional poet to fill this role but appropriated Statius instead.

18. See Levine for an excellent discussion of Joyce's use of preexisting discourse (especially clichés) for his own purposes.

19. This construction was brought to my attention by R. A. Shoaf.

20. For a modern discussion of the historicity of language in very much this same spirit, see Steiner.

21. Similarly, the titles of most of the stories from *Dubliners* are embedded in distorted form in pages 186–87 of the *Wake*. Note again that the appropriation is bidirectional. The mentions of *Dubliners*, *Portrait*, and *Ulysses* in the *Wake* add resonance to those previous texts as well as to the *Wake* itself.

22. Hart presents an extensive discussion of Joyce's leitmotiv technique in the *Wake*, noting that "Neither before nor since *Finnegans Wake* has the literary *leitmotiv* been used so consistently or to such brilliant effect" (*Structure* 161). Hart's appendix includes an extensive tabulation of leitmotivs from the *Wake*. Similarly, Schutte presents a compilation of repeated phrases in *Ulysses* (*Index*).

23. Candles do not figure directly in "A Little Cloud," but there is clearly an implied hint at phallic inadequacy in the designation of its protagonist as Little Chandler, especially in light of the sexual significance of candles in the rest of *Dubliners* and the "unmanly" characteristics displayed by Little Chandler himself.

24. I discuss the motif of repetition in *Dubliners* at more length in my essay "History and Language in Joyce's 'The Sisters'."

25. Augustine, upon discovering this striking passage, relates that "I had no wish to read more and no need to do so" (178). Similarly, Francesca, in *Inferno* V, tells Dante that she and Paulo read the story of Lancelot, which spoke to their own condition in such a way that "that day we read no more" (l. 138). Moreover, the passage quoted by Augustine, with its rejection of "nature's appetites," turns out to make a striking comment upon the sensual activities of Francesca and Paulo. Dante's strong reaction to Francesca's story can be taken as evidence that he is still at this point under the sway of Virgil, the author of Dido.

26. See the chapter "The Prose of the World" in Foucault, *The Order of Things* (17–44).

Chapter Four

1. These parallels are nicely summarized in Henry Hatfield's essay "The Walpurgis Night: Theme and Variations," which looks at the Walpurgisnacht motif in *Faust*, *Ulysses*, and Mikhail Bulgakov's *The Master and Margarita*.

2. The biography was originally published in 1959, prior to Ellmann's 1977 study of Joyce's library. However, a revised 1982 edition of the biography seems to have been affected surprisingly little by the intervening study.

3. For example, the wedding of Faust and Helen of Troy in *Faust* 2 is usually interpreted as an allegorical enactment of Goethe's dream of uniting the culture of ancient Greece with that of his contemporary Germany. For a useful but relatively conventional study of Goethe and the Greeks, see Trevelyan.

4. Here, Goethe seems to draw upon the neoplatonic interpretations of the Daedalus myth that I discussed in chapter 2. Incidentally, in *Faust* 2, Euphorion, the son of Faust and Helen of Troy, is explicitly identified as an Icarus figure before he plunges to his death while attempting to fly beyond the bounds of mortal capability (208). As the father of Icarus, Faust thus becomes a sort of Daedalus figure, and much of what Faust learns in the course of the two parts of *Faust* might be described as a maturation from the status of Icarus to that of Daedalus.

5. On the significance of *Mignon* as an intertext for "The Dead," see Kershner, *Joyce* 149–50.

6. Recall Joyce's reference in *Finnegans Wake* to the "Circe" episode of *Ulysses* as Walpurgas Nackt (229.16).

7. The abbreviation A. G. stands for Aktien-Gesellshaft, German for "joint stock company," suggesting that Joyce sees all three great poets as figures of bourgeois culture.

8. Ellmann concludes that Joyce in fact drew significantly upon both *Wilhelm Meister's Apprenticeship* and *Faust* in working out the theory of Shakespearean drama espoused by Stephen in this chapter (*Consciousness* 50–51). Meanwhile, the parallels between *Faust* 1 and *Hamlet* have been pointed out by numerous critics. See, for example, Fleissner.

9. For Bradley, Hamlet is a "heroic, terrible figure" who, if confronted by the "shrinking flower-like youth" depicted by Wilhelm, "would have hurled him from his path with one sweep of his arm" (102–3).

10. On the other hand, the same might be said for other characters in the play. See Elaine Showalter's "Representing Ophelia," a particularly suggestive study of the way various figurations of Ophelia over the centuries reflect contemporary social concerns.

11. Stephen acknowledges this reading of Hamlet in a passage in which he relates the violent ending of *Hamlet* to the violence and brutality of the Boer War—one of Shakespeare's many suggestions of a cultural complicity between Shakespeare and British imperialism (*Ulysses* 152).

12. Gerlach takes this same tack in a vigorous defense of reading Wilhelm's attitude toward *Hamlet* as Goethe's own.

13. Diamond and Blackall are, incidentally, among the critics supposedly refuted by Gerlach.

14. The real William Lyster, on whom Joyce's character is based, had published an English translation of Düntzler's *Life of Goethe* in 1883.

15. Kershner notes the strong influence of Wilde on Joyce, particularly in

Stephen's Shakespeare theory, which in many ways parallels that developed by Wilde in a story, "The Portrait of Mr. W. H." ("Artist" 216).

16. Joyce's composition of Stephen's theory, however, involved a complex combination of materials from numerous sources. For a survey of these, see Schutte 153–77.

17. Stephen is here conjugating the Latin verb meaning "to urinate."

18. On palinodic narration in Joyce, see my essay "History and Language in Joyce's 'The Sisters'."

19. The existing fragment refers several times to a detailed discussion of *Wilhelm Meister* that is to follow. Unfortunately, the portion of the manuscript that contains this discussion is not extant.

20. Wise lists Goethe as the sole author of the essay, though it was cosigned by Schiller.

21. See Blackall for an extended treatment of Goethe's novels that seeks to demonstrate that Goethe did not consider the genre an inferior form of literature and that Goethe's novels participate in the traditions of the genre in more important ways than has generally been recognized. For example, Goethe himself declared the novel a genre worthy of consideration as serious literature and even of comparison with the drama (Blackall 77–79).

22. Reiss describes the "unity of style" that characterizes *Wilhelm Meister's Apprenticeship*, noting that "the language of the last three books does not differ materially from that of the first five; even when letters of Wilhelm or conversations are reported, the tone hardly differs from that of the narrator" (94).

23. The contamination referred to in relation to Eileen is the fact that her Protestant background will interfere with Stephen's puerile plans to marry her.

24. In *Stephen Hero*, this reference to Stephen's aesthetics as "applied Aquinas" is made directly by the narrator in a mode that clearly links this suggestion to Stephen's own attitude (77).

25. Homer Brown notes the "exotic Oriental motif" of *Dubliners* (42). This motif runs throughout Joyce's work. For a treatment of the symbolic use of oriental motifs in *Ulysses*, see Kershner, "*Ulysses*."

26. Mahaffey does, however, usefully indicate the potential complexity of the attitudes of both Stephen and Molly, so that this motif is not as simple as it might appear.

Chapter Five

1. Moore is mentioned among the middlebrow *littérateurs* championed by the old josser in "An Encounter," and his ballads may be alluded to in the titles of both "Araby" and "Eveline." Gifford sardonically summarizes Moore's literary status by noting that "No properly sentimental Irish home was complete without its copy of Moore's *Irish Melodies*" ("*Ulysses*" *Annotated* 39). In *Ulysses*, Leopold Bloom alludes to Moore's song "The Meeting of the Waters" in noting that a statue of Moore has been appropriately erected over a urinal (133).

2. Shakespeare's disguised Duke notes that "music oft hath such a

charm/To make bad good, and good provoke to harm" (IV.i.14–15). Quotations from Shakespeare are taken from the Bevington edition.

3. I explore some of these, particularly in terms of the relationship between "The Dead" and *Twelfth Night*, in "Serendipitous Intertextuality."

4. Reynolds's view of Schutte's book as a pioneering work still holds, though it is worth mentioning that David Hayman's *Joyce et Mallarmé*, which was published one year earlier, can claim a certain priority as a comparative study. But Hayman's book, published in French, had little immediate impact on Anglo-American criticism.

5. Florence Walzl notes that interpretations of the ending of "The Dead" tend to fall into one of these two camps and she argues that, if one reads the story in isolation, the affirmative ending seems more appropriate, while a reading of the story in conjunction with the rest of *Dubliners* points toward the negative view in which Gabriel is "a dead member of a dead society" (424).

6. Compare Kershner's suggestion that the development of Stephen's consciousness in *Portrait* shows a gradual change from orientation toward the past to orientation (occidentation?) toward the future ("Time").

7. One might also compare the movement of "The Dead" to Webster and Dekker's Jacobean play *Westward Hoe*, with its plot of wives being unfaithful and then being reconciled to their husbands.

8. Thomas Dilworth usefully clears up some of this confusion, noting that the festival of Twelfth Night begins on the night of January 5 and ends at dawn the next day, while the feast of Epiphany begins at midnight on January 6. Thus, the two occasions overlap, but they are not, strictly speaking, synonymous (170).

9. Olivia, for example, later tells Cesario that she would rather hear a suit of love from him/her than "music from the spheres" (III.i.108–10). Compare Moseley's claim that the end of "The Dead" "indicates that Gabriel, like Dante, has become so transhumanized that he is now able to hear the music of the spheres" (433).

10. Gilbert herself consistently regards Joyce's work as a typical masculine effort to preserve conventional gender roles, but this reading seems peculiar, indeed. See my response to Gilbert on this score in "The Baby in the Bathwater."

11. For an excellent discussion of Shakespeare's predecessors in the literature of sexual metamorphosis, see Carroll.

12. See Richard Brown's discussion of Joyce's treatment of gender boundaries, supported by useful information on Joyce's own reading on the matter (96–107).

13. The link between mother and child, on the other hand, is more directly physical, as witnessed by the connecting navel cord on which Stephen muses: "The cords of all link back, strandentwining cable of all flesh" (32). But in *Ulysses* nothing is simple, especially where gender is concerned, and later we find Bloom becoming impossibly confused trying to unravel the question of Corley's *maternity* (504).

14. The use of "Eve and Adam's" also evokes "even Adam's," meaning before the time even of Adam. But everything has multiple meanings in the *Wake*.

15. Of course, both Dolan and Deasy are undermined by the quotations they choose, appearing unaware of the implications of the passages they cite. Dolan's blustery promise to return "tomorrow and tomorrow and tomorrow" is taken from the "sound and fury" passage, suggesting that his own posturing is a "tale told by an idiot." Meanwhile, Deasy's citation of Shakespeare as advising one to "put money in thy purse" inadvertently identifies Deasy with the evil Iago. Joyce thus suggests that the cultural misuse of Shakespeare is largely perpetrated by those with no real understanding of Shakespeare's work.

16. Compare Woolf's evocation of Anon as ancient singer to Eliot's suggestion that poetry begins "with a savage beating a drum in the jungle, and it retains the essential of percussion and rhythm" (*Use* 148).

17. In his review of the 1929 version of Bakhtin's Dostoevsky book, Anatoly Lunacharsky notes conventional figurations of Shakespeare's impersonality, citing Gundolf to the effect that Shakespeare differs from Goethe in that the latter derived his works from his own experience, while Shakespeare "was able to create human beings quite independent of himself and of his own experience" (86).

18. Fredric Jameson echoes Benjamin in his acknowledgment of the importance of the novel as a genre that expresses the growing alienation of the subject in bourgeois society. Jameson notes that the modern novel "expresses the increasing atomization of our societies, where the privileged meeting places of collective life and of the intertwining of collective destinies . . . have decayed, and with them, the vital sources of anecdote" ("Metacommentary" 13).

19. One might compare this with Joyce's remark in a notebook entry that *The Waste Land* ended the idea that poetry was for ladies (Ellmann, *James Joyce* 495).

20. During the reign of Elizabeth I, the Irish rebelled against English rule three different times, partially because the recent establishment of Protestantism in England had increased cultural tensions with Catholic Ireland. All three rebellions were brutally suppressed in a clear attempt to annihilate Irish Catholic culture, which was seen in England as little more than savagery. Compare, for example, Spenser's notoriously contemptuous views on the Irish as degenerate (see Cairns and Richards 3–7). This view had, moreover, moderated very little by the nineteenth century, when English visitors like Charles Kingsley likened the natives he encountered during an 1860 visit to Ireland to "white chimpanzees" (Lyons 12).

21. Bakhtin opposes to Brecht's grotesque realism the relatively degraded modernist grotesque of Alfred Jarry. One would guess that Bakhtin would have categorized Joyce with the former rather than the latter had it been possible to speak kindly of Joyce during the Stalinist years. It would, after all, have been perfectly acceptable for Bakhtin to discuss Joyce as long as he did so in the negative and critical fashion in which he discusses the modernist grotesque.

22. Brecht conducts this project through the technical subversion that informs his entire career. It also enters his plays as content, as when the gangster Arturo Ui (a cipher for Hitler) rehearses speeches from Shakespeare in an effort to learn rhetorical techniques that will aid his rise to power (*Resistible* 240–45).

Chapter Six

1. On the resonances between poststructuralism and the work of Joyce, see Attridge and Ferrer. Also see Lernout's review of the critical reaction to Joyce in France.

2. These are among the "disputed" texts of the Bakhtin circle. It is my position that available evidence does not warrant attributing these texts to Bakhtin rather than to Voloshinov, listed as the author upon initial publication. However, the ideas expressed in these texts are not fundamentally inconsistent with Bakhtin's own.

3. Leon Edel includes Joyce with writers like Proust and Woolf as practitioners of the "novel of subjectivity" or the "psychological novel."

4. One might compare here the work of Woolf, in which all the thoughts of different characters are typically presented in the same style.

5. See chapter 2, note 16. In addition to Brivic's, recent Lacan-influenced studies of Joyce include those by McGee, Leonard, Henke (*James Joyce and the Politics of Desire*), Rabaté (*James Joyce, Authorized Reader*), and MacCabe (*James Joyce and the Revolution of the Word*).

6. Voloshinov's notion of inner speech obviously recalls the psycholinguistic theories of Vygotsky. In fact, the models of subjectivity of Vygotsky and of the Bakhtin circle converge at many points. Caryl Emerson outlines some of these points and suggests that Lev Vygotsky's *Thought and Language* "can be read as an important predecessor and perhaps even as clinical underpinning to Bakhtin's philosophy of language" ("Outer" 27).

7. In *Finnegans Wake* the discourse is so convoluted that one would be hard pressed to identify anything as an interior monologue. But the general language of the *Wake* bears certain resemblances to Vygotsky's description of inner speech. He suggests, for example, that inner speech is characterized by a "prevalence of sense over meaning" and that words are often combined in inner speech so that the "senses of different words flow into one another—literally 'influence' one another—so that the earlier ones are contained in, and modify, the later ones" (Vygotsky 246–47). He also notes that inner speech has the frequent character of "omitting the subject of a sentence and all words connected with it, while preserving the predicate" (236), as Asenjo notes of the *Wake* (399).

8. Jameson himself elsewhere considers the process of narrative to be "the central function or *instance* of the human mind" (*Political* 13).

9. That Joyce saw his "characters" in this way is evidenced by the fact that he referred to them in his working notebooks by abstract symbols, or "sigla."

Interestingly, Joyce's sigla bear some striking resemblances to the system of symbols that Woolf foresees as someday replacing words ("Craftsmanship" 246–47). See McHugh for a discussion of Joyce's sigla.

10. This doubleness is especially well apprehended in Louis Althusser's discussion of interpellation—the way ideology acts to call each of us into a particular subject position (170–83). His paradigmatic example of this phenomenon is the ideology of Christianity, in which individuals are interpellated as subjects both in subjection to and in the specular image of a central Absolute Subject, i.e., God.

11. Kaus makes this argument in *Dostojewski und sein Schicksal*, which Bakhtin briefly reviews in *Problems of Dostoevsky's Poetics* (18–20). Bakhtin agrees with Kaus's analysis as far as it goes, but suggests that the polyphony of Dostoevsky's texts involves a conception of the novel the relevance of which goes far beyond capitalism.

12. Waugh's argument that women writers have a different perspective because they are marginal to official culture seems convincing. But gender is not the only criterion by which one can be marginalized, and Joyce himself was quite marginal to mainstream British culture—Woolf herself haughtily rejected him as a somewhat shabby and disreputable Irishman.

13. Holquist emphasizes this aspect of *The Brothers Karamazov* in *Dostoevsky and the Novel*.

14. For a detailed study of Dostoevsky's treatment of Catholicism, see Dirscherl.

15. As long ago as 1939 Helen Muchnic noted that the wide variety of critical responses to Dostoevsky's work suggests that Dostoevsky criticism often tells us more about the inclinations of the critics than about Dostoevsky himself. The parallel to Joyce criticism is obvious.

16. *Skaz* is a mode of narration (popular in Russian fiction), which achieves multiple voicing by making obvious potential differences in perspective between author and narrator. For a good discussion of *skaz* from a Bakhtinian perspective, see Titunik. Bakhtin himself discusses *skaz* in his Dostoevsky book, noting that Dostoevsky often employs a particularly sophisticated form of "parodistic *skaz*" (*Problems* 194). For a summary of some of the shenanigans of the narrator of *Devils*, see Jones (275–78).

17. See, for example, Shari Benstock's discussion of Stephen's narrative activities in her essay "The Dynamics of Narrative Performance." Stephen's most famous narratives, of course, are the "Parable of the Plums" and the Hamlet theory of *Ulysses*.

18. Silvio is the hero of Pushkin's story "The Shot." Narratives about duels are a particularly common motif in nineteenth-century Russian literature.

Conclusion

1. This conclusion is the one I reach in my recent study of the Peruvian writer Mario Vargas Llosa in a postmodernist context. See Patricia Caughie's reading of Woolf within a postmodernist context for a similar conclusion.

2. In *Vargas Llosa* I suggest that it is useful to consider modernism and the avant-garde as separate categories. Both share a belief in the ability of art to effect social change, but in modernism this change is expected to derive from the effective use of art, while the avant-garde pursues an "anti-art" strategy, seeking to dismantle certain social institutions and conventions by dismantling conventional notions of art itself.

3. For a useful review of Marxist reactions to Joyce's work, see Roughley (217–49). See also Segall for an interesting historical survey of left-wing attitudes toward Joyce in America, especially as they were influenced by Trotsky.

4. One might compare here Moretti's suggestion that the very structure of *Ulysses* mirrors the structure of capitalist society itself (190). Thus, *Ulysses* can be primarily about itself, yet it can comment on society at the same time.

5. See my *Vargas Llosa* for a discussion of this notion of modernist critical engagement seen through the optic of postmodernism.

6. Huyssen does, however, suggest that his criticisms are directed more at the "Flaubert-Thomas Mann-Eliot axis" of modernism than at the "Mallarmé-Lautréamont-Joyce axis" (49).

7. On Joyce's productive use of popular culture, see the studies by Herr and by Kershner.

8. See, for example, Ruth Nevo's reading of the poem as a postmodernist Ur-text of deconstruction, which includes a view of Eliot's notes as a "parody of academic footnoting" (459).

9. For a Derridean discussion of the significance of quotation from sources in the work of Brecht and Joyce, see Sartiliot.

10. In Brecht's case, of course, there is also an important critical engagement with German literature. For example, Benjamin Bennett suggests that Brecht is the modern writer who best represents "a synthesis of the modern tendencies to supersede and to preserve the Classical achievement" of predecessors like Goethe and Schiller (320).

11. See Bathrick for a good discussion of the implications of Brecht's use of high culture in *Arturo Ui*.

12. Note that the word *vandalism* comes from Brecht's own description of his technique of reworking the past in his plays, indicating an attitude of self-irony somewhat reminiscent of the late Joyce (*Gesammelte Werke* 15 179).

13. Kenner notes that some wags took to referring to the poem as "the piece that passes understanding" soon after its publication (*Invisible* 182).

14. Moreover, there are many parallels between *Ulysses* and *The Waste Land*, including some cases of a direct influence of Joyce's novel upon Eliot's poem. Stanley Sultan has published two books detailing the relationship between these two works.

15. Compare Eliot's suggestion that he is no more qualified to interpret *The Waste Land* than is anybody else: "But what a poem means is as much what it means to others as what it means to the author" (*Use* 122).

16. Josipovici's suggestion obviously has much in common with the formulations of "defamiliarization" by the Russian formalists and with the more explicitly political "estrangement" effect in Brecht.

17. Indeed, Ross suggests that Eliot's very "invisibility" as author of *The Waste Land*, combined with the canonical ascendancy of that poem during peak years of the New Criticism, resulted in a situation in which the fortunes of *The Waste Land* and of the New Criticism were "inextricably linked" (39).

18. Compare Woolf's contention that the goal of the artist should be to "practise anonymity" (*Writer's Diary* 119).

19. Eagleton presents such a distinction between structuralism and poststructuralism in his *Literary Theory: An Introduction*, though he himself suggests that modernism inspired both structuralism and poststructuralism (139–42). For a summary of various attempts to distinguish between modernism and postmodernism, see the appendix to my *Vargas Llosa*.

20. Just how successful Eliot was in avoiding autobiography in his poetry is open to debate. Recent analyses of *The Waste Land*, based on the evidence of the published manuscript versions, have emphasized its personal nature. See, for example, Moody.

21. For a representative discussion of feminist explorations of communal subjectivity, see Gardiner. These explorations resemble those of Voloshinov/Bakhtin in many ways.

22. Susan Suleiman, in a useful survey of some attempts to distinguish between modernism and postmodernism, also suggests that the modernism-postmodernism dichotomy is less clear for many female writers than for males. She asks: "Could it be that Postmodernism is an exclusively 'male' domain, both for critics and authors?" (268 n12).

23. Reinelt also cites the open-endedness of Brecht's plays and his penchant for constant revision as evidence of a postmodernist rejection of closure (350). On the other hand, she adds that "Brecht's certainty about truth, respect for the efficacy of science, and old-fashioned Marxist solutions, reinstate him within the precincts of modernism" (353).

24. Even more Eliotic is a statement of Jacques Lacan: "What is realized in my history is not the past definite of what was, since it is no more, or even the present perfect of what has been in what I am, but the future anterior of what I shall have been for what I am in the process of becoming" (*Écrits* 86). Lacan, of course, was significantly influenced by Heidegger, and here he may have even been influenced by Eliot, since later in the same essay he produces a description of the Damyata, Datta, and Dayadhyam of the god of thunder that must surely have *The Waste Land* in mind (106–7).

25. The fact that Eliot's lines may be a direct allusion to Ecclesiastes 3:15 is of no help, since we are given no indication of the attitude that the poem takes toward this source, and anyway the biblical verse is just as confusing as Eliot's poem: "That which has been is now; and that which is to be hath already been; and God requireth that which is past."

26. On Aristotle, Stephen, and history, see Schneider 54–56.

27. One might also argue that the growing availability of sophisticated explication made the difficulty of modernist works feasible. Ong notes that the New Critics were the first professional literary scholars: "The New Criticism was the

product of the first age when thousands of persons became intent on academic, and ultimately scholarly, analysis" (33). Of course, the New Critics dealt with a variety of literary works not just modernist ones. However, as Ong points out, their preoccupation with contemporary literature was unprecedented in the history of criticism (30). See also Spears for an extensive discussion of the importance of the New Critics and their successors (like Kermode and Frye) to the modernist movement (153–228).

Works Cited

Abrams, M. H. *Natural Supernaturalism: Tradition and Revolution in Romantic Literature*. New York: Norton, 1971.

Adorno, T. W. *Aesthetic Theory*. Trans. C. Lenhardt. Ed. Gretel Adorno and Rolf Tiedemann. London: Routledge and Kegan Paul, 1984.

Althusser, Louis. *Lenin and Philosophy and Other Essays*. Trans. Ben Brewster. New York: Monthly Review Press, 1971.

Arieti, Silvano. *Creativity: The Magic Synthesis*. New York: Basic Books, 1976.

Asenjo, F. G. "The General Problem of Sentence Structure: An Analysis Prompted by the Loss of Subject in *Finnegans Wake*." *Centennial Review of Arts and Science* 8 (1964): 398–408.

Atherton, James. "Shaun A." In *A Conceptual Guide to* Finnegans Wake. Ed. Michael H. Begnal and Fritz Senn. University Park: Pennsylvania State University Press, 1974, 149–72.

Attridge, Derek, and Daniel Ferrer, eds. *Post-structuralist Joyce*. Cambridge: Cambridge University Press, 1984.

Aubert, Jacques, ed. *Joyce avec Lacan*. Paris: Navarin, 1987.

Augustine, Saint. *Confessions*. Trans. R. S. Pine-Coffin. New York: Dorset, 1961.

Bakhtin, M. M. *The Dialogic Imagination*. Ed. Michael Holquist. Trans. Caryl Emerson and Michael Holquist. Austin: University of Texas Press, 1981.

Bakhtin, Mikhail. *Problems of Dostoevsky's Poetics*. Trans. and ed. Caryl Emerson. Minneapolis: University of Minnesota Press, 1984.

Bakhtin, M. M. *Rabelais and His World*. Trans. Helene Iswolsky. Bloomington: Indiana University Press, 1984.

Bakhtin, M. M. *Speech Genres and Other Late Essays*. Trans. Vern W. McGhee. Ed. Caryl Emerson and Michael Holquist. Austin: University of Texas Press, 1986.

Bakunin, Mikhail. *God and the State*. New York: Dover, 1970.

Barolini, Teodolinda. *Dante's Poets: Textuality and Truth in the Comedy*. Princeton, N. J.: Princeton University Press, 1984.

Barthes, Roland. "The Death of the Author." In *Image — Music — Text*. Trans. Stephen Heath. London: Collins, 1977, 142–48.

Barthes, Roland. *Mythologies*. Trans. Annette Lavers. New York: Hill and Wang, 1970.

Bataille, Georges. *Story of the Eye*. Trans. Joachim Neugroschel. San Francisco: City Lights, 1987.

Bathrick, David. "A One-Sided History: Brecht's Hitler Plays." In *Literature and History*. Ed. Leonard Schulze and Walter Wetzels. Lanham, Md.: University Press of America, 1983, 181–96.

Beckett, Samuel. "Dante... Bruno. Vico... Joyce." In *Our Exagmination Round his Factification for Incamination of* Work in Progress. London: Faber and Faber, 1929, 3–22.

Beebe, Maurice. "*Ulysses* and the Age of Modernism." In *Ulysses: Fifty Years*. Ed. Thomas Staley. Bloomington: Indiana University Press, 1974, 172–88.

Beebe, Maurice. "What Modernism Was." *Journal of Modern Literature* 3 (1974): 1065–80.

Belknap, Robert L. *The Structure of "The Brothers Karamazov."* Evanston, Ill.: Northwestern University Press, 1989.

Bell, Robert H. *Jocoserious Joyce: The Fate of Folly in "Ulysses."* Ithaca, N.Y.: Cornell University Press, 1991.

Belsey, Catherine. "Disrupting Sexual Difference: Meaning and Gender in the Comedies." In *Alternative Shakespeares*. Ed. John Drakakis. London and New York: Methuen, 1985, 166–90.

Benjamin, Walter. *Illuminations*. Trans. Harry Zohn. Ed. Hannah Arendt. New York: Harcourt, Brace, and World, 1955.

Bennett, Benjamin. *Modern Drama and German Classicism: Renaissance from Lessing to Brecht*. Ithaca, N.Y.: Cornell University Press, 1979.

Benstock, Shari. "The Dynamics of Narrative Performance: Stephen Dedalus as Storyteller." *ELH* 49 (1982): 707–38.

Berman, Russell A. *Modern Culture and Critical Theory: Art, Politics, and the Legacy of the Frankfurt School*. Madison: University of Wisconsin Press, 1989.

Bernstein, Michael André. *Bitter Carnival: Ressentiment and the Abject Hero*. Princeton, N. J.: Princeton University Press, 1992.

Berrong, Richard M. *Rabelais and Bakhtin: Popular Culture in "Gargantua and Pantagruel."* Lincoln: University of Nebraska Press, 1986.

Bishop, John. *Joyce's Book of the Dark: "Finnegans Wake."* Madison: University of Wisconsin Press, 1986.

Blackall, Eric A. *Goethe and the Novel*. Ithaca, N.Y.: Cornell University Press, 1976.

Booker, M. Keith. "The Baby in the Bathwater: Joyce, Gilbert, and Feminist Criticism." *Texas Studies in Literature and Language* 32 (1990): 446–67.

Booker, M. Keith. "*Finnegans Wake* and *The Satanic Verses*: Two Modern Myths of the Fall." *Critique* 32 (1991): 190–207.

Booker, M. Keith. "From the Sublime to the Ridiculous: Dante's Beatrice and Joyce's Bella Cohen." *James Joyce Quarterly* (Winter 1992): 357–68.

Booker, M. Keith. "History and Language in Joyce's 'The Sisters'." *Criticism* 33 (Spring 1991): 217–33.

Booker, M. Keith. "The Rats of God: Pynchon, Joyce, Beckett, and the Carnivalization of Religion." *Pynchon Notes* 24–25 (1989): 21–30.

Booker, M. Keith. "Serendipitous Intertextuality: Joyce's 'The Dead' and Shakespeare's *Twelfth Night*." *The Arkansas Quarterly* 1 (1992): 55–86.

Booker, M. Keith. *Techniques of Subversion in Modern Literature: Transgression, Abjection, and the Carnivalesque.* Gainesville: University of Florida Press, 1991.

Booker, M. Keith. *Vargas Llosa Among the Postmodernists: Commitment and Ambivalence.* Gainesville: University Press of Florida, 1994.

Booker, M. Keith. "Western Culture in the Wake of Joyce: From Egypt to Derrida (by Way of Nietzsche)." *College English* 53 (January 1991): 19–33.

Booker, M. Keith, and Dubravka Juraga. *Bakhtin, Stalin, and Modern Russian Fiction: Carnival, Dialogism, and Chronotope.* Westport, Conn.: Greenwood Press, 1995.

Booth, Wayne C. *The Rhetoric of Fiction.* 2d ed. Chicago: University of Chicago Press, 1983.

Bowen, Zack. *"Ulysses" as a Comic Novel.* Syracuse, N.Y.: Syracuse University Press, 1989.

Bradley, A. C. *Shakespearean Tragedy.* 2d ed. London: Macmillan, 1919.

Brecht, Bertolt. *Gesammelte Werke.* Vol. 15: *Schriften zum Theater 1.* Frankfurt: Suhrkamp Verlag, 1967.

Brecht, Bertolt. *A Man's a Man.* In *"Baal," "A Man's a Man," and "The Elephant Calf": Three Plays.* Trans. Eric Bentley. New York: Grove, 1964, 119–98.

Brecht, Bertolt. *The Resistible Rise of Arturo Ui.* In *Brecht: Collected Plays.* Vol. 6. Trans. Ralph Manheim. New York: Vintage, 1976, 195–303.

Brecht, Bertolt. *Roundheads and Peakheads.* Trans. N. Goold-Verschoyle. In *"Jungle of Cities" and Other Plays.* New York: Grove, 1966, 163–280.

Brivic, Sheldon. *Joyce Between Freud and Jung.* Port Washington, N.Y.: Kennikat, 1980.

Brivic, Sheldon. *Joyce the Creator.* Madison: University of Wisconsin Press, 1985.

Brown, Homer Obed. *James Joyce's Early Fiction.* Hamden, Conn.: Archon, 1975.

Brown, Richard. *James Joyce and Sexuality.* Cambridge: Cambridge University Press, 1985.

Budgen, Frank. *James Joyce and the Making of "Ulysses."* Bloomington: Indiana University Press, 1960.

Bürger, Peter. *Theory of the Avant-Garde.* Trans. Michael Shaw. Minneapolis: University of Minnesota Press, 1984.

Buttigieg, Joseph A. *"A Portrait of the Artist" in Different Perspective.* Athens: Ohio University Press, 1987.

Buttigieg, Joseph A. "The Struggle Against Meta(Phantasma)-physics: Nietzsche, Joyce and the Excess of History." In *Why Nietzsche Now?* Ed. Daniel O'Hara. Bloomington: Indiana University Press, 1985, 187–207.

Cairns, David, and Shaun Richards. *Writing Ireland: Colonialism, Nationalism, and Culture.* Manchester: Manchester University Press, 1988.

Calinescu, Matei. *Five Faces of Modernity.* Durham, N.C.: Duke University Press, 1987.

Callow, Heather Cook. "Exiles, Keys, and Salt Bread: Yet Another Note on Who Rented the Tower." *James Joyce Quarterly* 22 (1985): 425–27.

Campbell, Joseph, and Henry Morton Robinson. *A Skeleton Key to "Finnegans Wake."* 1944. New York: Penguin, 1977.

Carroll, William C. "The Ending of *Twelfth Night* and the Tradition of Metamorphosis." In *Shakespearean Comedy*. Ed. Maurice Charney. New York: New York Literary Forum, 1980, 49–61.

Caughie, Patricia. *Virginia Woolf and Postmodernism: Literature in Quest and Question of Itself.* Urbana: University of Illinois Press, 1991.

Cheng, Vincent. *Shakespeare and Joyce: A Study of "Finnegans Wake."* University Park: Pennsylvania State University Press, 1986.

Cheyfitz, Eric. *The Poetics of Imperialism: Translation and Colonization from "The Tempest" to "Tarzan."* New York: Oxford University Press, 1991.

Cixous, Hélène. "Joyce: The (R)use of Writing." In *Post-structuralist Joyce*. Ed. Derek Attridge and Daniel Ferrer. Cambridge: Cambridge University Press, 1984, 15–30.

Clark, Katerina, and Michael Holquist. *Mikhail Bakhtin.* Cambridge, Mass.: Belknap, 1984.

Cohn, Dorrit. *Transparent Minds: Narrative Modes for Presenting Consciousness in Fiction.* Princeton, N. J.: Princeton University Press, 1978.

Colie, Rosalie L. *Paradoxia Epidemica: The Renaissance Tradition of Paradox.* Hamden, Conn.: Archon, 1976.

Cross, Richard K. *Flaubert and Joyce: The Rite of Fiction.* Princeton, N. J.: Princeton University Press, 1971.

Culler, Jonathan. "The Call of the Phoneme: Introduction." *On Puns: The Foundation of Letters.* Ed. Jonathan Culler. London: Basil Blackwell, 1988, 1–16.

Curtius, E. R. *European Literature and the Latin Middle Ages.* Trans. Willard R. Trask. Princeton N. J.: Princeton University Press, 1953.

Dante Alighieri. *Inferno.* Trans. Allen Mandelbaum. Berkeley, Los Angeles, and London: University of California Press, 1980.

Dante Alighieri. *Paradiso.* Trans. Allen Mandelbaum. Berkeley, Los Angeles, and London: University of California Press, 1984.

Dante Alighieri. *Purgatorio.* Trans. Allen Mandelbaum. Berkeley, Los Angeles, and London: University of California Press, 1982.

Dante Alighieri. *De vulgari eloquentia.* Trans. Sally Purcell as *Literature in the Vernacular.* Manchester: Carcanet New Press, 1981.

Davis, Arthur G. *Hamlet and the Eternal Problem of Man.* New York: St. John's University Press, 1964.

Deane, Seamus. Introduction to *Nationalism, Colonialism, and Literature.* Minneapolis: University of Minnesota Press, 1990.

de Man, Paul. *The Resistance to Theory.* Minneapolis: University of Minnesota Press, 1986.

Derrida, Jacques. "Structure, Sign, and Play in the Discourse of the Human Sciences." In *The Languages of Criticism and the Sciences of Man*. Ed. Richard Macksey and Eugenio Donato. Baltimore and London: Johns Hopkins University Press, 1970, 247–65.

Derrida, Jacques. "Two Words for Joyce." In *Post-structuralist Joyce.* Ed. Derek

Attridge and Daniel Ferrer. Cambridge: Cambridge University Press, 1984, 145–59.

Diamond, William. "Wilhelm Meister's Interpretation of *Hamlet*." *Modern Philology* 23 (1925–26): 89–101.

DiBattista, Maria. *Virginia Woolf's Major Novels: The Fables of Anon*. New Haven and London: Yale University Press, 1980.

Dickson, Keith A. *Towards Utopia: A Study of Brecht*. Oxford: Clarendon, 1978.

Dilworth, Thomas. "Sex and Politics in 'The Dead.'" *James Joyce Quarterly* 23 (1986): 157–71.

Dirscherl, Denis, S. J. *Dostoevsky and the Catholic Church*. Chicago: Loyola University Press, 1986.

Dodds, E. R. *The Greeks and the Irrational*. Berkeley: University of California Press, 1951.

Doherty, Lillian E. "Joyce's Penelope and Homer's: Feminist Reconsiderations." *Classical and Modern Literature* 10.4 (1990): 343–49.

Dostoevsky, Fyodor. *The Brothers Karamazov*. Trans. Richard Pevear and Larissa Volokhonsky. San Francisco: North Point Press, 1990.

Dostoevsky, Fyodor. *Crime and Punishment*. Trans. David McDuff. New York: Penguin, 1991.

Dostoevsky, Fyodor. *Devils*. Trans. Michael R. Katz. Oxford: Oxford University Press, 1992.

Dostoevsky, Fyodor. *Notes from Underground*. Trans. Mirra Ginsburg. New York: Bantam, 1976.

Dunleavy, Janet Egleson, ed. *Re-Viewing Classics of Joyce Criticism*. Urbana: University of Illinois Press, 1991.

Eagleton, Terry. "Capitalism, Modernism and Postmodernism." *New Left Review* 152 (1985): 60–72.

Eagleton, Terry. *Criticism and Ideology: A Study in Marxist Literary Theory*. London: NLB, 1976.

Eagleton, Terry. *The Ideology of the Aesthetic*. Oxford: Basil Blackwell, 1990.

Eagleton, Terry. *Literary Theory: An Introduction*. Minneapolis: University of Minnesota Press, 1983.

Eagleton, Terry. *Walter Benjamin: Towards a Revolutionary Criticism*. London: Verso, 1981.

Eastman, Arthur. *A Short History of Shakespearean Criticism*. New York: Random House, 1968.

Eco, Umberto. *The Aesthetics of Chaosmos: The Middle Ages of James Joyce*. Trans. Ellen Esrock. Tulsa, Okla.: University of Tulsa Press, 1982.

Edel, Leon. *The Psychological Novel, 1900–1950*. New York: Lippincott, 1955.

Eliot, T. S. *Collected Poems, 1909–1962*. New York: Harcourt, Brace, and World, 1963.

Eliot, T. S. "Hamlet and His Problems." In *The Sacred Wood*. London: Methuen, 1964, 95–103.

Eliot, T. S. "The Metaphysical Poets." In *Selected Essays*. New York: Harcourt, Brace, 1950, 241–50.

Eliot, T. S. "Tradition and the Individual Talent." In *The Sacred Wood*. London: Methuen, 1960, 47–59.

Eliot, T. S. "*Ulysses*, Order, and Myth." *The Dial* 75 (1923): 480–83. Cited here as reprinted in *The Modern Tradition*. Eds. Richard Ellmann and Charles Feidelson, Jr. New York: Oxford University Press, 1965, 679–81.

Eliot, T. S. *The Use of Poetry and the Use of Criticism*. Cambridge, Mass.: Harvard University Press, 1933.

Ellmann, Richard. *The Consciousness of Joyce*. Toronto and New York: Oxford University Press, 1977.

Ellmann, Richard. *James Joyce*. New and rev. ed. New York: Oxford University Press, 1982.

Emerson, Caryl. "The Outer Word and Inner Speech: Bakhtin, Vygotsky, and the Internalization of Language." In *Bakhtin: Essays and Dialogues on His Work*. Ed. Gary Saul Morson. Chicago: University of Chicago Press, 1986, 21–40.

Esslin, Martin. *Brecht: The Man and His Work*. New York: Anchor, 1961.

Ewen, Frederic. *Bertolt Brecht: His Life, His Art, and His Times*. New York: Citadel, 1969.

Fiedler, Leslie. "Bloom on Joyce; or Jokey for Jacob." *Journal of Modern Literature* 1 (1970): 19–29.

Flaubert, Gustave. *The Temptation of St. Antony*. Trans. Kitty Mrosovsky. Harmondsworth, Middlesex: Penguin, 1983.

Fleissner, Robert F. *The Prince and the Professor: The Wittenberg Connection in Marlowe, Shakespeare, Goethe, and Frost*. Heidelberg: Carl Winter, 1986.

Foucault, Michel. *The History of Sexuality*. Vol. 1. *An Introduction*. Trans. Robert Hurley. New York: Vintage, 1980.

Foucault, Michel. *Language, Counter-Memory, Practice: Selected Essays and Interviews*. Ed. Donald F. Bouchard. Trans. Donald F. Bouchard and Sherry Simon. Ithaca, N. Y.: Cornell University Press, 1977.

Foucault, Michel. *Madness and Civilization: A History of Insanity in the Age of Reason*. Trans. Richard Howard. New York: Vintage, 1973.

Foucault, Michel. *The Order of Things*. Trans. anonymous. New York: Pantheon, 1970.

Foucault, Michel. *The Use of Pleasure*. Trans. Robert Hurley. New York: Vintage, 1986.

Frank, Joseph. "Spatial Form in Modern Literature." In *The Widening Gyre*. Bloomington: Indiana University Press, 1963, 3–62.

Freccero, John. *Dante: The Poetics of Conversion*. Ed. Rachel Jacoff. Cambridge, Mass.: Harvard University Press, 1986.

French, Marilyn. *The Book as World*. Cambridge and London: Harvard University Press, 1976.

Freud, Sigmund. "Psycho-Analytic Notes upon an Autobiographical Account of a Case of Paranoia (Dementia Paranoides)." In *Sigmund Freud: Collected Papers*. Trans. Alix Strachey and James Strachey. New York: Basic, 1959, 387–470.

Friedman, Melvin J. "Ellmann on Joyce." In *Re-Viewing Classics of Joyce Criti-*

cism. Ed. Janet Egleson Dunleavy. Urbana: University of Illinois Press, 1991, 131–41.

Friedrich, Gerhard. "Bret Harte as a Source for James Joyce's 'The Dead.'" *Philological Quarterly* 33 (1954): 442–44.

Gardiner, Judith Kegan. "On Female Identity and Writing by Women." In *Writing and Sexual Difference.* Ed. Elizabeth Abel. Chicago: University of Chicago Press, 1982, 177–91.

Gerlach, U. Henry. "Wilhelm Meister's Observations about Hamlet." *University of Dayton Review* 7 (1971): 25–33.

Ghiselin, Brewster. "The Unity of Joyce's *Dubliners.*" In James Joyce, *"Dubliners": Text, Criticism, and Notes.* Ed. Robert Scholes and A. Walton Litz. New York: Viking, 1969, 316–32.

Gifford, Don. *Joyce Annotated: Notes for* Dubliners *and* A Portrait of the Artist as a Young Man. Berkeley: University of California Press, 1982.

Gifford, Don, with Robert J. Seidman. *"Ulysses" Annotated.* 2d ed. Berkeley: University of California Press, 1988.

Gilbert, Sandra M. "Costumes of the Mind: Transvestism as Metaphor in Modern Literature." In *Writing and Sexual Difference.* Ed. Elizabeth Abel. Chicago: University of Chicago Press, 1982, 193–219.

Gilbert, Stuart. *James Joyce's "Ulysses": A Study.* New York: Vintage, 1955.

Gillespie, Michael Patrick. *Reading the Book of Himself: Narrative Strategies in the Works of James Joyce.* Columbus: Ohio State University Press, 1989.

Glasheen, Adaline. *Third Census of "Finnegans Wake."* Berkeley: University of California Press, 1977.

Goethe, Johann Wolfgang von. *Faust.* Pt. 1. Trans. Philip Wayne. London: Penguin, 1949.

Goethe, Johann Wolfgang von. *Faust.* Pt. 2. Trans. Philip Wayne. London: Penguin, 1959.

Goethe, Johann Wolfgang von. *The Sorrows of Young Werther.* Trans. Michael Hulse. London: Penguin, 1989.

Goethe, Johann Wolfgang von. *Wilhelm Meister's Apprenticeship.* Trans. Thomas Carlyle. New York: Heritage, 1959.

Greenblatt, Stephen. *Shakespearean Negotiations: The Circulation of Social Energy in Renaissance England.* Berkeley: University of California Press, 1988.

Grossman, Marshall. *"Authors to Themselves": Milton and the Revelation of History.* Cambridge and New York: Cambridge University Press, 1987.

Hardy, Barbara. "Joyce and Homer: Seeing Double." In *James Joyce: The Artist and the Labyrinth.* Ed. Augustine Martin. London: Ryan, 1990, 169–91.

Hart, Clive. *A Concordance to "Finnegans Wake."* Minneapolis: University of Minnesota Press, 1963.

Hart, Clive. *Structure and Motif in* Finnegans Wake. Evanston, Ill.: Northwestern University Press, 1962.

Hartman, Geoffrey. "Shakespeare's Poetical Character in *Twelfth Night.*" In *Shakespeare and the Question of Theory.* Ed. Patricia Parker and Geoffrey Hartman. London and New York: Methuen, 1985, 37–53.

Hassan, Ihab. "Ideas of Cultural Change." In *Innovation/Renovation: New Per-*

spectives on the Humanities. Ed. Ihab Hassan and Sally Hassan. Madison: University of Wisconsin Press, 1983, 15–39.

Hatfield, Henry. "The Walpurgis Night: Theme and Variations." *Journal of European Studies* 13 (1983): 56–74.

Hawthorn, Jeremy. "*Ulysses*, Modernism, and Marxist Criticism." In *James Joyce and Modern Literature*. Ed. W. J. McCormack and Alistair Stead. London: Routledge and Kegan Paul, 1982, 112–25.

Hayman, David. *Joyce et Mallarmé*. 2 vols. Paris: Cahiers des lettres modernes, 1956.

Hayman, David. "*Ulysses*": *The Mechanics of Meaning*. Rev. ed. Madison: University of Wisconsin Press, 1982.

Heath, Stephen. "Ambiviolences: Notes for Reading Joyce." In *Post-structuralist Joyce*. Ed. Derek Attridge and Daniel Ferrer. Cambridge: Cambridge University Press, 1984, 31–68.

Hegel, G. W. F. *Lectures on the Philosophy of History*. Trans. H. B. Nisbet. Cambridge: Cambridge University Press, 1975.

Heidegger, Martin. *Being and Time*. Trans. John Macquarrie and Edward Robinson. New York: Harper and Row, 1962.

Henke, Suzette. *James Joyce and the Politics of Desire*. New York and London: Routledge, 1990.

Herr, Cheryl. *Joyce's Anatomy of Culture*. Urbana and Chicago: University of Illinois Press, 1986.

Herrmann, Anne. *The Dialogic and Difference: "An/Other Woman" in Virginia Woolf and Christa Wolf*. New York: Columbia University Press, 1989.

Hoffman, Gerhard, Alfred Hornung, and Rudiger Kunow. "'Modern', 'Postmodern' and 'Contemporary' as Criteria for the Analysis of 20th Century Literature." *Amerikastudien* 22 (1977): 19–46.

Holland, Norman N. "*Hamlet*—My Greatest Creation." *Journal of the American Academy of Psychoanalysis* 3 (1975): 419–27.

Hollander, Robert. *Allegory in Dante's* Commedia. Princeton, N.J.: Princeton University Press, 1969.

Hollander, Robert. "Babytalk in Dante's *Commedia*." In *Studies in Dante*. Ravenna: Longo Editore, n.d., 115–29.

Holquist, Michael. "Bakhtin and Rabelais: Theory as Praxis." *Boundary 2* 11 (Fall-Winter 1982): 1–17.

Holquist, Michael. *Dostoevsky and the Novel*. Princeton, N.J.: Princeton University Press, 1977.

Hulse, Michael. Introduction to *The Sorrows of Young Werther* by Johann Wolfgang von Goethe. London: Penguin, 1989, 5–19.

Hussey, Mark, ed. *Virginia Woolf and War: Fiction, Reality, and Myth*. Syracuse, N.Y.: Syracuse University Press, 1991.

Huyssen, Andreas. *After the Great Divide: Modernism, Mass Culture, Postmodernism*. Bloomington and Indianapolis: Indiana University Press, 1986.

Jacquet, Claude. *Joyce et Rabelais: Aspects de la création verbale dans "Finnegans Wake"*. Paris: Didier, 1972.

Jameson, Fredric. *Marxism and Form: Twentieth-Century Dialectical Theories of Literature.* Princeton, N.J.: Princeton University Press, 1971.

Jameson, Fredric. "Metacommentary." *PMLA* 86 (1971): 9–18.

Jameson, Fredric. *The Political Unconscious: Narrative as a Socially Symbolic Act.* Ithaca, N.Y.: Cornell University Press, 1981.

Jameson, Fredric. "Postmodernism and Consumer Society." In *The Anti-Aesthetic: Essays on Postmodern Culture.* Ed. Hal Foster. Port Townsend, Wash.: Bay Press, 1983, 111–26.

Jameson, Fredric. *Postmodernism, or, The Cultural Logic of Late Capitalism.* Durham: Duke University Press, 1991.

Jameson, Fredric. "*Ulysses* in History." In *James Joyce and Modern Literature.* Ed. W. J. McCormack and Alistair Stead. London: Routledge and Kegan Paul, 1982, 126–41.

Jantz, Harold. "Discovering Goethe." In *Goethe Proceedings: Essays Commemorating the Goethe Sesquicentennial at the University of California, Davis.* Ed. Clifford A. Bernd, et al. Columbia, S.C.: Camden House, 1984, 35–50.

Jones, John. *Dostoevsky.* Oxford: Clarendon, 1983.

Josipovici, Gabriel. "The Lessons of Modernism." In *The Lessons of Modernism and Other Essays.* London: Macmillan, 1977, 109–23.

Josipovici, Gabriel. "Modernism and Romanticism." In *The World and the Book.* Stanford: Stanford University Press, 1971, 179–200.

Joyce, James. *The Collected Letters of James Joyce.* Vol. 1. Ed. Stuart Gilbert. London: Faber, 1957.

Joyce, James. *The Critical Writings of James Joyce.* Ed. Ellsworth Mason and Richard Ellmann. Ithaca, N.Y.: Cornell University Press, 1989.

Joyce, James. *"Dubliners": Text, Criticism, and Notes.* Ed. Robert Scholes and A. Walton Litz. New York: Viking, 1969.

Joyce, James. *Finnegans Wake.* New York: Viking, 1939.

Joyce, James. *"A Portrait of the Artist as a Young Man": Text, Criticism, and Notes.* Ed. Chester G. Anderson. New York: Viking, 1968.

Joyce, James. *Stephen Hero.* Ed., from manuscripts, by Theodore Spencer. Additional manuscript pages ed. John J. Slocum and Herbert Cahoon. New York: New Directions, 1963.

Joyce, James. *"Ulysses": The Corrected Text.* Ed. Hans Walter Gabler, with Wolfhard Steppe and Claus Melchior. New York: Random House, 1986.

Juraga, Dubravka, and M. Keith Booker. "Literature, Power, and Oppression in Stalinist Russia and Catholic Ireland: Danilo Kiš's Use of Joyce in *A Tomb for Boris Davidovich.*" *South Atlantic Review* 58.4 (1993): 39–58.

Kain, Richard. *Fabulous Voyager: A Study of James Joyce's "Ulysses."* New York: Viking, 1947.

Kaye, Julian. "The Wings of Dedalus: Two Stories in *Dubliners.*" *Modern Fiction Studies* 4 (1958): 31–41.

Kearney, Richard. *The Wake of Imagination: Toward a Postmodern Culture.* Minneapolis: University of Minnesota Press, 1988.

Kenner, Hugh. "The Cubist *Portrait.*" In *Approaches to Joyce's "Portrait."* Ed.

Thomas F. Staley and Bernard Benstock. Pittsburgh: University of Pittsburgh Press, 1976, 171–84.

Kenner, Hugh. *Dublin's Joyce*. 1956. New York: Columbia University Press, 1987.

Kenner, Hugh. *The Invisible Poet: T. S. Eliot*. New York: McDowell, Obolensky, 1959.

Kenner, Hugh. *Joyce's Voices*. Berkeley: University of California Press, 1978.

Kenner, Hugh. *Ulysses*. Rev. ed. Baltimore: Johns Hopkins University Press, 1987.

Kermode, Frank. *Romantic Image*. New York: Chilmark, 1963.

Kershner, R. B., Jr. "The Artist as Text: Dialogism and Incremental Repetition in Joyce's *Portrait*." *ELH* 53 (1986): 881–94.

Kershner, R. B., Jr. "Artist, Critic, and Performer: Wilde and Joyce on Shakespeare." *Texas Studies in Literature and Language* 20 (1978): 216–29.

Kershner, R. B., Jr. *Joyce, Bakhtin, and Popular Literature: Chronicles of Disorder*. Chapel Hill: University of North Carolina Press, 1989.

Kershner, R. B., Jr. "Time and Language in Joyce's *Portrait of the Artist*." *ELH* 43 (1976): 604–19.

Kershner, R. B., Jr. "*Ulysses* and the Orient." Unpublished manuscript.

Kidd, John. "Joyce, Rabelais, and Plutarch: The Deaths of Parnell and Pan." *James Joyce Quarterly* 21.3 (1984): 279–81.

Kinser, Samuel. *Rabelais's Carnival: Text, Context, and Metatext*. Berkeley: University of California Press, 1990.

Knapp, Jeffrey. *An Empire Nowhere: England, America, and Literature from "Utopia" to "The Tempest."* Berkeley: University of California Press, 1992.

Kristeva, Julia. *Desire in Language: A Semiotic Approach to Literature and Art*. Trans. Thomas Gora, Alice Jardine, and Leon S. Roudiez. Ed. Leon S. Roudiez. New York: Columbia University Press, 1980.

Kristeva, Julia. *Revolution in Poetic Language*. Trans. Margaret Waller. New York: Columbia University Press, 1984.

Lacan, Jacques. *Écrits: A Selection*. Trans. Alan Sheridan. New York: Norton, 1977.

LaCapra, Dominic. *Rethinking Intellectual History: Texts, Contexts, Language*. Ithaca, N.Y.: Cornell University Press, 1983.

Laclau, Ernesto, and Chantal Mouffe. *Hegemony and Socialist Strategy: Towards a Radical Democratic Politics*. London: Verso, 1985.

Lamb, M. E. "Ovid's *Metamorphoses* and Shakespeare's *Twelfth Night*." In *Shakespearean Comedy*. Ed. Maurice Charney. New York: New York Literary Forum, 1980, 63–77.

Langbaum, Robert. *The Mysteries of Identity: A Theme in Modern Literature*. New York: Oxford University Press, 1977.

Langbaum, Robert. "New Modes of Characterization in *The Waste Land*." In *Eliot in His Time: Essays on the Occasion of the Fiftieth Anniversary of* The Waste Land. Ed. A. Walton Litz. Princeton, N.J.: Princeton University Press, 1973, 95–128.

Larbaud, Valery. "James Joyce." *Criterion* 1 (October 1922): 94–103. Translated portion of Larbaud's "James Joyce." *La Nouvelle Revue Francaise* 18 (1922): 385–409.

Lawrence, Karen. *The Odyssey of Style in "Ulysses."* Princeton, N.J.: Princeton University Press, 1981.

Leonard, Garry Martin. *Reading "Dubliners" Again: A Lacanian Perspective.* Syracuse, N.Y.: Syracuse University Press, 1993.

Lernout, Geert. *The French Joyce.* Ann Arbor: University of Michigan Press, 1990.

Levin, Richard, and Charles Shattuck. "First Flight to Ithaca: A New Reading of Joyce's *Dubliners.*" In *James Joyce: Two Decades of Criticism.* Ed. Seon Givens. New York: Vanguard, 1963, 47–93.

Levine, Jennifer Schiffer. "Originality and Repetition in *Finnegans Wake* and *Ulysses.*" *PMLA* 94 (1979): 106–20.

Lévi-Strauss, Claude. *The Savage Mind.* Chicago: University of Chicago Press, 1969.

Litz, A. Walton. *The Art of James Joyce: Method and Design in "Ulysses" and "Finnegans Wake."* London: Oxford University Press, 1961.

Lodge, David. *After Bakhtin: Essays on Fiction and Criticism.* London: Routledge, 1990.

Lodge, David. "Double Discourses: Joyce and Bakhtin." *James Joyce Broadsheet* 11 (1983): 1.

Lowe-Evans, Mary. *Crimes Against Fecundity: Joyce and Population Control.* Syracuse, N.Y.: Syracuse University Press, 1989.

Lukács, Georg. *Realism in Our Time: Literature and the Class Struggle.* Trans. John Mander and Necke Mander. New York: Harper and Row, 1964.

Lunacharsky, Anatoly. *On Literature and Art.* Ed. K. M. Cook. Trans. Avril Pyman and Fainna Glagoleva. Moscow: Progress, 1973.

Lyons, F. S. L. *Culture and Anarchy in Ireland, 1890–1939.* Oxford: Clarendon, 1979.

MacCabe, Colin. *James Joyce and the Revolution of the Word.* London: Macmillan, 1978.

MacCabe, Colin. "The Voice of Esau: Stephen in the Library." In *James Joyce: New Perspectives.* Ed. Colin MacCabe. Bloomington: Indiana University Press, 1982, 111–28.

Maddox, James H. *Joyce's* Ulysses *and the Assault upon Character.* New Brunswick: Rutgers University Press, 1978.

Mahaffey, Vicki. *Reauthorizing Joyce.* New York: Cambridge University Press, 1988.

Manganiello, Dominic. *Joyce's Politics.* London: Routledge and Kegan Paul, 1980.

Mannoni, Octave. "Writing and Madness: *Schreber als Schreiber.*" In *Psychosis and Sexual Identity: Toward a Post-Analytic View of the Schreber Case.* Ed. David B. Allison, et al. Albany: State University of New York Press, 1988, 43–60.

Marchand, James W. "A Milestone in *Hamlet* Criticism: Goethe's *Wilhelm Meis-*

ter." In *Goethe as a Critic of Literature*. Ed. Karl J. Fink and Max L. Baeumer. Lanham, Md.: University Press of America, 1984, 140–59.

Martin, Rux. "Truth, Power, Self: An Interview with Michel Foucault." In *Technologies of the Self*. Ed. Luther H. Martin, Huck Gutman, and Patrick H. Hutton. Amherst: University of Massachusetts Press, 1988, 9–15.

Marx, Karl. *The Eighteenth Brumaire of Louis Bonaparte*. In *The Marx-Engels Reader*. Ed. Robert C. Tucker. 2d. ed. New York: Norton, 1978, 594–617.

Mazzotta, Giuseppe. *Dante, Poet of the Desert: History and Allegory in the* Divine Comedy. Princeton, N. J.: Princeton University Press, 1979.

McCarthy, Patrick A. "Stuart Gilbert's Guide to the Perplexed." In *Re-Viewing Classics of Joyce Criticism*. Ed. Janet Egleson Dunleavy. Urbana: University of Illinois Press, 1991, 23–35.

McDuff, David. Introduction to *Crime and Punishment* by Fyodor Dostoevsky. New York: Penguin, 1991, 9–29.

McGee, Patrick. *Paperspace: Style as Ideology in Joyce's "Ulysses."* Lincoln: University of Nebraska Press, 1988.

McHale, Brian. *Postmodernist Fiction*. New York and London: Methuen, 1987.

McHugh, Roland. *The Sigla of "Finnegans Wake."* Austin: University of Texas Press, 1976.

Mercier, Vivian. "James Joyce and the Macaronic Tradition." In *Twelve and a Tilly*. Ed. Jack P. Dalton and Clive Hart. Evanston, Ill.: Northwestern University Press, 1965, 26–38.

Mitchell, Breon. "*A Portrait* and the *Bildungsroman* Tradition." In *Approaches to Joyce's "Portrait."* Ed. Thomas F. Staley and Bernard Benstock. Pittsburgh: University of Pittsburgh Press, 1976, 61–76.

Monas, Sidney. "Verbal Carnival: Bakhtin, Rabelais, *Finnegans Wake*, and the Growthesk." Paper presented at the International Bakhtin Conference, Queen's University, Kingston, Ontario, October 8, 1983.

Moody, A. D. "'To fill all the desert with inviolable voice.'" In *The Waste Land in Different Voices*. Ed. A. D. Moody. New York: St. Martin's, 1974, 47–66.

Moretti, Franco. *Signs Taken for Wonders: Essays in the Sociology of Literary Forms*. Trans. Susan Fischer, David Forgacs, and David Miller. London: Verso, 1983.

Morson, Gary Saul, and Caryl Emerson. *Mikhail Bakhtin: Creation of a Prosaics*. Stanford: Stanford University Press, 1990.

Moseley, Virginia. "'Two Sights for Ever a Picture' in Joyce's 'The Dead.'" *College English* 6 (1965): 426–33.

Muchnic, Helen. "Dostoevsky's English Reputation (1881–1936)." *Smith College Studies in Modern Languages* 20.3–4 (1939).

Musil, Robert. *The Man Without Qualities*. Trans. Eithne Wilkins and Ernst Kaiser. New York: Perigee (Putnam), 1980.

Nänny, Max. "Ezra Pound and the Menippean Tradition." *Paideuma* 11 (1982): 395–405.

Nänny, Max. "*The Waste Land*: A Menippean Satire?" *English Studies* 66 (1985): 526–35.

Nevo, Ruth. *"The Waste Land*: Ur-Text of Deconstruction." *New Literary History* 13 (1982): 453–61.

Nietzsche, Friedrich. *The Birth of Tragedy*. In *Basic Writings of Nietzsche*. Trans. and ed. Walter Kaufmann. New York: Modern Library, 1968, 3–144.

Nietzsche, Friedrich. "On the Uses and Disadvantages of History." In *Untimely Meditations*. Trans. R. J. Hollingdale. Cambridge: Cambridge University Press, 1983, 57–123.

Nietzsche, Friedrich. "On Truth and Lies in a Nonmoral Sense." In *Philosophy and Truth: Selections from Nietzsche's Notebooks of the Early 1870's*. Trans. and ed. Daniel Breazeale. Atlantic Highlands, N.J.: Humanities Press, 1979, 79–97.

Norris, Margot. *The Decentered Universe of "Finnegans Wake": A Structuralist Analysis*. Baltimore: Johns Hopkins University Press, 1976.

O'Brien, Flann. *At Swim-Two-Birds*. 1939. New York: New American Library, 1976.

Ong, Walter J. *In the Human Grain*. New York: Macmillan, 1967.

Pater, Walter. *The Renaissance: Studies in Art and Poetry*. 1873. London: Macmillan, 1919.

Pecora, Vincent P. "'The Dead' and the Generosity of the Word." *PMLA* 101 (1986): 233–45.

Petronius. *The Satyricon*. In *Petronius: "The Satyricon," and Seneca: "The Apocolocyntosis."* Trans. J. P. Sullivan. New York: Penguin, 1986, 37–160.

Plato. *Phaedrus*. Trans. C. J. Rowe. Warminster: Aris and Phillips, 1986.

Poggioli, Renato. *The Theory of the Avant-Garde*. Trans. Gerald Fitzgerald. Cambridge, Mass.: Harvard University Press, 1968.

Poirier, Richard. "The Difficulties of Modernism and the Modernism of Difficulty." In *Images and Ideas in American Culture*. Ed. Arthur Edelstein. Hanover, N. H.: Brandeis University Press, 1979, 124–40.

Power, Arthur. *Conversations with James Joyce*. Ed. Clive Hart. Chicago: University of Chicago Press, 1974.

Purdy, Strother B. "Mind Your Genderous: Toward a *Wake* Grammar." In *New Light on Joyce from the Dublin Symposium*. Ed. Fritz Senn. Bloomington: Indiana University Press, 1972, 46–78.

Rabain, Jean-François. "Figures of Delusion." In *Psychosis and Sexual Identity: Toward a Post-Analytic View of the Schreber Case*. Ed. David B. Allison, et al. Albany: State University of New York Press, 1988, 61–69.

Rabaté, Jean-Michel. *James Joyce, Authorized Reader*. Baltimore: Johns Hopkins University Press, 1991.

Rabelais, François. *The Histories of Gargantua and Pantagruel*. Trans. J. M. Cohen. London: Penguin, 1955.

Rabelais, François. *Gargantua and Pantagruel*. Trans. Jacques Le Clerq. New York: Modern Library, 1944.

Radek, Karl. "Contemporary World Literature and the Tasks of Proletarian Art." In *Problems of Soviet Literature*. Trans. anonymous. Ed. H. G. Scott. Westport, Conn.: Greenwood Press, 1979, 73–162.

Rea, Joanne E. "Joyce and 'Master François Somebody.'" *James Joyce Quarterly* 18.4 (1981): 445–50.

Reinelt, Janelle. "Approaching the Postmodernist Threshold: Samuel Beckett and Bertolt Brecht." In *The Aesthetics of the Critical Theorists: Studies on Benjamin, Adorno, Marcuse, and Habermas.* Ed. Ronald Roblin. Lewiston, Pa.: Edwin Mellen, 1990, 337–58.

Reiss, Hans. *Goethe's Novels.* Coral Gables, Fla.: University of Miami Press, 1969.

Restuccia, Frances L. *Joyce and the Law of the Father.* New Haven: Yale University Press, 1989.

Reynolds, Mary T. *Joyce and Dante: The Shaping Imagination.* Princeton, N.J.: Princeton University Press, 1981.

Reynolds, Mary T. "Joyce's Shakespeare/Schutte's Joyce." In *Re-Viewing Classics of Joyce Criticism.* Ed. Janet Egleson Dunleavy. Urbana: University of Illinois Press, 1991, 169–85.

Ricoeur, Paul. *Time and Narrative.* Vol. 3. Trans. Kathleen Blamey and David Pellauer. Chicago: University of Chicago Press, 1988.

Riffaterre, Michael. "Syllepsis." *Critical Inquiry* 6 (1980): 625–38.

Riquelme, John Paul. *Teller and Tale in Joyce's Fiction: Oscillating Perspectives.* Baltimore: Johns Hopkins University Press, 1983.

Robinson, Lillian S., and Lise Vogel. "Modernism and History." *New Literary History* 3 (1971): 177–99.

Ross, Andrew. *The Failure of Modernism: Symptoms of American Poetry.* New York: Columbia University Press, 1986.

Roughley, Alan. *James Joyce and Critical Theory: An Introduction.* Ann Arbor: University of Michigan Press, 1991.

Rushdie, Salman. "The Empire Writes Back With a Vengeance." London *Times,* July 3, 1982, 8.

Rushdie, Salman. *The Satanic Verses.* New York: Viking, 1989.

Sacher-Masoch, Leopold von. *Venus in Furs.* Trans. Uwe Moeller and Laura Lindgren. New York: Blast, 1989.

Sartiliot, Claudette. *Citation and Modernity: Derrida, Joyce, and Brecht.* Norman: University of Oklahoma Press, 1993.

Schneider, Ulrich. "'An actuality of the possible as possible': Reflections on the Theme of History in 'Nestor.'" In *International Perspectives on Joyce.* Ed. Gottlieb Gaiser. Troy, N.Y.: Whitson, 1986, 44–58.

Schreber, Daniel Paul. *Memoirs of My Nervous Illness.* Trans. and ed. Ida MacAlpine and Richard A. Hunter. Cambridge: Harvard University Press, 1988.

Schutte, William. *Index of Recurrent Elements in James Joyce's "Ulysses."* Carbondale: Southern Illinois University Press, 1982.

Schutte, William. *Joyce and Shakespeare: A Study in the Meaning of "Ulysses."* New Haven: Yale University Press, 1957.

Segall, Jeffrey. "Between Marxism and Modernism, or How to Be a Revolutionist and Still Love *Ulysses.*" *James Joyce Quarterly* 25.4 (1988): 421–44.

Senn, Fritz. "Remodeling Homer." In *Light Rays: James Joyce and Modernism*. Ed. Heyward Ehrlich. New York: New Horizon, 1984, 70–92.

Shaffer, Brian. "Kindred by Choice: Joyce's 'Exiles' and Goethe's 'Elective Affinities.'" *James Joyce Quarterly* 26.2 (1989): 199–212.

Shakespeare, William. *The Complete Works of William Shakespeare*. Ed. David Bevington. 3d ed. London: Scott, Foresman, 1980.

Shoaf, R. A. *Dante, Chaucer, and the Currency of the Word: Money, Images, and Reference in Late Medieval Poetry*. Norman, Okla.: Pilgrim, 1983.

Shoaf, R. A. "Medieval Studies After Derrida After Heidegger." In *Sign, Sentence, Discourse: Language in Medieval Thought and Literature*. Ed. Julian N. Wasserman and Lois Y. Roney. Syracuse: Syracuse University Press, 1989, 9–30.

Shoaf, R. A. "The Play of Puns in Late Middle English Poetry: Concerning Juxtology." In *On Puns: The Foundation of Letters*. Ed. Jonathan Culler. London: Basil Blackwell, 1988, 44–61.

Showalter, Elaine. "Representing Ophelia: Women, Madness, and the Responsibilities of Feminist Criticism." In *Shakespeare and the Question of Theory*. Ed. Patricia Parker and Geoffrey Hartman. New York: Methuen, 1985, 77–94.

Singleton, Charles S. "'In Exitu Israel de Aegypto.'" In *Dante: A Collection of Critical Essays*. Ed. John Freccero. Englewood Cliffs, N.J.: Prentice-Hall, 1965, 102–21.

Sollers, Philippe. "Joyce & Co." *Triquarterly* 38 (1977): 107–21.

Spanos, William. "Modern Literary Criticism and the Spatialization of Time: An Existential Critique." *Journal of Aesthetics and Art Criticism* 29 (1970): 87–104.

Spanos, William V. "Postmodern Literature and Its Occasion: Retrieving the Preterite Middle." In *Repetitions: The Postmodern Occasion in Literature and Culture*. Baton Rouge and London: Louisiana State University Press, 1987, 189–276.

Spearing, A. C. *Criticism and Medieval Poetry*. New York: Barnes and Noble, 1972.

Spears, Monroe K. *Dionysius and the City: Modernism in Twentieth-Century Poetry*. New York: Oxford University Press, 1970.

Spitzer, Leo. "Linguistic and Literary History." In *Linguistics and Literary History: Essays in Stylistics*. New York: Russell and Russell, 1962, 1–39.

Spivak, Gayatri Chakravorty. "Translator's Preface." In *Of Grammatology*, by Jacques Derrida. Baltimore: Johns Hopkins University Press, 1976, ix–lxxxvii.

Steiner, George. *After Babel: Aspects of Language and Translation*. London, Oxford, and New York: Oxford University Press, 1975.

Steppe, Wolfhard, and Hans Walter Gabler. *A Handlist to James Joyce's "Ulysses": A Complete Alphabetical Index to the Critical Reading Text*. New York: Garland, 1985.

Suleiman, Susan Rubin. "Naming and Difference: Reflections on 'Modernism versus Postmodernism' in Literature." In *Approaching Postmodernism*. Ed. Douwe Fokkema and Hans Bertens. Amsterdam and Philadelphia: John Benjamins, 1986, 255–70.

Sultan, Stanley. *Eliot, Joyce, and Company*. New York: Oxford University Press, 1987.

Sultan, Stanley. *"Ulysses," "The Waste Land," and Modernism*. London and Port Washington, N.Y.: Kennikat, 1977.

Tambling, Jeremy. *Dante and Difference: Writing in the* Commedia. Cambridge: Cambridge University Press, 1988.

Thompson, Jon. "Joyce and Dialogism: Politics of Style in *Dubliners*." *Works and Days* 5.2 (1987): 79–95.

Thornton, Weldon. *Allusions in "Ulysses": An Annotated List*. Chapel Hill: University of North Carolina Press, 1968.

Titunik, I. R. "Mikhail Zoshchenko and the Problem of *Skaz*." *California Slavic Studies* 6 (1971): 83–96.

Topia, André. "The Matrix and the Echo: Intertextuality in *Ulysses*." In *Post-structuralist Joyce*. Ed. Derek Attridge and Daniel Ferrer. Cambridge: Cambridge University Press, 1984, 103–25.

Trevelyan, Humphrey. *Goethe and the Greeks*. New York: Octagon Books, 1972.

Ulmer, Gregory L. "The Object of Post-Criticism." In *The Anti-Aesthetic: Essays on Postmodern Culture*. Ed. Hal Foster. Port Townsend, Wash.: Bay Press, 1983, 83–110.

Valente, Joseph. "The Politics of Joyce's Polyphony." In *New Alliances in Joyce Studies: "When It's Aped to Foul a Delfian."* Ed. Bonnie Kime Scott. Newark: University of Delaware Press, 1988, 56–68.

Vance, Eugene. *Mervelous Signals: Poetics and Sign Theory in the Middle Ages*. Lincoln: University of Nebraska Press, 1986.

Voloshinov, V. N. *Freudianism: A Critical Sketch*. Trans. I. R. Titunik. Ed. I. R. Titunik and Neal H. Bruss. Bloomington: Indiana University Press, 1987.

Voloshinov, V. N. *Marxism and the Philosophy of Language*. Trans. Ladislav Matejka and I. R. Titunik. Cambridge, Mass.: Harvard University Press, 1986.

Vygotsky, Lev. *Thought and Language*. Trans. Alex Kozulin. Cambridge, Mass.: MIT Press, 1986.

Walzl, Florence. "Gabriel and Michael: The Conclusion of 'The Dead.'" In James Joyce. *Dubliners: Text Criticism, and Notes*. Ed. Robert Scholes and A. Walton Litz. New York: Viking, 1969, 423–43.

Watson, G. J. "The Politics of *Ulysses*." In *Joyce's "Ulysses": The Larger Perspective*. Ed. Robert D. Newman and Weldon Thornton. Newark: University of Delaware Press, 1987, 39–58.

Waugh, Patricia. *Feminine Fictions: Revisiting the Postmodern*. London and New York: Routledge, 1989.

Weisinger, Kenneth D. *The Classical Facade: A Nonclassical Reading of Goethe's Classicism*. University Park: Pennsylvania State University Press, 1988.

Werner, Craig. *Paradoxical Resolutions: American Fiction Since James Joyce*. Urbana: University of Illinois Press, 1982.

Wertsch, James V. *Vygotsky and the Social Formation of Mind.* Cambridge, Mass.: Harvard University Press, 1985.

White, Allon. "Bakhtin, Sociolinguistics and Deconstruction." In *The Theory of Reading.* Ed. Frank Gloversmith. New York: Barnes, 1984, 123–46.

White, Allon. "Pigs and Pierrots: The Politics of Transgression in Modern Fiction." *Raritan* 11 (1982): 51–70.

Wikander, Matthew. *The Play of Truth and State: Historical Drama from Shakespeare to Brecht.* Baltimore: Johns Hopkins University Press, 1986.

Wilde, Alan. *Horizons of Assent: Modernism, Postmodernism, and the Ironic Imagination.* Baltimore: Johns Hopkins University Press, 1981.

Wilde, Oscar. "The Critic as Artist." In *The Portable Oscar Wilde.* Ed. Richard Aldington and Stanley Weintraub. London: Penguin, 1946, 51–137.

Wilde, Oscar. *The Picture of Dorian Gray.* In *The Portable Oscar Wilde.* Ed. Richard Aldington and Stanley Weintraub. London: Penguin, 1946, 138–391.

Williams, Trevor L. "Dominant Ideologies: The Production of Stephen Dedalus." In *James Joyce: The Augmented Ninth.* Ed. Bernard Benstock. Syracuse, N.Y.: Syracuse University Press, 1988, 312–22.

Williams, William Carlos. "A Point for American Criticism." In *Our Exagmination Round his Factification for Incamination of Work in Progress.* London: Faber and Faber, 1929, 173–85.

Wise, Jennifer. "Marginalizing Drama: Bakhtin's Theory of Genre." *Essays in Theatre* 8.1 (1989): 15–22.

Woolf, Virginia. "'Anon' and 'The Reader': Virginia Woolf's Last Essays." Ed. Brenda R. Silver. *Twentieth-Century Literature* 25 (1979): 356–441.

Woolf, Virginia. "Craftsmanship." In *Collected Essays.* New York: Harcourt Brace Jovanovich, 1967, 2:245-51.

Woolf, Virginia. "Modern Fiction." In *The Common Reader.* New York: Harcourt, Brace, 1948, 207–18.

Woolf, Virginia. *Mrs. Dalloway.* New York: Harcourt, Brace, 1925.

Woolf, Virginia. *Orlando.* New York: Harcourt Brace Jovanovich, 1956.

Woolf, Virginia. *A Room of One's Own.* New York: Harcourt Brace Jovanovich, 1929.

Woolf, Virginia. *To the Lighthouse.* New York: Harcourt Brace Jovanovich, 1927.

Woolf, Virginia. *The Waves.* New York: Harcourt, Brace, Jovanovich, 1931.

Woolf, Virginia. *A Writer's Diary.* Ed. Leonard Woolf. New York: Harcourt, Brace, 1954.

Worringer, Wilhelm. *Abstraction and Empathy: A Contribution to the Psychology of Style.* Trans. Michael Bullock. New York: International Universities Press, 1953.

Zwerdling, Alex. *Virginia Woolf and the Real World.* Berkeley, Los Angeles, and London: University of California Press, 1986.

Index

psychoanalysis/feminism

Bakhtin - relates to
dominant discourse → post colonial.

But Bloom is the female man.